A
& Other Exciting News
from Frommer's!

In our continuing effort to publish the savviest, most up-to-date, and most appealing travel guides available, we've added some great new features.

Frommer's guides now include a new **star-rating system.** Every hotel, restaurant, and attraction is rated from 0 to 3 stars to help you set priorities and organize your time.

We've also added **seven brand-new features** that point you to the great deals, in-the-know advice, and unique experiences that separate travelers from tourists. Throughout the guide, look for:

Finds Special finds—those places only insiders know about

Fun Fact Fun facts—details that make travelers more informed and their trips more fun

Kids Best bets for kids—advice for the whole family

Moments Special moments—those experiences that memories are made of

Overrated Places or experiences not worth your time or money

Tips Insider tips—some great ways to save time and money

Value Great values—where to get the best deals

Here's what critics say about Frommer's:

"Amazingly easy to use. Very portable, very complete."

—*Booklist*

"Detailed, accurate, and easy-to-read information for all price ranges."

—*Glamour Magazine*

"Hotel information is close to encyclopedic."

—*Des Moines Sunday Register*

"Frommer's Guides have a way of giving you a real feel for a place."

—*Knight Ridder Newspapers*

Frommer's®

portable
Washington, D.C.

4th Edition

by Elise Hartman Ford

Wiley Publishing, Inc.

Published by:

WILEY PUBLISHING, INC.

909 Third Ave.
New York, NY 10022

ISBN 0-7645-6692-X
ISSN 1092-3918

Editor: Stephen Bassman
Production Editor: Bethany André
Photo Editor: Richard Fox
Cartographer: Nicholas Trotter
Production by Wiley Indianapolis Composition Services

For information on our other products and services or to obtain technical
support, please contact our Customer Care Department within the U.S. at
800-762-2974, outside the U.S. at 317-572-3993 or fax 317-572-4002.

Contents

List of Maps

ABOUT THE AUTHOR

Elise Hartman Ford has been a freelance writer in the Washington, D.C., area since 1985. Her writing has appeared in *The Washington Post*, *Washingtonian* magazine, the London-based *Bradman's North America Guide*, *The Essential Guide to Business Travel*, *Ladies' Home Journal*, and other national, regional, and trade publications. In addition to this guide, she is the author of *Frommer's Washington, D.C. from $80 a Day*, *Frommer's Memorable Walks in Washington, D.C.*, and *Unique Meeting, Wedding, and Party Places in Greater Washington*.

AN INVITATION TO THE READER

In researching this book, we discovered many wonderful places—hotels, restaurants, shops, and more. We're sure you'll find others. Please tell us about them, so we can share the information with your fellow travelers in upcoming editions. If you were disappointed with a recommendation, we'd love to know that, too. Please write to:

Frommer's Portable Washington, D.C., 4th Edition
Wiley Publishing, Inc. • 909 Third Ave. • New York, NY 10022

AN ADDITIONAL NOTE

Please be advised that travel information is subject to change at any time—and this is especially true of prices. We therefore suggest that you write or call ahead for confirmation when making your travel plans. The authors, editors, and publisher cannot be held responsible for the experiences of readers while traveling. Your safety is important to us, however, so we encourage you to stay alert and be aware of your surroundings. Keep a close eye on cameras, purses, and wallets, all favorite targets of thieves and pickpockets.

WHAT THE SYMBOLS MEAN

AE	American Express	DISC	Discover	V	Visa
DC	Diners Club	MC	MasterCard		

FROMMERS.COM

Now that you have the guidebook to a great trip, visit our website at **www.frommers.com** for travel information on nearly 2,500 destinations. With features updated regularly, we give you instant access to the most current trip-planning information available. At Frommers.com, you'll also find the best prices on airfares, accommodations, and car rentals—and you can even book travel online through our travel booking partners. At Frommers.com, you'll also find the following::

- Online updates to our most popular guidebooks
- Vacation sweepstakes and contest giveaways
- Newsletter highlighting the hottest travel trends
- Online travel message boards with featured travel discussions

Planning Your Trip to Washington, D.C.

As you prepare to visit the nation's capital, you'll want to make sure you pack certain essentials. Got your curiosity about American history? Good. How about your appreciation of our democratic society and for the government that ensures our freedoms? Great. OK, now do you have your interest in beautiful art and architecture? That's terrific. And an enthusiasm for the peoples, food, music, crafts, inventions, and theater, not just of the United States, but of the world? Yes? Well, then, Washington, D.C., in all its glory, awaits you. You're good to go.

Wait a second. It might help if you do a little practical planning, as well. Read on for tips to help make your trip here hassle-free.

1 Visitor Information

Before you leave, contact the **Washington, D.C. Convention and Tourism Corporation,** 1212 New York Ave. NW, Washington, DC 20005 (© **800/422-8644** or 202/789-7000; www.washington. org), and ask for a free copy of the *Washington, D.C. Visitors Guide,* which details hotels, restaurants, sights, shops, and more. The staff will also be happy to answer specific questions.

Also helpful is the *Washington Post* site, **www.washingtonpost. com**, which gives you up-to-the-minute news, weather, visitor information, restaurant reviews, and nightlife insights.

2 When to Go

The city's peak seasons generally coincide with two activities: the sessions of Congress and springtime, starting with the appearance of the cherry blossoms along the Potomac. Specifically, when Congress is "in," from about the second week in September until Thanksgiving, and again from about mid-January through June, hotels are full with guests whose business takes them to Capitol Hill or to conferences. Mid-March through June traditionally is the most

Destination: Washington, D.C.— Red Alert Checklist

- Have you packed a photo ID? You'll need one to board a plane, of course, but even if you are not flying, you may find yourself being asked for a photo ID, once you're here.

- And while we're on the subject of IDs: Did you bring your ID cards that could entitle you to discounts such as AAA and AARP cards, student IDs, etc.?

- Have you booked theater and restaurant reservations (two weeks in advance for hot spots)?

- Have you checked to make sure your favorite attraction is open?

- Would you like to avoid the wait of a long line or the ultimate disappointment of missing a tour altogether? A number of sightseeing attractions permit you to reserve a tour slot in advance. The Supreme Court, the Library of Congress, the Washington National Cathedral, and the Kennedy Center all direct you to your senator or representative's office to request advance reservations for "congressional" tours at each of their sites. In the past, it was possible also to reserve advance tickets for tours of

frenzied season, when families and school groups descend upon the city to see the cherry blossoms and enjoy Washington's sensational spring. This is also the season for protest marches. Hotel rooms are at a premium and airfares tend to be higher.

If crowds turn you off, consider visiting Washington at the end of August/early September, when Congress is still "out," and families return home to get their children back to school, or between Thanksgiving and mid-January, when Congress leaves again and many people are ensconced in their own holiday-at-home celebrations. Hotel rates are cheapest at this time, too, and many places offer attractive packages.

If you're thinking of visiting in July and August, be forewarned: The weather is very hot and humid. Many of Washington's stages go dark in summer, although outdoor arenas and parks pick up some of the slack by featuring concerts, festivals, parades, and more. There's something doing almost every night and day. And, of the Capitol, the White House, and the FBI; this policy still holds at the FBI, but was canceled after September 11 at the Capitol and the White House. It may have been reinstated by the time you read this—it's worth a call to your senator or representative.

The switchboard for the Senate is ℰ **202/224-3121;** for the House switchboard, call ℰ **202/225-3121.** You can also correspond by e-mail; check out the websites **www.senate.gov** and **www.house.gov** for e-mail addresses, individual member information, legislative calendars, and much more. Or you can write for information. Address requests to representatives as follows: name of your congressperson, U.S. House of Representatives, Washington, DC 20515; or name of your senator, U.S. Senate, Washington, DC 20510. Don't forget to include the exact dates of your Washington trip.

- If you purchased traveler's checks, have you recorded the check numbers, and stored the documentation separately from the checks?

course, Independence Day (July 4th) in the capital is a spectacular celebration.

WASHINGTON, D.C., CALENDAR OF EVENTS

January

Martin Luther King, Jr.'s, Birthday. Events include speeches by prominent civil rights leaders and politicians; readings; dance, theater, and choral performances; prayer vigils; a wreath-laying ceremony at the Lincoln Memorial (call ℰ **202/619-7222**); and concerts. Many events take place at the Martin Luther King Memorial Library, 901 G St. NW (ℰ **202/727-0321**). Third Monday in January.

February

Black History Month. Features numerous events, museum exhibits, and cultural programs celebrating the contributions of African Americans to American life, including a celebration of abolitionist Frederick Douglass's birthday. For details, check the *Washington Post* or call ℂ **202/357-2700.** For additional activities at the Martin Luther King Library, call ℂ **202/727-0321.** February.

Chinese New Year Celebration. A friendship archway, topped by 300 painted dragons and lighted at night, marks Chinatown's entrance at 7th and H streets NW. The celebration begins the day of the Chinese New Year and continues for 10 or more days, with traditional firecrackers, dragon dancers, and colorful street parades. Some area restaurants offer special menus. For details, call ℂ **202/789-7000.** Early February.

George Washington's Birthday. Similar celebratory events to Lincoln's birthday, centered around the Washington Monument. Call ℂ **202/619-7222** for details. Both presidents' birthdays also bring annual citywide sales. February 22. Mount Vernon also marks Washington's birthday with free admission and activities that include music and military performances on the bowling green. Call ℂ **703/780-2000.** The town of Alexandria holds the nation's largest parade celebrating Washington's birthday; call ℂ **703/838-4200.** Third Monday in February.

March

St. Patrick's Day Parade, on Constitution Avenue NW from 7th to 17th streets. A big parade with floats, bagpipes, marching bands, and the wearin' o' the green. For parade information, call ℂ **202/789-7000.** The Sunday before March 17.

Smithsonian Kite Festival. A delightful event if the weather cooperates—an occasion for a trip in itself. Throngs of kite enthusiasts fly their unique creations on the Washington Monument grounds and compete for ribbons and prizes. To compete, just show up with your kite and register between 10am and noon. Call ℂ **202/357-2700** or 202/357-3030 for details. A Saturday in mid- or late March, or early April.

April

Cherry Blossom Events. Washington's best-known annual event: the blossoming of the 3,700 famous Japanese cherry trees by the Tidal Basin in Potomac Park. Festivities include a major parade (marking the end of the festival) with floats, concerts, celebrity guests, and more. There are also special ranger-guided tours departing from the Jefferson Memorial. For information, call ℂ **202/547-1500.** See p. 138 for more information about the cherry blossoms. Early April (national news programs monitor the budding).

White House Easter Egg Roll. The biggie for little kids. This year's is the White House's 124th Easter Egg Roll (and before that, it took place on the Capitol grounds—until Congress banned it). In past years, entertainment on the White House South Lawn and the Ellipse has included clog dancers, clowns, Ukrainian egg-decorating exhibitions, puppet and magic shows, military drill teams, an egg-rolling contest, and a hunt for 1,000 or so wooden eggs, many of them signed by celebrities, astronauts, or the president. *Note:* Attendance is limited to children ages 3 to 6, who must be accompanied by an adult. Hourly timed tickets are issued at the National Parks Service Ellipse Visitors Pavilion just behind the White House at 15th and E streets NW beginning at 7am. Call ✆ **202/208-1631** for details. Between 10am and 2pm; enter at the southeast gate on East Executive Avenue, and arrive early, to make sure you get in, and also to allow for increased security procedures. One such new rule: Strollers are not permitted. Easter Monday.

African-American Family Day at the National Zoo. This tradition extends back to 1889, when the zoo opened. The National Zoo celebrates African-American families the day after Easter with music, dance, Easter egg rolls, and other activities. Free. Easter Monday.

Shakespeare's Birthday Celebration. Music, theater, children's events, food, and exhibits are all part of the afternoon's hail to the bard at the Folger Shakespeare Library. Call ✆ **202/544-7077.** Free admission. Mid-April.

Taste of the Nation. An organization called Share Our Strength (SOS) sponsors this fundraiser, for which 100 major restaurants and many wineries set up tasting booths and offer some of their finest fare. In 2002, the event was staged at the Ritz-Carlton Hotel. For the price of admission, you can do the circuit, sampling everything from barbecue to bouillabaisse. Wine flows freely, and there are dozens of great desserts. The evening also includes a silent auction. Tickets are $125 if purchased in advance, $150 at the door, and 100% of the profits go to feed the hungry. To obtain tickets and information, call ✆ **202/478-6578** or check out www.strength.org. Late April through early May.

Smithsonian Craft Show. Held in the National Building Museum, 401 F St. NW, this juried show features one-of-a-kind limited-edition crafts by more than 100 noted artists from all over the country. There's an entrance fee of about $12 per adult, free for children under 12, each day. For details, call ✆ **202/357-4000** (TDD 202/357-1729). Four days in late April.

May

Georgetown Garden Tour. View the remarkable private gardens of one of the city's loveliest neighborhoods. Admission (about $25) includes light refreshments. Some years there are related events such as a flower show at a historic home. Call ✆ 202/789-7000 or browse the website, www.gtowngarden.org for details. Early to mid-May.

Washington National Cathedral Annual Flower Mart. Now in its 64th year, the flower mart takes place on cathedral grounds, featuring displays of flowering plants and herbs, decorating demonstrations, ethnic food booths, children's rides and activities (including an antique carousel), costumed characters, puppet shows, and other entertainment. Admission is free. Call ✆ 202/537-6200 for details. First Friday and Saturday in May.

Memorial Day. At 11am, a wreath-laying ceremony takes place at the Tomb of the Unknowns in Arlington National Cemetery, followed by military band music, a service, and an address by a high-ranking government official (sometimes the president); call ✆ 202/685-2851 for details. There's also a ceremony at 1pm at the Vietnam Veterans Memorial, including a wreath-laying, speakers, and the playing of taps (✆ 202/619-7222 for details), and activities at the U.S. Navy Memorial (✆ 202/737-2300). On the Sunday before Memorial Day, the National Symphony Orchestra performs a free concert at 8pm on the West Lawn of the Capitol to officially welcome summer to Washington; call ✆ 202/619-7222 for details. Last Sunday and Monday of May.

June

Shakespeare Theatre Free For All. This free theater festival presents a different Shakespeare play each year for a 2-week run at the Carter Barron Amphitheatre in upper northwest Washington. Tickets are required, but they're free. Call ✆ 202/334-4790. Evenings in mid-June.

Smithsonian Festival of American Folklife. A major event with traditional American music, crafts, foods, games, concerts, and exhibits, staged the length of the National Mall. All events are free; most events take place outdoors. Call ✆ 202/357-2700, or check the listings in the *Washington Post* for details. For 5 to 10 days, always including July 4.

July

Independence Day. There's no better place to be on the Fourth of July than in Washington, D.C. The festivities include a massive National Independence Day Parade down Constitution

Avenue, complete with lavish floats, princesses, marching groups, and military bands. There are also celebrity entertainers and concerts. (Most events take place on the Washington Monument grounds.) A morning program in front of the National Archives includes military demonstrations, period music, and a reading of the Declaration of Independence. In the evening, the National Symphony Orchestra plays on the west steps of the Capitol with guest artists (for example, Leontyne Price). And big-name entertainment also precedes the fabulous fireworks display behind the Washington Monument. You can also attend a free 11am organ recital at Washington's National Cathedral. Consult the *Washington Post* or call ✆ **202/789-7000** for details. July 4, all day.

September

Labor Day Concert. West Lawn of the Capitol. The National Symphony Orchestra closes its summer season with a free performance at 8pm; call ✆ **202/619-7222** for details. Labor Day. (Rain date: Same day and time at Constitution Hall.)

Kennedy Center Open House Arts Festival. A day-long festival of the performing arts, featuring local and national artists on the front plaza and river terrace (which overlooks the Potomac), and throughout the stage halls of the Kennedy Center. Past festivals have featured the likes of Los Lobos, Mary Chapin Carpenter, and Washington Opera soloists. Kids' activities usually include a National Symphony Orchestra "petting zoo," where children get to bow, blow, drum, or strum a favorite instrument. Admission is free, although you may have to stand in a long line for the inside performances. Check the *Washington Post* or call ✆ **800/444-1324** or 202/467-4600 for details. A Sunday in early to mid-September, noon to 6pm.

Black Family Reunion. Performances, food, and fun are part of this celebration of the African-American family and culture, held on the Mall. Free. Call ✆ **202/737-0120.** Mid-September.

Hispanic Heritage Month. Various museums and other institutions host activities celebrating Hispanic culture and traditions. Call ✆ **202/789-7000.** Mid-September to mid-October.

Washington National Cathedral's Open House. Celebrates the anniversary of the laying of the foundation stone in 1907. Events include demonstrations of stone carving and other crafts utilized in building the cathedral; carillon and organ demonstrations; and performances by dancers, choirs, strolling musicians, jugglers, and puppeteers. This is the only time visitors are allowed to ascend to the top of the central tower to see the bells; it's a tremendous climb, but you'll be rewarded with a spectacular view. For details, call © **202/537-6200.** A Saturday in late September or early October.

October

Taste of D.C. Festival. Pennsylvania Avenue, between 9th and 14th streets NW. Dozens of Washington's restaurants offer food tastings, along with live entertainment, dancing, storytellers, and games. Admission is free; purchase tickets for tastings. Call © **202/789-7000** for details. Three days, including Columbus Day weekend.

White House Fall Garden Tours. For 2 days, visitors have an opportunity to see the famed Rose Garden and South Lawn. Admission is free. A military band provides music. For details, call © **202/208-1631.** Mid-October.

800/RUN-USMC or 703/784-2225 for details. Anyone can enter; register online at www.marinemarathon.com. Fourth Sunday in October.

Halloween. There's no official celebration, but costumed revels seem to get bigger every year. Giant block parties take place in the Dupont Circle area and Georgetown. Check the *Washington Post* for special parties and activities. October 31.

November

Veterans Day. The nation's war dead are honored with a wreath-laying ceremony at 11am at the Tomb of the Unknowns in Arlington National Cemetery followed by a memorial service. The president of the United States or a very high-ranking government personage officiates. Military music is provided by a military band. Call © **202/685-2951** for information. At the Vietnam Veterans Memorial (© **202/619-7222**), observances include speakers, wreath placement, a color guard, and the playing of taps. November 11.

December

Christmas Pageant of Peace/National Tree Lighting. At the northern end of the Ellipse, the president lights the national Christmas tree to the accompaniment of orchestral and choral music. The lighting inaugurates the 3-week Pageant of Peace, a tremendous holiday celebration with seasonal music, caroling, a nativity scene, 50 state trees, and a burning yule log. Call © **202/ 208-1631** for details. A select Wednesday or Thursday in early December at 5pm.

White House Candlelight Tours. On 3 evenings after Christmas from 5 to 7pm, visitors can see the president's Christmas holiday decorations by candlelight. String music enhances the tours. Lines are long; arrive early. Call ℂ **202/208-1631** for dates and details.

3 Tips for Travelers with Special Needs

TRAVELERS WITH DISABILITIES

Washington, D.C., is one of the most accessible cities in the world for travelers with disabilities. The best overall source of information about accessibility at specific Washington hotels, restaurants, shopping malls, and attractions is the nonprofit organization Access Information. You can read the information (including restaurant reviews) online at **www.disabilityguide.org**, or order a free copy of *The Access Entertainment Guide for the Greater Washington Area* by calling ℂ **301/528-8591,** or by writing to Access Information, 21618 Slidell Rd., Boyds, MD 20841.

The **Washington Metropolitan Transit Authority** publishes accessibility information on its website **www.wmata.com**, or you can call ℂ **202/962-1245** with questions about Metro services for travelers with disabilities, including how to obtain a Disabled ID card that entitles you to discounted fares. (Make sure you call at least 3 weeks ahead to allow enough time to obtain an ID card.) For up-to-date information about how Metro is operating on the day you're using it, for instance, to verify that the elevators are operating at the stations you'll be traveling to, call ℂ **202/962-6464.**

All **Smithsonian museum buildings** are accessible to wheelchair visitors. A comprehensive free publication called "Smithsonian Access" lists all services available to visitors with disabilities, including parking, building access, sign-language interpreters, and more. To obtain a copy, call ℂ **202/357-2700** or TTY 202/357-1729, or find the information online, at www.si.edu/resource/faq/access.htm. You can also use the TTY number to get information on all Smithsonian museums and events.

The **Lincoln, Jefferson, and Vietnam memorials** and the **Washington Monument** are also equipped to accommodate visitors with disabilities and keep wheelchairs on the premises. There's limited parking for visitors with disabilities on the south side of the Lincoln Memorial. Call ahead to other sightseeing attractions for accessibility information and special services: ℂ **202/426-6842.**

Call your senator or representative to arrange wheelchair-accessible tours of **the Capitol;** they can also arrange special tours for the blind or deaf. For further information, call ℂ **202/224-4048.**

GAY & LESBIAN TRAVELERS

Washington, D.C., has a strong gay and lesbian community, and clearly welcomes gay and lesbian visitors, as evidenced by the fact that the Washington Convention and Tourism Corporation publishes a guide, "The Gay and Lesbian Traveler's Guide to Washington, D.C.," which you can download from its website, www.washington.org, or order by calling ✆ 202/789-7000.

While in Washington, you'll want to get your hands on the *Washington Blade,* a comprehensive weekly newspaper distributed free at about 1,000 locations in the District. Every issue provides an extensive events calendar and a list of hundreds of resources, such as crisis centers, health facilities, switchboards, political groups, religious organizations, social clubs, and student activities; it puts you in touch with everything from groups of lesbian bird-watchers to the Asian Gay Men's Network. Gay restaurants and clubs are, of course, also listed and advertised. You can subscribe to the *Blade* for $45 a year, check out **www.washingtonblade.com**, or pick up a free copy at Olsson's Books/Records, 1307 19th St. NW; Borders, 18th and L streets; and Kramerbooks, 1517 Connecticut Ave. NW, at Dupont Circle. Call the *Blade* office at ✆ 202/797-7000 for other locations.

Washington's gay bookstore, **Lambda Rising,** 1625 Connecticut Ave. NW (✆ 202/462-6969), also informally serves as an information center for the gay community, which centers in the Dupont Circle neighborhood.

SENIOR TRAVEL

Mention the fact that you're a senior when you first make your travel reservations. All major airlines and many hotels offer discounts for seniors. Major airlines also offer coupons for domestic travel for seniors over sixty. Typically, a book of four coupons costs less than $700, which means you can fly anywhere in the continental United States for under $350 round-trip.

Washington, like most cities, offers discounted admission to seniors at theaters, at those few museums that charge for entry, and for discounted travel on Metro, although the designated "senior" age differs slightly from place to place. For instance, discount eligibility requires that you must be 60 or older at Arena Stage, older than 62 at the Phillips Collection, and 65 or older for the Metro. Some places, such as Arena Stage, take you at your word that you qualify for a discount, so you may order your tickets over the phone, without showing proof of your age. To obtain discounted fare cards to ride the Metro, you must first apply for a Senior ID card, well in advance of your trip; call ℂ **202/962-2136** for more information.

Members of **AARP** (formerly known as the American Association of Retired Persons), 601 E St. NW, Washington, DC 20049 (ℂ **800/424-3410** or 202/434-2277; www.aarp.org), get discounts on hotels, airfares, and car rentals. AARP offers members a wide range of benefits, including *Modern Maturity* magazine and a monthly newsletter. Anyone over 50 can join.

4 Getting There

BY PLANE

All three of Washington, D.C.'s airports, Washington Dulles International Airport (Dulles), Ronald Reagan Washington National Airport (National), and Baltimore-Washington International Airport (BWI), are operating up to speed once again, though with added security procedures, following the terrorist attacks of September 11, 2001.

Note: At these three airports, as at all American airports now, only ticketed passengers are permitted to go through security to the gates, which means that if people are meeting you at the airport they will no longer be allowed to greet you at the gate; you should agree beforehand on some other designated rendezvous site.

SHUTTLE SERVICE FROM NEW YORK, BOSTON & CHICAGO

Delta and US Airways continue to dominate the lucrative D.C.–East Coast shuttle service. Between the two of them, the airlines operate hourly or almost hourly shuttle service between Boston's Logan Airport and Washington, and New York's La Guardia Airport and Washington. The **Delta Shuttle** (ℂ **800/ 221-1212**) travels daily between New York and Washington, while the **US Airways Shuttle** (ℂ **800/428-4322**) operates weekdays, between Boston and Washington, and New York and Washington. Both airlines fly into and out of Ronald Reagan Washington National Airport. Southwest Airlines, known for its low fares, offers nearly hourly service daily between BWI and Chicago's Midway Airport, Providence, Hartford, and Nashville.

D.C.'S AREA AIRPORTS

Ronald Reagan Washington National Airport (or simply "National") lies across the Potomac River in Virginia, a few minutes by car, 15 to 20 minutes by Metro from downtown in non-rush-hour traffic. Its proximity to the District and its direct access to the Metro rail system are reasons why you might want to fly into National.

Washington Dulles International Airport (Dulles) lies 26 miles outside the capital, in Chantilly, Virginia, a 35- to 45-minute ride to downtown in non-rush-hour traffic. Of the three airports, Dulles handles more daily flights—about 1,000, although by the time you read this, the number may have returned to its pre-September 11 average of 1,200—and its airlines fly to more destinations, about 69 U.S. and 23 foreign cities. For information about National and Dulles, call © **703/572-2700** or go to www.metwashairports.com.

Last but not least is **Baltimore–Washington International Airport** (BWI), which is located about 45 minutes from downtown, a few miles outside of Baltimore. Two factors especially recommend BWI to travelers: Southwest Airlines, with its bargain fares, commands a major presence here, pulling in about one-third of BWI's business.

The other big benefit to using BWI concerns security. The airport is the primary screening site for the Transportation Security Administration's field testing of possible new security measures; the best and brightest security procedures will be tried here first. If you're extremely anxious about traveling, you may want to choose to fly into and out of BWI. Call © **800/435-9294** for airport information, or point your browser to www.bwiairport.com.

GETTING INTO TOWN FROM THE AIRPORT

Taxi service: For a trip to downtown D.C., you can expect a taxi to cost anywhere from $8 to $15 for the 10- to 15-minute ride from National Airport; $35 to $47 for the 30- to 40-minute ride from Dulles Airport; and $55 for the 45-minute ride from BWI.

SuperShuttle buses (© **800/258-3826;** www.supershuttle.com) offer shared-ride, door-to-door service between the airport and your destination, whether in the District or in a suburban location. No need to reserve seats; however, if you arrive after midnight, call the toll-free number above to summon a van. This 24-hour service bases its fares on ZIP code, so, to reach downtown, expect to pay about $10, plus $8 for each additional person, from National; $22, plus $10 per additional person, from Dulles; and $26 to $32, plus $8 per additional person, from BWI.

Individual transportation options at each airport are as follows:

FROM RONALD REAGAN WASHINGTON NATIONAL AIRPORT
If you are not too encumbered with luggage, you should

take **Metrorail** (*℗* **202/637-7000**) into the city. Metro's Yellow and Blue lines stop at the airport and connect via an enclosed walkway to level two, the concourse level, of the main terminal, adjacent to terminals B and C.

FROM WASHINGTON DULLES INTERNATIONAL AIR-PORT   The **Washington Flyer Express Bus** runs between Dulles and the West Falls Church Metro station, where you can board a train for D.C. Buses to the West Falls Church Metro station run daily, every 30 minutes, and cost $8 one way.

FROM BALTIMORE–WASHINGTON INTERNATIONAL AIRPORT   In late 2001, BWI initiated an Express Metro Bus service that runs between the Greenbelt Metro station and the airport. The service operates daily, departs every 40 minutes, and costs $2. At the Greenbelt Metro station, you purchase a Metro fare card and board a Metro train, which takes you into the city.

BY CAR

Major highways approach Washington, D.C., from all parts of the country. Specifically, these are I-270, I-95, and I-295 from the north; I-95 and I-395, Route 1, and Route 301 from the south; Route 50/301 and Route 450 from the east; and Route 7, Route 50, I-66, and Route 29/211 from the west.

No matter which road you take, there's a good chance you will have to navigate some portion of the **Capital Beltway** (I-495 and I-95) to gain entry to D.C. The Beltway girds the city, 66 miles around, with 56 interchanges or exits, and is nearly always congested, but especially during weekday morning and evening rush hours, roughly between 7 to 9am and 3 to 7pm. Commuter traffic on the Beltway now rivals that of major L.A. freeways, and drivers can get a little crazy, weaving in and out of traffic.

If you're planning to drive to Washington, get yourself a good map before you do anything else. The **American Automobile Association (AAA;** *℗* **800/222-4357** for emergency road service, or **703/222-6000** for the mid-Atlantic office; www.aaa.com) provides its members with maps and detailed Trip-Tiks that give precise directions to a destination, including up-to-date information about areas of construction. AAA also provides towing services should you have car trouble during your trip. If you are driving to a hotel in D.C. or its suburbs, contact the establishment to find out the best route to the hotel's address and other crucial details concerning parking availability and rates.

The District is 240 miles from New York City, 40 miles from Baltimore, 700 miles from Chicago, nearly 500 miles from Boston, and about 630 miles from Atlanta.

BY TRAIN

Amtrak (© 800/USA-RAIL; www.amtrak.com) offers daily service to Washington from New York, Boston, Chicago, and Los Angeles (you change trains in Chicago). Amtrak also travels daily from points south of Washington, including Raleigh, Charlotte, Atlanta, cities in Florida, and New Orleans.

Metroliner service—which costs a little more but provides faster transit and roomier, more comfortable seating than regular trains—is available between New York and Washington, D.C., and points in between.

Even faster, roomier, and more expensive than Metroliner service are Amtrak's high-speed **Acela** trains. The trains, which travel as fast as 150 miles per hour, navigate the Northeast Corridor, linking Boston, New York, and Washington.

Amtrak trains arrive at historic **Union Station,** 50 Massachusetts Ave. NE (© **202/371-9441;** www.unionstationdc.com), a short walk from the Capitol, across the circle from several hotels, and a short cab or Metro ride from downtown. Union Station is a turn-of-the-20th-century beaux arts masterpiece that was magnificently restored in the late 1980s. Offering a three-level marketplace of shops and restaurants, this stunning depot is conveniently located and connects with Metro service. There are always taxis available there.

2

Getting to Know
Washington, D.C.

On the one hand, Washington, D.C., is an easy place to get to know. It's a small city, where walking will actually get you places, but also with a model public transportation system that travels throughout D.C.'s neighborhoods, and to most tourist spots. A building height restriction creates a landscape in which the lost tourist can get his bearings from tall landmarks—the Capitol, the Washington Monument—that loom into view from different vantage points.

On the other hand, when you do need help, it's hard to find. The city lacks a single, large, comprehensive, and easily found visitor center. Signage to tourist attractions and Metro stations, even street signs, are often missing or frustratingly inadequate. In the wake of September 11, touring procedures at individual sightseeing attractions are constantly changing, as new security precautions take effect, and these changes can be disorienting.

The District is always in the process of improving the situation, it seems. But in the meantime, you can turn to the following small visitors and information centers, helpful publications, and information phone lines.

1 Orientation

VISITOR INFORMATION
INFORMATION CENTERS
The Washington, D.C., Visitor Information Center (© 202/328-4748; www.dcvisit.com) is a small visitors center inside the immense Ronald Reagan Building and International Trade Center, at 1300 Pennsylvania Ave. NW. To enter the federal building, you need to show a picture ID. The visitor center lies on the ground floor of the building, a little to your right as you enter from the Wilson Plaza, near the Federal Triangle Metro. It's open Monday through Friday, 8am to 6pm and on Saturday from 11am to 5pm.

There are two other excellent tourist-information centers in town, and though each focuses on a specific attraction, they can also tell you about other popular Washington sights.

The **White House Visitor Center,** on the first floor of the Herbert Hoover Building, Department of Commerce, 1450 Pennsylvania Ave. NW (between 14th and 15th sts.; ℂ **202/208-1631,** or 202/456-7041 for recorded information), is open daily from 7:30am to 4pm.

The **Smithsonian Information Center,** in the "Castle," 1000 Jefferson Dr. SW (ℂ **202/357-2700,** or TTY 202/357-1729; www. si.edu), is open every day but Christmas from 9am to 5:30pm. Call for a free copy of the Smithsonian's "Planning Your Smithsonian Visit," which is full of valuable tips, or stop at the Castle for a copy. A calendar of Smithsonian exhibits and activities for the coming month appears the third Friday of each month in the *Washington Post*'s "Weekend" section.

The **American Automobile Association (AAA)** has a large central office near the White House, at 701 15th St. NW, Washington, DC 20005-2111 (ℂ **202/331-3000**). Hours are 8:30am to 5:30pm Monday through Friday.

PUBLICATIONS

At the airport, pick up a free copy of *Washington Flyer* magazine (www.fly2dc.com), which is handy as a planning tool.

Washington has two daily newspapers: the *Washington Post* (www.washingtonpost.com) and the *Washington Times* (www. washingtontimes.com). The Friday "Weekend" section of the *Post* is essential for finding out what's going on, recreation-wise. *City Paper,* published every Thursday and available free at downtown shops and restaurants, covers some of the same material but is a better guide to the club and art gallery scene.

Also on newsstands is *Washingtonian,* a monthly magazine with features, often about the "100 Best" this or that (doctors, restaurants, and so on) in Washington; the magazine also offers a calendar of events, restaurant reviews, and profiles of Washingtonians.

HELPFUL TELEPHONE NUMBERS & WEBSITES

- **National Park Service** (ℂ **202/619-7222;** www.nps.gov/ nacc). You reach a real person and not a recording when you call the phone number with questions about the monuments, the National Mall, national park lands, and activities taking place at these locations. National Park Service information kiosks are located near the Jefferson, Lincoln, Vietnam

Veterans, and Korean War memorials, and at several other locations in the city.

- **Dial-A-Park** (© 202/619-7275). This is a recording of information regarding park-service events and attractions.
- **Dial-A-Museum** (© 202/357-2020; www.si.edu). This recording informs you about the locations of the 14 Washington Smithsonian museums and of their daily activities.

CITY LAYOUT

The U.S. Capitol marks the center of the city, which is divided into quadrants: **northwest (NW), northeast (NE), southwest (SW),** and **southeast (SE).** Almost all the areas of interest to tourists are in the northwest. If you look at your map, you'll see that some addresses—for instance, the corner of G and 7th streets—appear in all quadrants. Hence you must observe the quadrant designation (NW, NE, SW, or SE) when looking for an address.

MAIN ARTERIES & STREETS   The primary artery of Washington is **Pennsylvania Avenue,** scene of parades, inaugurations, and other splashy events. Pennsylvania runs northwest in a direct line between the Capitol and the White House—if it weren't for the Treasury Building, the president would have a clear view of the Capitol—before continuing on a northwest angle to Georgetown, where it becomes M Street.

Since May 1995, Pennsylvania Avenue between 15th and 17th streets NW has been closed to cars for security reasons. H Street is now one-way eastbound between 19th and 13th streets NW; I Street is one-way westbound between 11th and 21st streets NW.

Constitution Avenue, paralleled to the south most of the way by Independence Avenue, runs east-west, flanking the Capitol and the Mall. If you hear Washingtonians talk about the "House" side of the Hill, they're referring to the southern half of the Capitol, the side closest to Independence Avenue, and home to Congressional House offices and the House Chamber. Conversely, the Senate side is the northern half of the Capitol, where Senate offices and the Senate Chamber are found, closer to Constitution Avenue.

Washington's longest avenue, **Massachusetts Avenue,** runs parallel to Pennsylvania (a few avenues north). Along the way, you'll find Union Station and then Dupont Circle, which is central to the area known as Embassy Row. Farther out are the Naval Observatory (the vice president's residence is on the premises), Washington National Cathedral, American University, and, eventually, Maryland.

Connecticut Avenue, which runs more directly north (the other avenues run southeast to northwest), starts at Lafayette Square, intersects Dupont Circle, and eventually takes you to the National Zoo, on to the charming residential neighborhood known as Cleveland Park, and into Chevy Chase, Maryland, where you can pick up the Beltway to head out of town. Downtown Connecticut Avenue, with its posh shops and clusters of restaurants, is a good street to stroll.

Wisconsin Avenue originates in Georgetown; its intersection with M Street forms Georgetown's hub. Antiques shops, trendy boutiques, nightclubs, restaurants, and pubs all vie for attention. Wisconsin Avenue basically parallels Connecticut Avenue.

FINDING AN ADDRESS   Once you understand the city's layout, it's easy to find your way around. As you read this, have a map handy.

Each of the four corners of the District of Columbia is exactly the same distance from the Capitol dome. The White House and most government buildings and important monuments are west of the Capitol (in the northwest and southwest quadrants), as are major hotels and tourist facilities.

Numbered streets run north-south, beginning on either side of the Capitol with First Street. Lettered streets run east-west and are named alphabetically, beginning with A Street. (Don't look for a B, a J, an X, a Y, or a Z Street, however.) After W Street, street names of two syllables continue in alphabetical order, followed by street names of three syllables; the more syllables in a name, the farther the street is from the Capitol.

Avenues, named for U.S. states, run at angles across the grid pattern and often intersect at traffic circles. For example, New Hampshire, Connecticut, and Massachusetts avenues intersect at Dupont Circle.

With this in mind, you can easily find an address. On lettered streets, the address tells you exactly where to go. For instance, 1776 K St. NW is between 17th and 18th streets (the 1st 2 digits of 1776 tell you that) in the northwest quadrant (NW). *Note:* I Street is often written Eye Street to prevent confusion with 1st Street.

To find an address on numbered streets, you'll probably have to use your fingers. For instance, 623 8th St. SE is between F and G streets (the 6th and 7th letters of the alphabet; the 1st digit of 623 tells you that) in the southeast quadrant (SE). One thing to remember: You count B as the second letter of the alphabet even though no

B Street exists today (Constitution and Independence aves. were the original B sts.), but since there's no J Street, K becomes the 10th letter, L the 11th, and so on.

THE NEIGHBORHOODS IN BRIEF

Capitol Hill   Everyone's heard of "the Hill," the area crowned by the Capitol. When people speak of Capitol Hill, they refer to a large section of town, extending from the western side of the Capitol to the D.C. Armory going east, bounded by H Street to the north and the Southwest Freeway to the south. It contains not only the chief symbol of the nation's capital, but the Supreme Court building, the Library of Congress, the Folger Shakespeare Library, Union Station, and the U.S. Botanic Garden. Much of it is a quiet residential neighborhood of tree-lined streets and Victorian homes. There are a number of restaurants in the vicinity and a smattering of hotels, mostly close to Union Station.

The Mall   This lovely, tree-lined stretch of open space between Constitution and Independence avenues, extending for 2½ miles from the Capitol to the Lincoln Memorial, is the hub of tourist attractions. It includes most of the Smithsonian Institution museums and many other visitor attractions. The 300-foot-wide Mall is used by natives as well as tourists—joggers, food vendors, kite-flyers, and picnickers among them. As you can imagine, hotels and restaurants are located on the periphery.

Downtown   The area roughly between 7th and 22nd streets NW going east to west, and P Street and Pennsylvania Avenue going north to south, is a mix of the Federal Triangle's government office buildings, K Street (Lawyer's Row), Connecticut Avenue restaurants and shopping, historic hotels, the city's poshest small hotels, **Chinatown,** and the White House. You'll also find the historic **Penn Quarter,** a part of downtown that continues to flourish, since the opening of the MCI Center, trendy restaurants, boutique hotels, and art galleries. The total downtown area takes in so many blocks and attractions that I've divided discussions of accommodations (chapter 3) and dining (chapter 4) into two sections: "Downtown, 16th Street NW and West," and "Downtown, East of 16th Street NW." 16th Street and the White House form a natural point of separation.

U Street Corridor   D.C.'s avant-garde nightlife neighborhood between 12th and 15th streets NW is rising from the ashes of nightclubs and theaters frequented decades ago by African Americans. At two renovated establishments, the Lincoln Theater and the Bohemian Caverns jazz club, where Duke Ellington, Louis Armstrong, and Cab Calloway once performed, patrons today can enjoy performances by leading artists. The corridor offers many nightclubs and several restaurants (see chapter 7 for details). Go here to party, not to sleep—there are no hotels along this stretch.

Adams-Morgan   This ever-trendy, multiethnic neighborhood is about the size of a postage stamp, though crammed with boutiques, clubs, and restaurants. Everything is located on either 18th Street NW or Columbia Road NW. You won't find any hotels here, although there are a couple of B&Bs; nearby are the Dupont Circle and Woodley Park neighborhoods, each of which has several hotels (see below). Parking during the day is okay, but forget it at night. But you can easily walk (be alert—the neighborhood is edgy) to Adams-Morgan from the Dupont Circle or Woodley Park Metro stops, or taxi here. Weekend nightlife rivals that of Georgetown and Dupont Circle.

Dupont Circle   My favorite part of town, Dupont Circle is fun day or night. It takes its name from the traffic circle minipark, where Massachusetts, New Hampshire, and Connecticut avenues collide. Washington's famous **Embassy Row** centers on Dupont Circle, and refers to the parade of grand embassy mansions lining Massachusetts Avenue and its side streets. The streets extending out from the circle are lively with all-night bookstores, really good restaurants, wonderful art galleries and art museums, nightspots, movie theaters, and Washingtonians at their loosest. It is also the hub of D.C.'s gay community. There are plenty of hotels.

Foggy Bottom   The area west of the White House and southeast of Georgetown, Foggy Bottom was Washington's early industrial center. Its name comes from the foul fumes emitted in those days by a coal depot and gasworks, but its original name, Funkstown (for owner Jacob Funk), is perhaps even worse. There's nothing foul (and not much funky) about the area today. This is a low-key part of town, enlivened by the presence of the Kennedy Center, George Washington University, small and medium-size hotels, and a mix of restaurants on the main drag, Pennsylvania Avenue, and residential side streets.

Georgetown   This historic community dates from colonial times. It was a thriving tobacco port long before the District of Columbia was formed, and one of its attractions, the Old Stone House, dates from pre-Revolutionary days. Georgetown action centers on M Street and Wisconsin Avenue NW, where you'll find the luxury Four Seasons hotel and less expensive digs, numerous boutiques, chic restaurants, and popular pubs (lots of nightlife here). But get off the main drags and see the quiet, tree-lined streets of restored colonial row houses; stroll through the beautiful gardens of Dumbarton Oaks; and check out the C&O Canal. Georgetown is also home to Georgetown University. Note that the neighborhood gets pretty raucous on the weekends, which won't appeal to everyone.

Woodley Park Home to Washington's largest hotel (the Marriott Wardman Park), Woodley Park boasts the National Zoo, many good restaurants, and some antiques stores. Washingtonians are used to seeing conventioneers wandering the neighborhood's pretty residential streets with their name tags still on.

2 Getting Around

Washington is one of the easiest U.S. cities to navigate. Only New York rivals its comprehensive transportation system; but even with their problems, Washington's clean, efficient subways put the Big Apple's underground nightmare to shame. A complex bus system covers all major D.C. arteries as well, and it's easy to hail a taxi anywhere at any time. But because Washington is of manageable size and marvelous beauty, you may find yourself shunning transportation and choosing to walk.

BY METRORAIL

Metrorail's system of 83 stations and 103 miles of track includes locations at or near almost every sightseeing attraction and extends to suburban Maryland and northern Virginia. (Construction underway now will add 3 miles and 3 stations by late 2004.) There are five lines in operation—Red, Blue, Orange, Yellow, and Green—with extensions planned for the future. The lines connect at several points, making transfers easy. All but Yellow and Green Line trains stop at Metro Center; all except Red Line trains stop at L'Enfant Plaza; all but Blue and Orange Line trains stop at Gallery Place/Chinatown.

Metro stations are indicated by discreet brown columns bearing the station's name and topped by the letter M. Below the M is a colored stripe or stripes indicating the line or lines that stop there. When entering a Metro station for the first time, go to the kiosk and ask the station manager for a free **"Metro System Pocket Guide."** It contains a map of the system, explains how it works, and lists the

Major Metro Stops

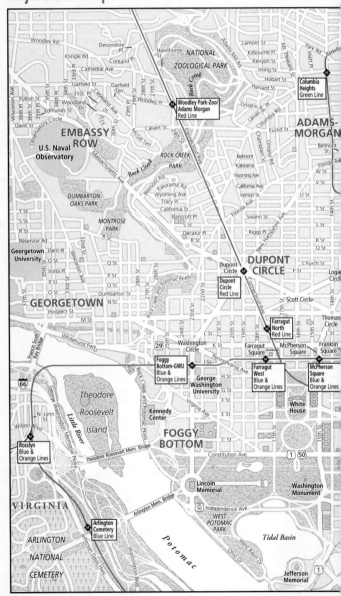

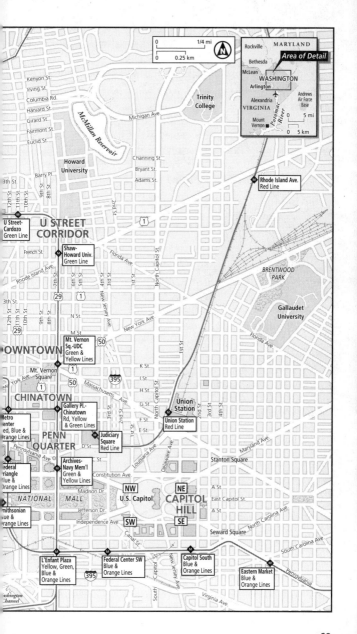

closest Metro stops to points of interest. The station manager can also answer questions about routing or purchase of fare cards.

To enter or exit a Metro station, you need a computerized **fare card,** available at vending machines near the entrance. The minimum fare to enter the system is $1.10, which pays for rides to and from any point within 7 miles of boarding during nonpeak hours; during peak hours (Mon–Fri 5:30–9:30am and 3–7pm), $1.10 takes you only 3 miles. The machines take nickels, dimes, quarters, and bills from $1 to $20; they can return up to $4.95 in change (coins only). If you plan to take several Metrorail trips during your stay, put more value on the farecard to avoid having to purchase a new card each time you ride. Up to two children under 5 can ride free with a paying passenger. Seniors (65 and older) and people with disabilities (with valid proof) ride Metrorail and Metrobus for a reduced fare.

Discount passes, called "One-Day Rail passes," cost $5 per person and allow you unlimited passage for the day, after 9:30am weekdays, and all day on Saturday, Sunday, and holidays. You can buy them at most stations; at WMATA headquarters, 600 5th St. NW (© **202/637-7000;** www.wmata.com), and at its sales office at Metro Center, 12th and G streets NW; or at retail stores, like Giant or Safeway grocery stores. Other passes are available—check out the website or call the main number for further information.

When you insert your card in the entrance gate, the time and location are recorded on its magnetic tape, and your card is returned. Don't forget to snatch it up and keep it handy; *you have to reinsert your farecard in the exit gate at your destination,* where the fare will automatically be deducted. The card will be returned if there's any value left on it. If you arrive at a destination and your fare card doesn't have enough value, add what's necessary at the Exitfare machines near the exit gate.

Tips Getting to Georgetown

Metrorail doesn't go to Georgetown but a special shuttle bus, called the Georgetown Metro Connection, links three Metro stations, Rosslyn, Foggy Bottom, and Dupont Circle, to Georgetown. The shuttle travels between the 3 stations and Georgetown every 10 minutes from 7am to midnight weekdays and until 2am weekends. One-way fares cost 50¢, or 25¢ with a Metrorail transfer.

> *Tips* **Safety for Pedestrians**
>
> Be careful crossing streets, especially in the downtown area,
> especially at rush hour. Though this may seem like obvious
> and silly advice, it's worth a mention here, as there's been an
> alarming increase lately in the number of pedestrians being
> hit by cars. Drivers in a hurry run red lights, turn corners too
> quickly, and so on, so be sure to take your time and check
> for oncoming traffic when crossing streets, and to use the
> crosswalks.

Metrorail opens at 5:30am weekdays and 8am Saturday and
Sunday, operating until midnight Sunday through Thursday, and
until 2am Friday and Saturday. Call © **202/637-7000,** or visit
www.wmata.com, for holiday hours and for information on Metro
routes.

BY BUS

While a 10-year-old can understand the Metrorail system, the
Metrobus system is considerably more complex. The 12,490 stops
on the 1,489-square-mile route (it operates on all major D.C. arteries as well as in the Virginia and Maryland suburbs) are indicated by
red, white, and blue signs. However, the signs tell you only what
buses pull into a given stop, not where they go. Furthermore, the
bus schedules posted at bus stops are often way out of date, so don't
rely on them. Instead, for routing information, call © **202/
637-7000.** Calls are taken Monday through Friday from 6am to
10:30pm, weekends and holidays from 8am to 10:30pm. This is the
same number you call to request a free map and time schedule,
information about parking in Metrobus fringe lots, and for locations and hours of the places where you can purchase bus tokens.

Base fare in the District is $1.10; bus transfers are free and valid
for 2 hours from boarding. There may be additional charges for
travel into the Maryland and Virginia suburbs. Bus drivers are not
equipped to make change, so be sure to carry exact change or
tokens. If you'll be in Washington for a while and plan to use the
buses a lot, consider buying a 1-week pass ($10), also available at the
Metro Center station and other outlets.

Most buses operate daily almost around the clock. Service is quite
frequent on weekdays, especially during peak hours. On weekends
and late at night, service is less frequent.

Up to two children under 5 ride free with a paying passenger on Metrobus, and there are reduced fares for seniors (℄ **202/637-7000**) and people with disabilities (℄ **202/962-1245** or 202/962-1100; see "Tips for Travelers with Special Needs," in chapter 1 for transit information for travelers with disabilities). If you should leave something on a bus, a train, or in a station, call Lost and Found at ℄ **202/962-1195.**

BY CAR

More than half of all visitors to the District arrive by car; but once you get here, my advice is to park your car and either walk or use Metrorail for getting around. If you must drive, be aware that traffic is always thick during the week, parking spaces are often hard to find, and parking lots are ruinously expensive.

Outside of the city, you'll want a car to get to most attractions in Virginia and Maryland. All the major car-rental companies are represented here, including Alamo, Avis, Budget, Dollar, Enterprise, Hertz, National, and Thrifty. In addition to locations at all three airports, car rental locations within the District include **Avis,** 1722 M St. NW (℄ 202/467-6585) and 4400 Connecticut Ave. NW (℄ 202/686-5149); **Budget,** Union Station (℄ 202/289-5374); **Enterprise,** 3307 M St. NW (℄ 202/338-0015); **Hertz,** 901 11th St. NW (℄ 202/628-6174); **National,** Union Station (℄ 202/842-7454); and **Thrifty,** 12th and K streets NW (℄ 202/371-0485).

BY TAXI

At the time of this writing, District cabs continue to operate on a zone system instead of using meters, and the cabbies hope to keep it that way. By law, basic rates are posted in each cab. If you take a trip from one point to another within the same zone, you pay just $5 (during non-rush hour) regardless of the distance traveled. So it would cost you $5 to travel a few blocks from the U.S. Capitol to the National Museum of American History, but the same $5 could take you from the Capitol all the way to Dupont Circle. They're both in Zone 1, as are most other tourist attractions: the White House, most of the Smithsonian, the Washington Monument, the FBI, the National Archives, the Supreme Court, the Library of Congress, the Bureau of Engraving and Printing, the Old Post Office, and Ford's Theatre. If your trip takes you into a second zone, the price is $8.40, $9.60 for a third zone, $10.10 for a fourth, and so on. These rates are based on the assumption that you are hailing a cab. If you telephone for a cab, you will be charged an additional

$1.50. During rush hour, between 7 and 9:30am and 4 and 6:30pm weekdays, you pay a surcharge of $1 per trip, plus a surcharge of $1.50 when you telephone for a cab, which brings that surcharge to $2.50.

Other charges might apply, as well: There's a $1.50 charge for each additional passenger after the first, so a $5 Zone 1 fare can become $10.50 for a family of four (though 1 child under 5 can ride free). Surcharges are also added for luggage (from 50¢ to $2 per piece, depending on size). Try **Diamond Cab Company** (© 202/387-6200), **Yellow Cab** (© 202/544-1212), or **Capitol Cab** (© 202/546-2400).

The zone system is not used when your destination is an out-of-District address (such as an airport); in that case, the fare is based on mileage—$2.65 for the first half-mile or part thereof and 80¢ for each additional half-mile or part. You can call © **202/331-1671** to find out the rate between any point in D.C. and an address in Virginia or Maryland. Call © **202/645-6018** to inquire about fares within the District.

It's generally easy to hail a taxi, although even taxis driven by black cabbies often ignore African Americans to pick up white passengers. Unique to the city is the practice of allowing drivers to pick up as many passengers as they can comfortably fit, so expect to share (unrelated parties pay the same as they would if they were not sharing). To register a complaint, note the cab driver's name and cab number and call © **202/645-6010.** You will be asked to file a written complaint either by fax (© **202/889-3604**) or mail (Commendations/Complaints, District of Columbia Taxicab Commission, 2041 Martin Luther King Jr. Ave. SE, Room 204, Washington, DC 20020).

 FAST FACTS: Washington, D.C.

American Express There's an American Express Travel Service office at 1150 Connecticut Ave. NW (© 202/457-1300) and another in upper northwest Washington at 5300 Wisconsin Ave. NW, in the Mazza Gallerie (© 202/362-4000).

Area Codes Within the District of Columbia, it's 202. In suburban Virginia, it's 703. In suburban Maryland, it's 301. You must use the area code when dialing any number, even local calls within the District or to nearby Maryland or Virginia suburbs.

Congresspersons To locate a senator or congressional representative, call the Capitol switchboard (© 202/225-3121). Point your Web browser to www.senate.gov and www.house.gov to contact individual senators and congressional representatives by e-mail, find out what bills are being worked on, the calendar for the day, and more.

Drugstores **CVS,** Washington's major drugstore chain (with more than 40 stores), has two convenient 24-hour locations: 14th Street and Thomas Circle NW, at Vermont Avenue (© 202/628-0720), and at Dupont Circle (© 202/785-1466), both with round-the-clock pharmacies. Check your phone book for other convenient locations.

Hospitals In case of a life-threatening emergency, call © **911.** If you don't require immediate ambulance transportation but still need emergency-room treatment, call one of the following hospitals (and be sure to get directions): **Children's Hospital National Medical Center,** 111 Michigan Ave. NW © 202/884-5000); **George Washington University Hospital,** 23rd St. NW at Washington Circle © 202/715-4000; **Georgetown University Medical Center,** 3800 Reservoir Rd. NW © 202/784-2000; or **Howard University Hospital,** 2041 Georgia Ave. NW (© 202/865-6100).

Hot Lines To reach a 24-hour poison-control hot line, call © **800/222-1222;** to reach a 24-hour crisis line, call © **202/561-7000;** and to reach the drug and alcohol abuse hot line, which operates from 8am to midnight daily, call © **888/294-3572.**

Internet Access You have free Internet access at the **Martin Luther King Jr. Memorial Library,** 901 G St. NW (© 202/727-1111; www.dclibrary.org), where you choose either a computer limited to 15 minutes' use or one limited to 1 hour's use; these are in high demand. Or try **Cyberstop Cafe,** 1513 17th St. NW (© 202/234-2470), where you can get a bite to eat while you surf one of nine computers for $6 per half hour, $8 per hour; the cafe is open from 7am to midnight daily. In Dupont Circle, the bookstore **Kramerbooks and Afterwords,** 1517 Connecticut Ave. NW (© 202/387-1400), has one computer available for free Internet access, 15 minute-limit.

Liquor Laws The legal age for purchase and consumption of alcoholic beverages is 21. Liquor stores are closed on Sunday. District gourmet grocery stores, mom-and-pop grocery stores, and 7-11 convenience stores often sell beer and wine, even on Sunday. Do not carry open containers of alcohol in your car in any public area that isn't zoned for alcohol consumption; police can fine you on the spot.

Maps Free city maps are often available at hotels and throughout town at tourist attractions. You can also contact the **Washington, D.C. Convention and Tourism Corporation,** 1212 New York Ave. NW, Washington, DC 20005 (© **202/789-7000**).

Newspapers & Magazines See "Visitor Information," in section 1 of this chapter.

Police In an emergency, dial © **911**. For a nonemergency, call © **202/727-1010**.

Taxes The sales tax on merchandise in 5.75% in the District, 5% in Maryland, and 4.5% in Virginia. The tax on restaurant meals in 10% in the District, 5% in Maryland, and 4.5% in Virginia. In the District, you pay 14.5% hotel tax. The hotel tax in Maryland varies by county but averages 12%. The hotel tax in Virginia also varies by county, averaging about 9.75%.

Time Washington is in the Eastern time zone. Clocks are advanced 1 hour April through October. For the correct time, call © **202/844-2525**.

Weather Call © **202/936-1212**.

3

Where to Stay

Most of Washington's 100-plus hotels center on the downtown and Dupont Circle neighborhoods, with a handful scattered in Georgetown, on Capitol Hill, and northward on Connecticut Avenue. Each of these communities has a distinct personality, which you should consider in choosing a location in which to base yourself. See the "Neighborhoods in Brief" section of chapter 2 to help you decide which location best suits you.

Within each neighborhood heading, this chapter further organizes hotels by rate categories, based on their lowest high-season rates for double rooms: Very Expensive (from about $250 and up), Expensive (from about $185), Moderate (from about $120), and Inexpensive (anything under $100). But these categories are intended as a general guideline only—rates can rise and fall dramatically, depending on how busy the hotel is. It's often possible to obtain a premium deal or better rate by asking the hotel whether special promotions or discounts are available for families, retirees, automobile or travel club participants, or for some other group of which you are a member.

1 Capitol Hill/The Mall

VERY EXPENSIVE

Hotel George ✮✮   Until the boutique hotels Rouge (p. 44) and Topaz (p. 50) came along the Hotel George was Washington's hippest place to stay. Well, it's still pretty rad. The hotel's facade is of stainless steel, limestone, and glass; the lobby is done in a sleek white, splashed with red, blue, and black furnishings; posters throughout the hotel depict a modern-day George Washington, sans wig; and clientele tends toward celebs (everyone from Christina Aguilera to Muhammad Ali). The oversize guest rooms sport a minimalist look, all creamy white and modern. Fluffy vanilla-colored comforters rest on oversize beds; slabs of granite top the desks and bathroom counters; and nature sounds (of the ocean, forest, and wind) emanate from the stereo CD/clock radios. A speaker in the spacious, mirrored, marble bathroom broadcasts TV sounds from the other room; other amenities include cordless phones, umbrellas, and terry-cloth robes. All rooms have high-speed Internet access; eighth-floor rooms also have fax machines, at no extra cost. The hotel has three one-bedroom suites.

Contributing to the hotel's hipness is the presence of its restaurant, **Bistro Bis,** which serves (duh) French bistro food to hungry lobbyists and those they are lobbying. (Capitol Hill is a block away.) See p. 63 for a full review.

15 E St. NW (at N. Capitol St.), Washington, DC 20001. ℂ **800/576-8331** or 202/ 347-4200. Fax 202/347-4213. www.hotelgeorge.com. 139 units. Weekdays $265–$350 double; weekends from $149 double; $950 suite. Ask about seasonal and corporate rates. Extra person $25. Children under 16 stay free in parents' room. AE, DC, DISC, MC, V. Parking $24. Metro: Union Station. **Amenities:** Restaurant (an excellent French bistro); small 24-hr. fitness center with steam rooms; cigar-friendly billiard room; 24-hr. concierge; business services; room service (7am–11pm); same-day laundry/dry cleaning; VCR rentals; 4 rooms for guests with disabilities. *In room:* A/C, TV w/pay movies, 2-line phone w/dataport, minibar, coffeemaker, hair dryer, iron, safe.

MODERATE

Capitol Hill Suites 🐾   Hotels frequently undergo refurbishments, though the changes may be barely noticeable to guests. But the $3 million renovation completed at this well-run, all-suite property in spring 2000 produced remarkable results. The old, outmoded decor has been replaced with panache. Bedroom walls are painted cobalt blue, heavy velvet drapes keep out morning sun, lamps and mirrors are from Pottery Barn, desks are long, desk chairs are ergonomically correct, and beds are firm. Bathrooms are tiny, but sparkling. The lobby, which features an enclosed fireplace, leather chairs, and an antique credenza where self-serve coffee is laid out, is inviting enough for lingering. (Sit here long enough and you might spy a congressman or senator—a number of members reserve suites for 100 days at a time.)

The location is another plus: Capitol Hill Suites is the only hotel truly *on* the Hill (on the House side of the Capitol). It stands on a residential street across from the Library of Congress, a short walk from the Capitol and Mall attractions, a food market, and more than 20 restaurants (many of which deliver to the hotel).

The term *suite* denotes the fact that every unit has a kitchenette with coffeemaker, toaster oven, microwave, refrigerator, flatware, and glassware. Most units are efficiencies, with the kitchenette, bed, and sofa all in the same room. The best choices are one-bedroom units, in which the kitchenette and living room are separate from

Washington, D.C., Accommodations

See "Adams-Morgan & Dupont Circle Accommodations" Map

Columbia Heights Green Line

NATIONAL ZOOLOGICAL PARK

Woodley Park-Zoo/ Adams Morgan Red Line

ADAMS-MORGAN

EMBASSY ROW

U.S. Naval Observatory

ROCK CREEK PARK

DUMBARTON OAKS PARK

MONTROSE PARK

Georgetown University

Dupont Circle Red Line

DUPONT CIRCLE

Farragut North Red Line

GEORGETOWN

Washington Circle

Farragut Square

McPherson Square

Franklin Square

Theodore Roosevelt Island

Foggy Bottom-GWU Blue & Orange Lines

George Washington University

Farragut West Blue & Orange Lines

McPherson Square Blue & Orange Lines

Rosslyn Blue & Orange Lines

Kennedy Center

FOGGY BOTTOM

White House

VIRGINIA

Arlington Cemetery Blue Line

Lincoln Memorial

Washington Monument

ARLINGTON NATIONAL CEMETERY

Potomac

WEST POTOMAC PARK

Tidal Basin

Jefferson Memorial

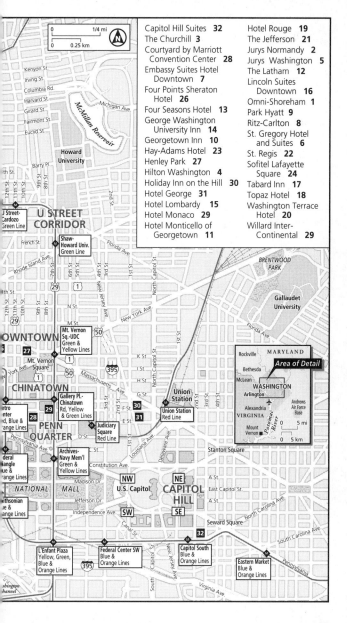

Capitol Hill Suites **32**
The Churchill **3**
Courtyard by Marriott
Convention Center **28**
Embassy Suites Hotel
Downtown **7**
Four Points Sheraton
Hotel **26**
Four Seasons Hotel **13**
George Washington
University Inn **14**
Georgetown Inn **10**
Hay-Adams Hotel **23**
Henley Park **27**
Hilton Washington **4**
Holiday Inn on the Hill **30**
Hotel George **31**
Hotel Lombardy **15**
Hotel Monaco **29**
Hotel Monticello of
Georgetown **11**

Hotel Rouge **19**
The Jefferson **21**
Jurys Normandy **2**
Jurys Washington **5**
The Latham **12**
Lincoln Suites
Downtown **16**
Omni-Shoreham **1**
Park Hyatt **9**
Ritz-Carlton **8**
St. Gregory Hotel
and Suites **6**
St. Regis **22**
Sofitel Lafayette
Square **24**
Tabard Inn **17**
Topaz Hotel **18**
Washington Terrace
Hotel **20**
Willard Inter-
Continental **29**

33

(Kids) Family-Friendly Hotels

Embassy Suites Hotel Downtown *(p. 51)*   You're close to both a Red line and a Blue line Metro station (the zoo is on the Red line; the Smithsonian museums are on the Blue line) and within walking distance of Georgetown. Your kids can sleep on the pullout sofa in the separate living room. You've got some kitchen facilities, but you might not use them, since the complimentary breakfast in the atrium is unbelievable. And there's an indoor pool and a free game room.

Holiday Inn on the Hill *(p. 35)*   Children receive a free toy and a book on arrival during summer promotions. Kids 12 and under eat free in the restaurant with an adult dining. The hotel is near Union Station, Capitol Hill, and the Mall and Smithsonian museums, and the kitchen will pack a picnic for you to enjoy on the Mall. Connecting rooms are available. Kids ages 4 to 14 can participate in the hotel's Discovery Zone program of activities 4 to 10pm daily in summer ($5 per child). The hotel has a rooftop outdoor pool.

Omni Shoreham *(p. 60)*   Adjacent to Rock Creek Park, the Omni is also within walking distance of the zoo and Metro and is equipped with a large outdoor pool and kiddie pool. The hotel gives children a goodie bag on check-in and the concierge has a supply of board games at the ready (no charge to borrow, just remember to return).

Hilton Washington *(p. 48)*   A large heated outdoor pool, a wading pool, three tennis courts, shuffleboard, and a goodie bag at check-in—what more does a kid need?

the bedroom. A third option is a "studio double," with two queen beds and a kitchenette, but no living room area. Some rooms in each category have pullout sofas.

Guests have privileges to dine at the nearby Capitol Hill Club, a members-only social club for Republicans, and can charge their meals and drinks to their hotel bill.

200 C St. SE (at 2nd St.), Washington, DC 20003. ℂ **800/424-9165** or 202/543-6000. Fax 202/547-2608. www.capitolhillsuites.com. 152 units. $119–$239 double. Weekend and long-term rates may be available. Extra person $22. Rates include

continental breakfast. Children under 18 stay free in parents' room. AE, DC, DISC, MC, V. Valet parking $20. Metro: Capitol South. **Amenities:** Breakfast room, dining privileges at Capitol Hill Club; free use of nearby Washington Sports and Health Club; business services; coin-op washer/dryers; same-day laundry/dry cleaning; 10 rooms for visitors with disabilities, all with roll-in showers. *In room:* A/C, TV w/pay movies, 2-line phone w/dataport, fridge, coffeemaker, hair dryer, iron.

INEXPENSIVE

Holiday Inn on the Hill *Kids Value*   Business travelers without bottomless expense accounts and families on a budget will likely find this hotel's rates the most reasonable on Capitol Hill. Several labor union headquarters are nearby, making the hotel a popular choice among the "labor" folks doing business with one of them. Amenities, like the free 24-hour fitness center, seasonal (outdoor) pool, and the "kids 12 and under eat free" restaurant policy, increase the value of a stay here. Best of all for families is the Discovery Zone—available from 4 to 10pm daily in summer for a charge of $5 per kid per day— a supervised program offering fun but educational activities for children ages 4 to 14. (See the Holiday Inn entry in the "Family-Friendly Hotels" box on p. 34 for more details on their perks for kids.)

A major renovation completed in 1999 added new bedspreads, drapes, shower curtains, 25-inch TVs with Nintendo, and individually controlled thermostats. The staff aims to make you feel at home here. Rooms are standard size, though bathrooms are larger than expected, with a small vanity ledge just outside the bathroom for overflow counter space.

To get the best deals and perks, ask about summer promotions, the "Great Rates" package, and the hotel's "Priority Club" frequent guest membership.

415 New Jersey Ave. NW (between D and E sts.). (C) **800/638-1116** or 202/638-1616. Fax 202/638-0707. www.basshotels.com/was-onthehill. 343 units. $109–$225 double (Mon and Tues are the most expensive days). Extra person $20. Children under 19 stay free in parents' room. Ask about special promotions and packages. AE, DC, DISC, MC, V. Parking $18. Metro: Union Station. **Amenities:** Restaurant (American), where kids ages 12 and under eat free with an adult; bar; outdoor (unheated) rooftop pool; 24-hr. fitness room; children's program and game room in summer; concierge; business center; room service (6am–11pm); same-day laundry/dry cleaning service; large ballroom; ATM in the lobby; 8 rooms for guests with disabilities, including 4 with roll-in showers. *In room:* A/C, TV w/pay movies, 2-line phone w/dataport, coffeemaker, hair dryer, iron.

2 Downtown, East of 16th Street NW

VERY EXPENSIVE

Hotel Monaco Washington, DC *★★★*   You may mistake this hotel for a museum. The Monaco occupies a four-story, all marble mid-19th-century building, half of which was designed by Robert Mills, the architect for the Washington Monument, the other half designed by Thomas Walter, one of the architects for the U.S. Capitol. The two halves connect seamlessly, enclosing a large interior, landscaped courtyard—picture a square within a square. (As a matter of fact, this is the same design as that of the two Smithsonian museums directly across the street from the Monaco; the Smithsonian American Art Museum and the National Portrait Gallery, both closed for renovations until 2005, join to form a central courtyard, too.) The hotel takes up an entire block, between 7th and 8th streets, and E and F streets. Superlatives are in order: The hotel is truly magnificent.

Constructed originally as the General Post Office, and later used to house the Tariff Commission, the building is a designated National Historic Landmark, and it remains a federal building. The Kimpton Hotel and Restaurant Group has leased the building for 60 years, performing an extensive renovation, which retains many original features, as required by its historic status, that blend creatively with the hotel's humming, hip, upscale decor. So you've got 19th-century columns uplit by Italian chrome and alabaster torchieres in the lobby, grand spiral staircases at each of the four corners, and high vaulted ceilings along corridors lit with whimsical, lantern-like red lamps.

The spacious guest rooms, similarly, combine historic and hip. Their vaulted ceilings are high (12 ft.–18 ft.) and windows are long, hung with charcoal and white patterned drapes. Each guest room has a removable bathroom module (its modular status is only apparent when you stand in your guest room and note that the bathroom ceiling lies a couple of feet below the overall ceiling of the room). A stand-alone headboard, upholstered in a funky black and white bull's-eye pattern, also screens a door behind the bed, which, in the building's former life, led to the next office. Eclectic furnishings include neoclassic armoires and three-legged desks. A color scheme successfully marries creamy yellow walls with periwinkle blue lounge chairs, with orange damask pillows. Interior rooms overlook the courtyard and the restaurant; you'll see the charming arched passageway through which horse and carriage came a century ago. Exterior rooms view the MCI Center and the Smithsonian's National Portrait Gallery on the north side, and downtown sights on the south side. This is a great location.

Need more? The Hotel Monaco gives you a complimentary goldfish at check-in; offers specially designed "Tall Rooms" with

18-foot-high ceilings, 96-inch-long beds, and raised shower heads, for tall guests. Its restaurant, **Poste**, is gaining attention. Though it only just opened in summer 2002, the Hotel Monaco is already a winner.

700 F St. NW (at 7th St.), Washington, DC 20004. 📞 **877/202-5411** or 202/628-7177. Fax 202/628-7277. www.monaco-dc.com. 184 units. Weekdays $295 double, weekends $199 double; suites from $825 weekdays, $469 weekends. Extra person $20. Children under 18 stay free in parents' room. Rates include complimentary Starbucks coffee in morning and wine receptions in evening. AE, DC, DISC, MC, V. Parking $27. Pets allowed with $50 deposit: gets VIP treatment, with its own registration card at check-in, maps of neighborhood fire hydrants and parks, gourmet puppy and kitty treats. Metro: Gallery Place. **Amenities:** Restaurant (modern American); bar; spacious fitness center with flat screen TVs; 24-hr. concierge; full-service business center; 24-hr. room service; same-day laundry/dry cleaning; 9 rooms for guests with disabilities, 4 with roll-in showers. *In room:* A/C, TV w/pay movies and Nintendo, CD player, 2-line phones w/high-speed Internet access and dataports, minibar, hair dryer, iron, safe, robes.

Sofitel Lafayette Square, Washington, D.C. 🖈🖈

The Hay-Adams faces some competition with the summer 2002 opening of this luxury hotel, which, like the Hay-Adams, borders Lafayette Square and is just minutes from the White House. The Hay-Adams offers White House views, and the Sofitel does not, it's true, but the Sofitel's other appealing features may make up for that.

This handsome, 12-story limestone building was erected in the early 20th century, and its distinctive facade includes decorative bronze corner panels, bas-relief sculptural panels at ground-floor level, and a 12th-floor balcony that travels the length of both the H and 15th street-sides of the structure (decorative, not accessible, alas). Inside, hotel staff dressed in designer uniforms greet you with *"Bonjour!,"* small hints that a French company (Accor Hotels) owns the Sofitel. Noted French designer Pierre-Yves Rochon styled the interior; a Michelin three-star chef is behind the contemporary French cuisine served in Café 15, the hotel's restaurant; and the gift shop sells such specialty items as French plates and porcelain dolls.

Because of its corner location and exceptionally large windows, guest rooms are bright with natural light; second- and third-floor rooms facing 15th or H street bring in more light still, because their windows extend nearly from floor to ceiling. Each room sports an elegantly modern decor that includes a long desk, creamy duvet with a colorful throw on a king-size bed (about 17 rooms have 2 double beds instead of kings), a much-marbled bathroom with tub separate from the shower stall, fresh flowers, and original artwork, including dramatic photographs of Washington landmarks. The

11th floor has been designed with visiting heads of state in mind, and can be easily secured. In each of the 17 suites, the bedroom is separate from the living room.

806 15th St. NW (at H St.), Washington, DC 20005. ℂ **800/763-4835** or 202/737-8800. Fax 202/639-4677. www.sofitel.com. 254 units. Weekdays $275–$480 double; weekends, call for rates, which can start as low as $199 for a double; from $495 suite. For lowest rates at any time, call directly to the hotel and ask about specials or packages; also check out the website. Extra person $25. Children under 12 stay free in parents' room. AE, DC, DISC, MC, V. Parking $24. Pets allowed. Metro: McPherson Square, Farragut West, or Farragut North. **Amenities:** Restaurant (contemporary French); bar; fitness center with 14 pieces of state-of the art equipment; 24-hr. concierge; business services; 24-hr. room service; same-day laundry/dry cleaning; 8 rooms for guests with disabilities, all with roll-in showers. *In room:* A/C, TV with pay movies and Nintendo, CD player, 2-line phones w/high-speed Internet access and dataports, minibar, hair dryer, iron, safe, robes and slippers.

Willard Inter-Continental 𝄃𝄃𝄃   If you're lucky enough to stay here, you'll be a stone's throw from the White House and the Smithsonian museums, in the heart of downtown near plenty of excellent restaurants, down the block from the National Theater, and down the avenue from the Capitol. The Willard is definitely the classiest hotel in this neighborhood, among the best in the city, and also, naturally, one of the most expensive. Heads of state favor the Willard (the hotel offers 1 floor as "Secret Service–cleared"), as do visitors from other countries (the gift shop sells newspapers from around the world) and movie directors (who like to shoot scenes in the famously ornate lobby and restaurant).

A renovation completed in late 2000 spruced up the guest rooms' handsome, if staid, decor, which is heavy on reproduction Federal- and Edwardian-style furnishings. The rooms with the best views are the oval suites overlooking Pennsylvania Avenue to the Capitol and the rooms fronting Pennsylvania Avenue. Rooms facing the courtyard are the quietest. Best of all is the "Jenny Lind" suite, perched in the curve of the 12th floor's southeast corner; its round bull's-eye window captures glimpses of the Capitol.

The Willard's designation as a National Historic Landmark in 1974 and magnificent restoration in the 1980s helped revitalize Pennsylvania Avenue and this part of town. Stop in at the Round Robin Bar for a mint julep (introduced here), and listen to bartender and manager Jim Hewes spin tales about the history of the 1901 Willard and its predecessor, the City Hotel, built on this site in 1815.

Always inquire about off-season and weekend packages, when rates are sometimes halved and come with one of five complimentary options, including an upgrade to a suite, valet parking, or a second room at half price.

1401 Pennsylvania Ave. NW (at 14th St.), Washington, DC 20004. ℂ **800/327-0200** or 202/628-9100. Fax 202/637-7326. www.washington.interconti.com. 341 units. Weekdays $480 double, weekends from $199; $850–$4,200 suite. Extra person $30. Children under 18 stay free in parents' room. Ask about special promotions and packages. AE, DC, DISC, MC, V. Parking $23. Metro: Metro Center. Small pets allowed if guest signs waiver. **Amenities:** Restaurant (the excellent Willard Room); cafe; fabulous bar (The Round Robin); modest-size but state-of-the-art fitness center; children's programs; concierge; business center; 24-hr. room service; babysitting; same-day laundry/dry cleaning; currency exchange; airline/train ticketing. *In room:* A/C, TV, 2-line phone w/dataport, minibar, hair dryer, iron, safe, robes.

EXPENSIVE

Courtyard by Marriott Convention Center ℝ   Downtown
Washington needs more places like this—a conveniently situated, reasonably priced, medium-size property with a better-than-average restaurant on site. The hotel itself is only a few years old, but the eight-story building, with its handsome stonework and many arches, is a historic landmark, constructed in 1891 to house a bank. The bank's safe-deposit vault, with its original 2-foot-thick circular door, now holds a boardroom, and the marble-floored, columned space that was once the bank's lobby has been reincarnated as the upscale brewery restaurant, Gordon Biersch. Rooms have firm mattresses, chairs and ottomans, large desks, good-size bathrooms, and lots of windows with views of downtown. (The best views—including glimpses of the Washington Monument and the Capitol—are on the Ninth Street side, the higher up the better.) Rooms 715 and 1015 are especially recommended; each is exceptionally large and has a sofa and many oval-shaped windows. You'll be across the street from the MCI Center, around the corner from Ford's Theatre, 1 block from the FBI, and 2½ blocks from the convention center. Lots of really good restaurants are nearby, and if you don't feel like going out, they'll deliver.

900 F St. NW (at 9th St. NW), Washington, DC 20004. ℂ **800/321-2211** or 202/638-4600. Fax 202/638-4601. www.courtyard.com/wascn. 188 units. Weekdays $219 double, weekends $129–$189 double; from $265 suite. No charge for extra person in room. AE, DC, DISC, MC, V. Parking $22. Metro: Gallery Place or Metro Center. **Amenities:** Restaurant (American) and brewery; small fitness center with pool and whirlpool; small business center; room service (during dinner hours only); coin-op washer/dryers; same-day dry cleaning; 6 rooms for guests with disabilities, some with roll-in showers. *In room:* A/C, TV w/pay movies, 2-line phone w/dataport, coffeemaker, hair dryer, iron.

Henley Park ℝ   This intimate English-style hotel with 119 gargoyles on its facade was originally an apartment house. Built in

1918, the stunning building retains many of its Tudor-style features, including the lobby's exquisite ceiling, archways, and leaded windows. The hotel's popular restaurant, bar, and parlor received facelifts in late 2000, while an ongoing renovation recently replaced wallpaper, linens, and other items in all the guest rooms. Luxurious appointments make this a good choice for upscale romantic weekends, although these lodgings fill up with corporate travelers on weekdays. Rooms are decorated in the English country house mode, with Hepplewhite-, Chippendale-, and Queen Anne–style furnishings, including lovely period beds. Rooms and bathrooms are of standard size. A handful of suites are either one-bedroom or junior (combined living room and bedroom). Look in the Sunday *New York Times* "Travel" section for ads posting low rates.

926 Massachusetts Ave. NW (at 10th St.), Washington, DC 20001. © **800/ 222-8474** or 202/638-5200. Fax 202/638-6740. www.henleypark.com. 96 units. Weekdays $185–$245 double, summer and weekends $99–$159 double; suites from $325 weekdays, look for much lower rates on weekends. Extra person $20. Children under 14 stay free in parents' room. AE, DC, DISC, MC, V. Parking $16. Metro: Metro Center, Gallery Place, or Mt. Vernon Square. Very small pets allowed; you must call in advance. **Amenities:** Restaurant (New American); pub (with pianist Tues–Thurs evenings, live jazz and dancing on weekends), afternoon tea (daily 4–6pm); access to a fitness room in the Morrison-Clark Historic Inn across the street; 24-hr. concierge; complimentary weekday-morning sedan service to downtown and Capitol Hill; business services; room service during restaurant hours; same-day laundry/dry cleaning. *In room:* A/C, TV, 2-line speaker phone w/dataport, minibar, coffeemaker, hair dryer, iron, safe, robes.

MODERATE

Washington Terrace Hotel ⭐ For all intents and purposes, this is a new hotel, the transformation of the former Doubletree property being so utterly complete. Beautifully landscaped terraces front and back help create a buffer for this urban hotel. The flow of the public spaces leading back to the garden courtyard, and abundant use of earth tones and sandstone in decor accentuate the hotel's theme of "bringing the outdoors in." This theme resonates in the guest rooms, whose light golden wallcoverings feature an abstract botanical pattern, and whose windows are larger than the hotel norm, delivering lots of natural light. Ask for a room at the front of the house for a view of Scott Circle, the park across the street, and the city; request a room at the back for a view of the garden terrace. Best rooms are those on floors six through eight, all of which are spacious suites and have small wet bars, a dining table and sleeper sofa, high-speed Internet access, and larger bathrooms. Though the Washington Terrace calls itself an "upscale boutique hotel," I think its large size and its practical amenities, like ergonomic chairs in the guest rooms and extensive conference and party facilities, disqualify it. Still, the guest rooms do have a boutiquey feel, thanks to imaginative touches such as granite-topped desks, circular nightstands, and a blueberry toned wall behind the bed (the suites feature other colors: aubergine, nectar, and sienna), contrasting with the light toned coverings on the other walls.

1515 Rhode Island Ave. NW (at Scott Circle), Washington, DC 20005. © **866/984-6835** or 202/232-7000. Fax 202/332-8436. www.washingtonterracehotel.com. 220 units. Weekdays $139–$189, weekends $119–$149 double and suite. Extra person $30. Children 16 and under stay free in parents' room. AE, DC, DISC, MC, V. Parking $22. Metro: Dupont Circle or McPherson Square. **Amenities:** Restaurant (contemporary American with Southern flair); bar; fitness center with universal gym, free weights, treadmills, and life cycles; 24-hr. concierge; full-service business center; 24-hr. room service; same-day laundry/dry cleaning; 10 rooms for guests with disabilities, 2 with roll-in showers. *In room:* A/C, TV w/pay movies, radio/CD player, 2-line phones w/dataport, minibar, hair dryer, iron, safe, robes.

INEXPENSIVE

Four Points Sheraton, Washington, D.C. Downtown ⍟ *Value*

This former Days Inn has been totally transformed into a contemporary property that offers all the latest gizmos, from high-speed Internet access in all the rooms to a 2,000-square-foot fitness center. A massive renovation undertaken by a new owner essentially gutted the old building, but the location is still as terrific as ever (close to the Convention Center, MCI Center, and downtown). Best of all, the rates are reasonable, and spectacular hotel amenities make this a good choice for both business and leisure visitors.

Five types of rooms are available: units with two double beds, with one queen bed, or with one king bed; junior suites; or one-bedroom suites. Corner rooms (there are only about 10) are a little more spacious than others, which are of standard size. While guest rooms offer city views, the rooftop pool and lounge boasts a sweeping vista of the city that includes the Capitol. Under separate ownership from the hotel is a recommended restaurant, Corduroy.

1201 K St. NW (at 12th St.), Washington, DC 20005. © **888/481-7191** or 202/289-7600. Fax 202/289-3310. www.fourpointswashingtondc.com. 265 units. In season $99–$275 double, off-season $99–$245 double; from $400 suite. Extra person $20. Children under 18 stay free in parents' room. AE, DC, DISC, MC, V. Parking $22. Metro: McPherson Square or Metro Center. **Amenities:** Restaurant (seasonal American); bar; indoor heated pool on rooftop; fitness center; business center; room service (6am–midnight); same-day laundry/dry cleaning; executive-level rooms; 5 rooms for guests with disabilities, 3 with roll-in showers. *In room:* A/C, TV w/pay movies, 2-line phone w/dataport, minibar, coffeemaker, hair dryer, iron, safe.

3 Downtown, 16th Street NW & West

VERY EXPENSIVE

Hay-Adams Hotel 🏨🏨 An extensive $18 million renovation completed in spring 2002 was the Hay-Adams's first major refurbishment in its 75 year history. Some improvements, like the new heating and air-conditioning system and structural changes that make the hotel accessible to guests with disabilities, were long overdue. Other improvements, like the modernized kitchen, will be invisible to guests. Most of the changes will be obvious to anyone who has visited the hotel in the past: the custom-fitted staff uniforms; an elegant decor of sage green, off-white, beige, and gold tones; and CD players, high-speed Internet access, custom European linens, new furnishings (the hotel donated its old furniture to local homeless shelters), and thermostats in each room.

But the best of the Hay-Adams remains much the same. The hotel still offers the best views in town. Reserve a room on the sixth through eighth floors on the H Street side of the hotel (or as low as the 2nd floor in winter, when the trees are bare), pull back the curtains from the windows, and *voilà!*—you get a full frontal view of Lafayette Square, the White House, and the Washington Monument in the background. (You'll pay more for rooms with these views.) The view from rooms facing 16th Street isn't bad, either: Windows overlook the yellow-painted exterior of St. John's Episcopal Church, built in 1815, and known as the "church of the presidents."

The Hay-Adams is one in the triumvirate of exclusive hotels built by Harry Wardman in the 1920s (the Jefferson and the St. Regis are the other two). Its architecture is Italian Renaissance and much of the original features, such as ornate plaster moldings and ornamental fireplaces, the walnut-paneled lobby, and high-ceilinged guest rooms, are still in place. The hotel has about 15 one-bedroom suites (the living room and bedroom are separate) and seven junior suites (living room and bedroom are together in one space).

One Lafayette Square (at 16th and H sts. NW), Washington, DC 20006. ✆ **800/ 424-5054** or 202/638-6600. Fax 202/638-2716. www.hayadams.com. 145 units. Weekdays $345–$545 double, weekends $259–$425 double; from $1,000 suite. Extra person $30. Children under 17 stay free in parents' room. AE, DC, DISC, MC, V. Valet parking $28. Metro: Farragut West or McPherson Square. Small dogs accepted. **Amenities:** Restaurant (American); bar; access to local health club ($15 per day); 24-hr. concierge; complimentary morning car service; secretarial and business services; 24-hr. room service; same-day laundry/dry cleaning, 9 rooms for guests with disabilities. *In room:* A/C, TV with pay movies, 2-line phone w/dataport, minibar, hair dryer, iron, safe, umbrella, robes.

The Jefferson, a Loews Hotel 🐾🐾   Opened in 1923 just 4 blocks from the White House, the Jefferson is one of the city's three most exclusive hotels (along with the Hay-Adams and the St. Regis). Those looking for an intimate hotel, with excellent service, a good restaurant, sophisticated but comfortable accommodations, inviting public rooms (should you want to hang out), and proximity to attractions and restaurants (should you not want to hang out) will find that the Jefferson satisfies on all scores. About one-third of the lodgings are suites: junior, one- and two-bedroom size. The hotel's largest rooms are located in the "carriage house," an attached town house with its own elevator, which you reach by passing through the pub/lounge in the main building. Guest rooms were last upgraded in 2000 and are individually decorated with antiques and lovely fabrics, evoking a European feel.

The lobby was refurbished in 2001; a fine art collection, including original documents signed by Thomas Jefferson, graces the public areas as well as the guest rooms. Many local foodies like to dine at the hotel's acclaimed **Restaurant at the Jefferson.** And the paneled pub/lounge is another popular stopping place for Washingtonians; here you can sink into a red-leather chair and enjoy a marvelous high tea or cocktails.

1200 16th St. NW (at M St.), Washington, DC 20036. ✆ **800/235-6397** or 202/347-2200. Fax 202/331-7982. www.loewshotels.com. 100 units. Weekdays $319–$339 double, $350–$1,200 suite; weekends from $199 double, from $289 suite. Extra person $25. Children under 12 stay free in parents' room. AE, DC, DISC, MC, V. Parking $20. Metro: Farragut North. Pets welcomed and pampered. **Amenities:** Restaurant (American); bar/lounge (serving high tea 3–5pm); access to nearby health club (with pool) at the University Club across the street ($20 per visit); children's program (care package at check-in); 24-hr. concierge; 24-hr. room service; 24-hr. butler service; in-room massage; babysitting; same-day laundry/dry cleaning; 2 rooms for guests with disabilities, both with roll-in showers; video and CD rentals. *In room:* A/C, TV w/pay movies and VCR, CD player, 2-line phone w/dataport, minibar, hair dryer, safe, robes.

St. Regis 🐾🐾   If all goes according to plan, by the time you read this the St. Regis will be the most technologically advanced hotel on the East Coast. Think plasma televisions (the flat-screen TVs that are set in the wall), which you can program to play tomorrow's scheduled shows today, or to pick up a movie where you left off when you last stayed at the hotel. The hotel is undergoing a top-to-bottom renovation that will make it a marvel of technology, while enhancing its palace-like accommodations. The decor specifics are still being decided at this writing, but you can be sure that luxury will be the order of the day. Some St. Regis amenities that will carry on include the concierge level (called the "Astor Floor"), where a butler unpacks and packs your suitcase, presses two items upon your arrival, and generally sees to your needs. The best rooms (other than those on the Astor Floor) probably will still be the grand deluxe units, which are oversize traditional rooms with a sitting area. The number of one-bedroom suites most likely will increase to about 26. The hotel will continue to offer a top-notch restaurant, as well as its Library Lounge, a contender for the title of best hotel bar in Washington, with a working fireplace and paneled walls lined with bookcases.

923 16th St. NW (at K St.), Washington, DC 20006. ℭ 800/562-5661 or 202/638-2626. Fax 202/638-4231. www.stregis.com. 193 units. Weekdays $220–$460 double, weekends $189–$405 double; from $600 suite. For best rates, check the website or call the hotel directly to ask about special promotions. Children under 16 stay free in parents' room. AE, DC, DISC, MC, V. Parking $24. Metro: Farragut West or McPherson Square. Small pets allowed for $25 per night. **Amenities:** Restaurant (American); 1 bar/lounge; 24-hr. state-of-the-art fitness room (plus access, for $25 fee, to either of 2 nearby health clubs, 1 of which has an indoor lap pool); bike rentals; concierge; complimentary 1-way transportation within 8 blocks of hotel (7–9:30am weekdays); business center; 24-hr. room service; in-room massage; babysitting; same-day laundry/dry cleaning; concierge-level rooms; 8 rooms for guests with disabilities, all with roll-in showers. *In room:* A/C, TV w/pay movies, fax, 2-line phone w/dataport, minibar, coffeemaker, hair dryer, iron, safe, robes.

EXPENSIVE

Hotel Rouge⚝ High-energy rock music dances out onto the sidewalk. A red awning extends from the entrance. A guest with sleepy eyes and brilliant blue hair sits diffidently upon the white tufted leather sofa in the small lobby. Attractive, casually dressed patrons come and go, while an older couple roosts at a table just inside the doorway of the adjoining Bar Rouge sipping martinis at 2 in the afternoon. Shades of red are everywhere: in the staff's funky shiny shirts, in the accent pillows on the retro furniture, and in the artwork. This used to be a Quality Hotel: It's come a long way, baby.

The Kimpton Hotel Group (known for its offbeat but upscale boutique accommodations) has transformed five old D.C. buildings into these cleverly crafted and sexy hotels (see the Topaz and Hotel Monaco reviews in this chapter; hotels Helix and Madeira were expected to open in late 2002). In the case of Rouge, this means that your guest room will have deep crimson drapes at the window, a floor-to-ceiling red "pleather" headboard for your comfortable, white-with-red piping duvet-covered bed, and, in the dressing room, an Orange Crush–colored dresser, whose built-in minibar holds all sorts of red items, such as Hot Tamales candies, rex wax lips, and Red Bull. Guest rooms in most boutique hotels are notoriously cramped; not so here, where the rooms are spacious enough to easily accommodate several armchairs and a large ottoman (in shades of red and gold), a number of funky little lamps, a huge, mahogany framed mirror leaning against a wall, and a 10-foot-long mahogany desk. The Rouge has no suites but does offer 15 specialty guest rooms, including "Chill Rooms," which have DVD players and Sony PlayStation, "Chat Rooms," which have high-speed Internet access and computer/printers, and "Chow Rooms," which have a microwave and refrigerator. If you look at Rouge's website, you'll see that the hotel embraces the idea of "indulgence," a theme born out in the complimentary morning bloody mary bar set up in the lobby 10am to 11am, and in the Bar Rouge, where you can settle into thronelike armchairs and order drinks like "Sin on the Rocks" (blackberry schnapps, passion fruit Alize, and lime juice) and the Love Gun (ingredients a secret), as well as seductive bar food. See p. 161 for more info about Bar Rouge.

1315 16th St. NW (at Massachusetts Ave. NW and Scott Circle), Washington, DC 20036. ✆ **800/368-5689** or 202/232-8000. Fax 202/667-9827. www.rougehotel. com. 137 units. Weekdays $220–$255 double; weekends $125 double;. $260 for specialty rooms weekdays, $165 specialty rooms weekends. Best rates available by calling the 800-number and asking for promotional rate. Extra person $20. Rates include complimentary bloody marys from 10–11am. Children under 16 stay free in parents' room. AE, DC, DISC, MC, V. Parking $20. Metro: Dupont Circle. Refundable security deposit of $50 with pets, who are pampered here. **Amenities:** Bar/restaurant (innovative American, with a Latin flair); modest size fitness center with treadmill, stationary bikes; 24-hr. concierge; business center; room service (7am–11pm); same-day laundry/dry cleaning; 6 rooms for guests with disabilities, 1 with roll-in showers; *In room:* A/C, 27-in. flat-screen TV with pay movies, CD player, 2-line cordless phones w/dataport, minibar, coffeemaker (with Starbucks coffee), hair dryer, iron, robes.

MODERATE

Lincoln Suites Downtown ★★ ⟨Value⟩   This is a little hotel with a big heart. It tries hard to do right by its guests and, judging from feedback I've received from readers who've stayed here, I would say it succeeds. (Check out the website, where the hotel's can-do personality shines through.) Key elements include the hotel's location, in the heart of downtown, near Metro stops, restaurants, and the White House; a congenial staff; the complimentary milk and homemade cookies served each evening; and daily complimentary continental breakfast in the lobby. Lincoln Suites also has direct access to **Mackey's,** an Irish pub right next door (a second on-site restaurant is expected to open by the time you read this), and room service for lunch and dinner is delivered from **Luigi's** ✦, an Italian restaurant and veritable Washington institution (p. 81), which is right around the corner.

The all-suite 10-story hotel is quite nice, in a nothing-fancy sort of way. Lots of long-term guests bunk here. Suites are large and comfortable; about 28 offer full kitchens, while the rest have kitchenettes. An ongoing renovation has slowly but surely overhauled the hotel, replacing all the furniture, appliances, carpeting, and wall coverings. Most recently, the previously cramped lobby was transformed into a hip two-story lobby/lounge.

1823 L St. NW, Washington, DC 20036. ✆ **800/424-2970** or 202/223-4320. Fax 202/223-8546. www.lincolnhotels.com. 99 suites. Weekdays $129–$199, weekends $99–$139. Rates include continental breakfast. Discounts available for long-term stays. Children under 16 stay free in parents' room. AE, DC, DISC, MC, V. Parking $16 (in adjoining garage). Metro: Farragut North or Farragut West. Pets under 25 lb. accepted, second floor only, for $15 a day. **Amenities:** Bar/restaurant (Irish); free passes to the well-equipped Bally's Holiday Spa nearby; 24-hr. front desk/concierge; room service (11am–11pm); coin-op washer/dryers; same-day laundry/dry cleaning; 2 rooms for guests with disabilities, 1 with roll-in shower. *In room:* A/C, TV w/pay movies, dataport, kitchen or kitchenette, fridge, coffeemaker, microwave, wet bar, hair dryer, iron.

4 Adams-Morgan

Note: The hotels listed here are situated just north of Dupont Circle, more at the mouth of Adams-Morgan than within its actual boundaries.

EXPENSIVE

The Churchill ✦ This 1906 building, a registered historic property, sits on a hill a short walk from lively Dupont Circle; its elevated position allows for great city views from upper-floor rooms. You're also just a short walk from trendy Adams-Morgan (just cross Connecticut and walk up Columbia Rd.). The former Sofitel hotel underwent a thorough renovation in 2001–02 to emphasize its historic qualities and replaced all furnishings with custom-made pieces, including five-layer feather beds in every guest room. You can still count on the rooms being spacious, each with a breakfast/study alcove and many with sitting areas. You can choose from one of 84 regular guest rooms, each with a study but no parlor; 24 suites, with bedroom and parlor in one room, study separate; and 36 deluxe suites, in which the bedroom, study, and parlor are all separate rooms. The hotel welcomes an international clientele of diplomats, foreign delegations, and corporate travelers.

Adams-Morgan & Dupont Circle Accommodations

The Churchill **3**
Embassy Suites Hotel
  Downtown **7**
The George Washington
  University Inn **16**
Hilton Washington **4**
Hotel Lombardy **17**
Hotel Rouge **14**
The Jefferson **13**
Jurys Normandy **2**
Jurys Washington **5**

Lincoln Suites Hotel
  Downtown **10**
Omni Shoreham **1**
Park Hyatt **9**
Ritz-Carlton **8**
St. Gregory Hotel
  and Suites **6**
Tabard Inn **12**
Topaz Hotel **11**
Washington Terrace **15**

1914 Connecticut Ave. NW (between Wyoming Ave. and Leroy Place), Washington, DC 20009. (©) **800/424-2464** or 202/797-2000. Fax 202/462-0944. www.the churchillhotel.com. 144 units. Weekdays $199–$249 double, $279–$329 suite, $319–$369 deluxe suite; weekends $129–$149 double, $209–$229 suite, $249–$269 deluxe suite. Extra person $30. Children under 12 stay free in parents' room. AE, DISC, DC, MC, V. Valet parking $19 plus tax ($9 plus tax just for the day). Metro: Dupont Circle. **Amenities:** Restaurant (Continental); lounge/bar; fitness center; concierge; room service (5:30am–11pm); same-day laundry/dry cleaning; 3 rooms for guests with disabilities. *In room:* A/C, TV with pay movies, 3 phones, dataport, hair dryer, iron, robes.

Hilton Washington (𝓕 (Kids)   This sprawling hotel, built in 1965, occupies 7 acres and calls itself a "resort"—mostly on the basis of having landscaped gardens and tennis courts on its premises, unusual amenities for a D.C. hotel. The Hilton caters to corporate groups, which may have their families in tow (there's a kiddie pool and, from Memorial Day to Labor Day, children receive a goodie bag at check-in), and is accustomed to coordinating meetings for thousands of attendees. Its vast conference facilities include one of the largest hotel ballrooms on the East Coast (it accommodates nearly 4,000). By contrast, guest rooms are on the small side. A renovation of all guest rooms will be complete in 2003, installing elegant dark wood furnishings in every room. From the fifth floor up, city-side, you'll have panoramic views of Washington (as well as the Olympic-size pool).

The two designated concierge level rooms usually go for about $30 more than the standard room rate. The hotel has 53 suites, in all kinds of configurations, from the junior executive (in which parlor and bedroom are combined) to the huge Presidential suite.

The Hilton puts you within an easy stroll of embassies, great restaurants, museums, and the charming neighborhoods of Adams-Morgan, Kalorama, and Woodley Park (all up the hill), and Dupont Circle (down the hill).

1919 Connecticut Ave. NW (at T St.), Washington, DC 20009. (©) **800/HILTONS** or 202/483-3000. Fax 202/797-5755. www.washington-hilton.com. 1,119 units. Weekdays $169–$374 double, weekends (and some weekdays and holidays) $119–$314 double; $300–$1,500 suite. Look for deals on the website or by calling Hilton's 800-number. Extra person $20. Children 18 and under stay free in parents' room. AE, DISC, MC, V. Self-parking $15. Metro: Dupont Circle. **Amenities:** 2 restaurants (both American); deli; 2 bars (lobby bar featuring a pianist nightly and a pub); Olympic-size heated outdoor pool, children's pool; 3 lighted tennis courts; shuffleboard; extensive health-club facilities; concierge; transportation/sightseeing desk; comprehensive business center; lobby shops; room service (until 2am); same-day laundry/dry cleaning; concierge-level rooms; 28 rooms for guests with disabilities, some with roll-in showers. *In room:* A/C, TV w/pay movies; 2-line phone w/dataport, coffeemaker, hair dryer, iron.

INEXPENSIVE

Jurys Normandy *R* *Finds* This gracious hotel is a gem—a small gem, but a gem nonetheless. Situated in a neighborhood of architecturally impressive embassies, the hotel hosts many embassy-bound guests. You may discover this for yourself on a Tuesday evening, when guests gather in the charming Tea Room to enjoy complimentary wine and cheese served from the antique oak sideboard. This is also where you'll find daily continental breakfast (for about $6), complimentary coffee and tea after 10am, and cookies after 3pm. You can lounge or watch TV in the conservatory, or, in nice weather, you can move outside to the garden patio.

The six-floor Normandy has small but pretty twin and queen guest rooms (all remodeled in 1998), with tapestry-upholstered mahogany and cherry-wood furnishings in 18th-century style, and pretty floral-print bedspreads covering firm beds. Rooms facing Wyoming Avenue overlook the tree-lined street, while other rooms mostly offer views of apartment buildings. The Normandy is an easy walk from both Adams-Morgan and Dupont Circle, where many restaurants and shops await you.

2118 Wyoming Ave. NW (at Connecticut Ave.), Washington, DC 20008. © 800/ 424-3729 or 202/483-1350. Fax 202/387-8241. www.jurysdoyle.com. 75 units. $79–$175 double. Extra person $10. Children under 12 stay free in parents' room. AE, DC, DISC, MC, V. Parking $10. Metro: Dupont Circle. **Amenities:** Access to the neighboring Courtyard by Marriott's pool and exercise room; room service at breakfast; coin-op washer/dryers; same-day laundry/dry cleaning (Mon–Sat); 4 rooms for guests with disabilities, 1 with roll-in shower. *In room:* A/C, TV with pay movies, 2-line phone w/dataport, minibar, coffeemaker, hair dryer, iron, safe.

5 Dupont Circle

EXPENSIVE

St. Gregory Hotel and Suites *RR* The St. Gregory, open since June 2000, is an affordable luxury property, with marble floors and chandeliers. The hotel is well situated at the corner of 21st and M streets, not far from Georgetown, Dupont Circle, Foggy Bottom, and the White House, and with many good restaurants within a literal stone's throw.

Most of the guest rooms are one-bedroom suites, with a separate living room and bedroom, and with a pullout sofa in the living room. The best rooms are the 16 "sky" suites on the ninth floor, each with terrace and city views. All of the 100 suites have fully appointed kitchens, including microwaves, ovens, and full-size refrigerators. The remaining units are deluxe double rooms. Decor throughout the hotel is an attractive mélange of olive green and gold, with un-hotel-like lamps, mirror frames, and fabrics. Three whole floors of the hotel are reserved for club-level rooms.

The St. Gregory offers special rates to long-term and government guests, and to those from the diplomatic community. If you don't fall into one of those categories, check the hotel's website for great deals like the "One Dollar Summer Clearance Sale" posted in 2002: You pay $169 the first night and only $1 for the second night, for Friday and Saturday, or Saturday and Sunday stays.

2033 M St. NW (at 21st St.), Washington, DC 20036. ℭ **800/829-5034** or 202/530-3600. Fax 202/466-7353. www.stgregoryhotelwdc.com. 154 units. Weekdays $189–$269 double or suite, weekends $149–$249 double or suite. Extra person $20. Children under 16 stay free in parents' room. Ask about discounts, long-term stays, and packages. AE, DC, MC, V. Parking $12 weekends, $19 weekdays. Metro: Dupont Circle or Farragut North. **Amenities:** Cafe and coffee bar (American) with sidewalk seating seasonally; state-of-the-art fitness center, as well as access to the nearby and larger LA Sports Club (p. 55 for full description); concierge; tour desk; business center; room service (6:30am–10:30pm); massage; babysitting; coin-op laundry room; same-day laundry/dry cleaning; concierge-level rooms; 6 rooms for guests with disabilities, 2 with roll-in showers. *In room:* A/C, TV w/pay movies, CD player, 2-line phone w/dataport, fridge, coffeemaker, hair dryer, iron.

Topaz Hotel ⟳   Like the Hotel Rouge (p. 44), the Topaz is an upscale boutique hotel for those who think young. This hotel seems tamer than the Rouge, but it still has a buzz about it, a pleasant, interesting sort of buzz. The reception area, lobby and bar flow together, so if you arrive in the evening, you may feel like you've arrived at a party: The Topaz Bar and the Bar Rouge have fast become favorite hangouts for the after-work crowd. At the Topaz, they're liking drinks called "Blue Nirvana" (champagne mixed with vodka and blueberry liqueur) and "Pop" (6-oz. single servings of Pommery champagne), the better-than-bar-food cuisine with an Asian accent, and the decor of velvety settees, zebra-patterned ottomans, and a lighting system that fades in and out. (See p. 165 for more information about the Topaz Bar.)

Upstairs are guest rooms appealingly, whimsically decorated with striped lime green wallpaper; a polka dot padded headboard for the down-comforter-covered bed; a bright blue, curved-back settee; a big, round mirror set in a sunburst frame; a light green and yellow painted armoire with fabric panels; and a red, with gold star-patterned cushioned chair. The rooms are unusually large (in its former life as the Canterbury Hotel, these were "junior suites" and held kitchenettes), and each has an alcove where the desk is placed, and a separate dressing room that holds a dressing table and cube-shaped ottoman. The Topaz pursues a sort of New Age wellness motif; do note the spill of smooth stones arranged just so upon your bed ("Through time people have carried special stones called totems to bring them energy and empowerment . . ." reads a little card accompanying the stones.) You also have the option to book a specialty room: one of four "energy" guest rooms, which include a piece of exercise equipment (either a treadmill or a stationary bike), and fitness magazines; or one of three "yoga" rooms, which come with an exercise mat, an instructional tape, padded pillows, special towels, and yoga magazines.

The Topaz lies on a quiet residential street, whose front-of-the-house windows overlook picturesque town houses.

1733 N St. NW (right next to the Tabard Inn, see below, between 17th and 18th sts.), Washington, DC 20036. (©) **800/424-2950** or 202/393-3000. Fax 202/785-9581. www.topazhotel.com. 99 units. Weekdays $240–$275 double, $280 specialty room; weekends $145 double; $185 specialty rooms. Extra person $20. Children under 16 stay free in parents' room. Rates include complimentary morning energy potions. AE, DC, DISC, MC, V. Parking $20. Pets welcome. Metro: Dupont Circle. **Amenities:** Bar/restaurant (innovative American with an Asian influence); access to nearby health club ($5 per guest); 24-hr. concierge; business services; room service (7am–11pm); same-day laundry/dry cleaning; 5 rooms for guests with disabilities, 2 with roll-in showers. *In room:* A/C, TV w/pay movies, 2-line cordless phones w/dataports, minibar, teapot with exotic teas, hair dryer, iron, safe, robes.

MODERATE

Embassy Suites Hotel Downtown *(Kids* This hotel offers unbelievable value and a convenient location, within walking distance of Foggy Bottom, Georgetown, and Dupont Circle. You enter into a tropical and glassy eight-story atrium with two waterfalls constantly running. This is where you'll enjoy an ample complimentary breakfast—not your standard cold croissant and coffee, but stations from which you can choose omelets made to order, waffles, bacon, fresh fruit, juices, bagels, and pastries. Tables are scattered in alcoves throughout the atrium to allow for privacy. Each evening, the atrium is the setting for complimentary beverages (including cocktails) and light cold snacks.

The accommodations are nicer than your average hotel room, with better amenities. Every unit is a two-room suite, with a living room that closes off completely from the rest of the suite. The living room holds a queen-size sofa bed, TV, easy chair, and large table with four comfortable chairs around it. The bedroom lies at the back of the suite, overlooking a quiet courtyard of brick walkways or the street. A king-size bed or two double beds, TV, sink, easy chair, and chest of drawers furnish this space. Between the living room and the bedroom are the bathroom, small closet, and a kitchenette. It's worth requesting one of the eighth- or ninth-floor suites with views of Georgetown and beyond, as far as Washington National Cathedral (the hotel will note your request, but won't be able to guarantee you such a suite). For the roomiest quarters, ask for an "executive corner suite," the slightly larger, slightly more expensive suites situated in the corners of the hotel.

1250 22nd St. NW (between M and N sts.), Washington, DC 20037. © **800/ EMBASSY** or 202/857-3388. Fax 202/293-3173. www.embassysuitesdcmetro.com. 318 suites. Rates include full breakfast and evening reception. $169–$309 double. Ask for AAA discounts or check the website for best rates. Extra person $25. Children 18 under stay free in parents' room. AE, DC, DISC, MC, V. Parking $19. Metro: Foggy Bottom. **Amenities:** Restaurant (northern Italian); state-of-the-art fitness center with indoor pool, whirlpool, sauna, game room; concierge; business center; room service (11am–11pm); coin-op washer/dryers; same-day laundry/dry cleaning; 8 rooms for guests with disabilities, 2 with roll-in showers. *In room:* A/C, TV w/pay movies, 2-line phone w/dataport, kitchenette with fridge and microwave, coffeemaker, hair dryer, iron.

Jurys Washington Hotel ⓡ *Value*   This hotel gets high marks for convenience (it's located right on Dupont Circle), service, and comfort. Open since 2000, the hotel is favored by business groups especially, who like its reasonable rates. Each of the large rooms is furnished with two double beds with firm mattresses, an armoire with TV, a desk, a wet-bar alcove, and a tiny but attractive bathroom. Decor is Art Deco–ish, with lots of light-wood furniture. All guest rooms offer free, high-speed Internet access. Despite its prime location in a sometimes raucous neighborhood, the hotel's rooms are insulated from the noise. Rooms on higher floors offer the best views of the city and of Dupont Circle. An Irish management company owns this hotel (along with 2 other properties in Washington), which explains the Irish influence. You'll occasionally detect an Irish accent from the staff, and the comfortable and attractive hotel pub, Biddy Mulligan's, proudly features a bar imported from the Emerald Isle. Claddaghs, the hotel restaurant, serves an American buffet breakfast every morning and American fare with an Irish flair at other meals. To get the best rates, check the website or call the hotel directly.

1500 New Hampshire Ave. NW (across from Dupont Circle), Washington, DC 20036. © **800/42-DOYLE** or 202/483-6000. Fax 202/232-1130. www.jurysdoyle.com. 314 units. $145–$235 double; from $600 suite. Extra person $15. Children 17 and under stay free in parents' room. AE, DC, DISC, MC, V. Parking $17. Metro: Dupont Circle. **Amenities:** Restaurant (Irish/American); bar; exercise room; 24-hr. concierge; business center; room service (6:30am–midnight); same-day laundry/dry cleaning; 11 rooms for guests with disabilities, 4 with roll-in showers. *In room:* A/C, TV w/pay movies, 2-line phone w/dataport, minibar, coffeemaker, hair dryer, iron, safe.

Tabard Inn Hotel   If you favor the offbeat and the personal over brand names and cookie-cutter chains, this might be the place for you. The Tabard Inn, named for the hostelry in Chaucer's *Canterbury Tales,* is actually three Victorian town houses that were joined in 1914 and have operated as an inn ever since. Situated on a quiet street of similarly old dwellings, the Tabard is a well-worn, funky hotel that's looked after by a chummy, peace-love-and-understanding sort of staff who clearly cherish the place.

The heart of the ground floor is the dark-paneled lounge, with worn furniture, a wood-burning fireplace, the original beamed ceiling, and bookcases. This is a favorite spot for Washingtonians to come for a drink, especially in winter, or to linger before or after dining in the charming **Tabard Inn restaurant** ✦. From the lounge, the inn leads you up and down stairs, along dim corridors, and through nooks and crannies to guest rooms. Can you dig chartreuse? (Ask for room 3.) How about aubergine? (Ask for room 11.) Each is different, but those facing N Street are largest and brightest, and some have bay windows. Furnishings are a mix of antiques and flea-market finds. Perhaps the most eccentric room is the top-floor "penthouse," which has skylights, exposed brick walls, its own kitchen, and a deck accessed by climbing out a window. The inn is not easily accessible to guests with disabilities.

1739 N St. NW (between 17th and 18th sts.), Washington, DC 20036. ✆ **202/785-1277.** Fax 202/785-6173. www.tabardinn.com. 40 units, 27 with private bathroom (6 with shower only). $100–$120 double with shared bathroom; $125–$190 double with private bathroom. Extra person $15. Rates include continental breakfast. AE, DC, DISC, MC, V. Limited street parking, plus 2 parking garages on N St. Metro: Dupont Circle. Small and confined pets allowed ($20 fee). **Amenities:** Restaurant (regional American) with lounge (free live jazz Sun evenings); free access to nearby YMCA (with extensive facilities that include indoor pool, indoor track, and racquetball/basketball courts); laundry service; fax, iron, hair dryer and safe available at front desk. *In room:* A/C, dataport.

6 Foggy Bottom/West End
VERY EXPENSIVE

Park Hyatt ✦✦   This luxury hotel across the street from the Monarch Hotel wrapped up a full renovation in 2000. The large guest rooms now have goose-down duvets on the beds, and new furniture, wall coverings, and fabrics. Specially commissioned artwork hangs throughout the hotel. More than half of the rooms are suites (meaning the parlor and bedroom are separate), and the remaining rooms are deluxe kings. The suites also have dressing rooms with full vanities. Each bathroom has a TV, a radio, and a telephone, along with the usual amenities. The 15-year-old 10-story hotel hosts big names, royal families (who use the Presidential Suite, with its fireplace and grand piano), lobbyists, and tourists. Rooms are handsome and service is superb.

The bright and lovely Melrose dining room offers four-star cuisine with an emphasis on seafood (see p. 90 for a full review); the amiable chef, Brian McBride, pops into the dining room personally from time to time to make sure all is well. Adjoining the Melrose is a bar, where there's swing dancing to live jazz every weekend.

1201 24th St. NW (at M St.), Washington, DC 20037. © **800/778-7477** or 202/789-1234. Fax 202/419-6795. www.parkhyatt.com. 223 units. Weekdays $320–$450 double; weekends $215–$289 double. Extra person $25. Children 18 and under stay free in parents' room. AE, DC, DISC, MC, V. Valet parking $24. Metro: Foggy Bottom or Dupont Circle. Pets allowed. **Amenities:** Restaurant (American); bar/lounge (with live entertainment Fri–Sat); health club (with indoor pool, whirlpool, and sauna and steam rooms); spa with hair and skin salon; concierge; business center; 24-hr. room service; in-room massage; same-day laundry/dry cleaning; 10 rooms for guests with disabilities, 3 with roll-in showers. *In room:* A/C, TV w/pay movies, 2-line phone w/dataport, minibar, hair dryer, iron, safe, robes.

The Ritz-Carlton &&&   This new Ritz-Carlton, which opened in October 2000, surpasses all other Washington hotels for service and amenities. From the cadre of doormen and valet parking attendants who greet you effusively when you arrive, to the graceful young women in long dresses who swan around you serving cocktails in the bar and lounge, the Ritz staff is always looking after you.

The hotel is built around a multi-tiered Japanese garden and courtyard with reflecting pools and cascading waterfall; guest rooms on the inside of the complex overlook the waterfall or terraced garden, while guest rooms on the outside perimeter view landmarks and cityscapes. The woman who showed me to my terrace-view room inadvertently, but appropriately, kept referring to the hotel as the "Rich-Carlton." My standard room was very large, and richly furnished with a firm king-size bed covered in both duvet and bedspread, decorative inlaid wooden furniture, a comfy armchair and ottoman, and very pretty artwork. The marble bathroom was immense, with long counter space, separate bathtub and shower stall, and the toilet in its own room behind a louvered door. The clock radio doubles as a CD player and the phone features a button for summoning the "technology butler" (a complimentary, 24/7 service for guests with computer questions). Other nice touches in the rooms include an umbrella, windows that open, and an outlet for recharging laptops. Don't make the same mistake that I did when I passed up the evening turndown—the maid places a warm, freshly baked brownie upon your pillow instead of the usual mint.

Among the different versions of suites available, most are "executives," which include a sitting room and separate bedroom.

Guests enjoy free use of the hotel's fitness center, the two-level, 100,000-square-foot Sports Club/LA, which officially leaves all other hotel health clubs in the dust with its state-of-the-art weight-training equipment and free weights, two regulation-size basketball courts and four squash courts, an indoor heated swimming pool and an aquatics pool with a sun deck, exercise classes, personal trainers, the full-service Splash Spa and Salon, and its own restaurant and cafe.

The Ritz's bar and lounge are also exceptionally inviting, with lots of plush upholstered couches and armchairs, a fire blazing in the fireplace in winter, and a pianist playing every day. Afternoon tea is served in the lounge daily.

The Ritz's restaurant, The Grill, is still getting its feet wet. My guess is that by the time you read this, the restaurant will have ironed out its kinks and be a place worth trying.

1150 22nd St. NW (at M St.), Washington, DC 20037. ℰ 800/241-3333 or 202/835-0500. Fax 202/835-1588. www.ritzcarlton.com. 300 units. $450 double; from $595 suite. No charge for extra person in the room. Ask about discount packages. AE, DC, DISC, MC, V. Valet parking $18, self-parking $15. Metro: Foggy Bottom or Dupont Circle. Pets accepted (no fee). **Amenities:** Restaurant (American); lounge; fabulous health club and spa (the best in the city; see above); 24-hr. concierge; business center (open weekdays); 24-hr.fax and currency-exchange services; salon; 24-hr. room service; in-room massage; babysitting; same-day laundry/dry cleaning; 1-hr. pressing; club level with 5 complimentary food presentations throughout the day (including a chef station each morning to prepare individual requests); 10 rooms for guests with disabilities. *In room:* A/C, TV w/pay movies, 2-line phone w/high-speed Internet access, minibar/fridge, hair dryer, iron, safe, robes, umbrella.

EXPENSIVE

Hotel Lombardy ℱ   From its handsome walnut-paneled lobby with carved Tudor-style ceilings to its old-fashioned manual elevator (fasten your seat belts—it's going to be a bumpy ride), the 11-story Lombardy offers a lot of character and comfort for the price. Originally built in 1929, it's located about 5 blocks west of the White House. George Washington University's campus is just across Pennsylvania Avenue, so this area remains vibrant long after other downtown neighborhoods have rolled up the sidewalks. Peace Corps, World Bank, and corporate guests make up a large part of the clientele, but other visitors will also appreciate the Lombardy's warm, welcoming ambience and the attentive service of the multi-lingual staff.

The decor in each spacious room has a unique touch. All are entered via pedimented louver doors, and are furnished with original artwork and Chinese and European antiques. All rooms have large desks, precious dressing rooms, and roomy walk-in closets; new drapes, bedspreads, and carpeting were installed in the spring of 2001. Most of the 38 one-bedroom suites have small kitchens with dining areas. Front rooms overlook Pennsylvania Avenue and the small triangular park across the street, named for Pres. James Monroe. Back rooms are quieter; some overlook the garden of the hotel's next-door neighbor, the Arts Club of Washington, where Monroe once lived. Coming in 2003: an on-site fitness center.

2019 Pennsylvania Ave. NW (between 20th and 21st sts.), Washington, DC 20006. ✆ 800/424-5486 or 202/828-2600. Fax 202/872-0503. www.hotellombardy.com. 130 units. Weekdays $149–$199 double, weekends and some off-season weekdays $119–$149 double; weekdays $199–$239 suite for 2, weekends $169–$219 suite for 2. Extra person $20. Children under 16 stay free in parents' room. AE, DC, DISC, MC, V. Self-parking $17. Metro: Farragut West or Foggy Bottom. **Amenities:** Restaurant (American); lounge (shares a menu with the restaurant, as well as offering an appetizer menu); concierge; room service (6:30am–10pm); same-day laundry/dry cleaning. *In room:* A/C, TV w/pay movies, 2-line phone w/dataport, kitchens (in some rooms), minibar, coffeemaker, hair dryer, iron, robes.

MODERATE

George Washington University Inn   Rumor has it that this whitewashed brick inn, another former apartment building, used to be a favorite spot for clandestine trysts for high-society types. These days you're more likely to see Kennedy Center performers and visiting professors. The university purchased the hotel (formerly known as the Inn at Foggy Bottom) in 1994 and renovated it. The most recent refurbishment, in 2001, replaced linens, drapes, and the like in the guest rooms.

Rooms are a little larger and corridors are a tad narrower than those in a typical hotel, and each room includes a roomy dressing chamber. More than one-third of the units are one-bedroom suites. These are especially spacious, with living rooms that hold a sleeper sofa and a TV hidden in an armoire (there's another in the bedroom). The suites, plus the 16 efficiencies, have kitchens. The spaciousness and the kitchen facilities make this a popular choice for families and for long-term guests.

This is a fairly safe and lovely neighborhood, within easy walking distance to Georgetown, the Kennedy Center, and downtown. But keep an eye peeled—you have to pass through wrought-iron gates into a kind of cul-de-sac to find the inn.

Off the lobby is the restaurant (a new one will be in place by the time you read this).

If it's not full, the inn may be willing to offer reduced rates. Mention prices quoted in the inn's *New York Times* ad, if you've seen it; or your affiliation with George Washington University, if you have one.

824 New Hampshire Ave. NW (between H and I sts.), Washington, DC 20037. ℰ 800/426-4455 or 202/337-6620. Fax 202/298-7499. www.gwuinn.com. 95 units. Weekdays $130–$175 double, weekends $99–$135 double; weekdays $140–$185 efficiency, weekends $110–$155 efficiency; weekdays $155–$220 1-bedroom suite, weekends $125–$170 1-bedroom suite. Children under 12 stay free in parents' room. AE, DC, MC, V. Limited parking $18. Metro: Foggy Bottom. **Amenities:** Restaurant (hadn't opened yet, so cuisine still undecided); complimentary passes to nearby fitness center; room service; coin-op washer/dryers; same-day laundry/dry cleaning; 5 rooms for guests with disabilities, 1 with roll-in shower. *In room:* A/C, TV, 2-line phone w/dataport, fridge, coffeemaker, microwave, hair dryer, iron.

7 Georgetown

VERY EXPENSIVE

Four Seasons ✦✦✦   Although the Four Seasons now has a spectacular rival in the new and nearby Ritz-Carlton (p. 54), the hotel continues to attract the rich and famous, who appreciate the superb service. Staff members are trained to know the names, preferences, and even allergies of guests, and repeat clientele rely on this discreet attention.

The hotel sits at the mouth of Georgetown, backing up against Rock Creek Park and the C&O Canal. Accommodations, many of which overlook the park or canal, are newly renovated and have an upscale, homey feel. Beds are outfitted with down-filled bedding, dust ruffles, and scalloped spreads; and rooms have large desks and plump cushioned armchairs with hassocks. An adjoining building that opened in 1999 holds 25 rooms and 35 suites for clients who want state-of-the-art business amenities (each is soundproof and has an office equipped with a fax machine, at least 3 telephones with 2-line speakers, portable telephones, and headsets for private TV listening). These rooms are also larger than those in the main hotel. Three of the suites have kitchenettes. Original avant-garde artwork from the personal collection of owner William Louis-Dreyfus (yes, Julia's dad) hangs in every room and public space. Transmitters installed throughout the hotel allow you wireless connection to the Internet on your laptop, wherever you go in the hotel. In 2002, the hotel introduced its "Travel Light" service, which allows a guest to leave at the hotel a garment bag of clothing and personal items, which the hotel stores securely until the guest returns for another visit; upon arrival, the guest checks in and finds the garment bag hanging in his/her guest room closet.

2800 Pennsylvania Ave. NW (which becomes M St. a block farther along), Washington, DC 20007. ℂ **800/332-3442** or 202/342-0444. Fax 202/944-2076. www.fourseasons.com. 260 units. Weekdays $455–$615 double, weekends from $295 double; weekdays $695–$5,150 suite, weekends from $550 suite. Extra person $40. Children under 16 stay free in parents' room. AE, DC, MC, V. Parking $26, plus tax. Metro: Foggy Bottom. Pets allowed, up to 15 lb. **Amenities:** Formal restaurant (seasonal American); lounge (for afternoon tea, and cocktails); extensive state-of-the-art fitness club and spa with personal trainers, lap pool, Vichy shower, hydrotherapy, and synchronized massage (2 people work on you at the same time); bike rentals; children's program (various goodies provided, but no organized activities); 24-hr. concierge; complimentary sedan service weekdays within the District; business center; salon; 24-hr. room service; in-room massage; babysitting; same-day laundry/dry cleaning; 7 rooms for guests with disabilities. *In room:* A/C, TV w/pay movies and Web access, high-speed Internet access, high-tech CD player, minibar, hair dryer, iron, safe, robes.

EXPENSIVE

Georgetown Inn 𝄐   Like its sister inn, the Latham (see below), this hotel is in the thick of Georgetown. Most guests are here on business, but come Memorial Day weekend, the hotel is full of the proud parents of graduating Georgetown University students. (The hotel books up 2 years in advance for graduation weekend.)

The Georgetown is smaller than the Latham, but has larger rooms. Furnishings are European-handsome, heavy on the dark woods. Half of the rooms hold two double beds, although a couple of rooms have twin single beds, connecting with suites, helpful to families traveling with children. Ask for an "executive room" if you'd like a sitting area with pullout sofa, and extra conveniences like a reading lamp over the bed. Even better are the 10 one-bedroom suites, in which bedroom and large living room are separate. The bathrooms have only showers (some also have bidets), no tub.

The **Daily Grill** has an outpost here, offering the same generous portions of American food served at its original D.C. location, at 1200 18th St. NW.

1310 Wisconsin Ave. NW (between N and O sts.), Washington, DC 20007. ℂ **800/ 368-5922** or 202/333-8900. Fax 202/333-8308. www.georgetowninn.com. 96 units. Weekdays $195–$245 double, weekends $139–$245 double. Suites from $345. Ask about promotional rates. Extra person $20. Children under 12 stay free in parents' room. AE, DC, DISC, MC, V. Valet parking $22. Metro: Foggy Bottom, with a 30-minute walk, or take a cab. **Amenities:** 1 restaurant (American) and bar; outdoor pool (at the Latham; see below); exercise room, plus free access to Monarch

Hotel's extensive health club and spa; concierge; room service during restaurant hours; same-day laundry/dry cleaning; 4 rooms for guests with disabilities, all with roll-in showers. *In room:* A/C, TV w/pay movies and Nintendo, 2-line phones w/dataport and high-speed Internet access, hair dryer, iron.

Hotel Monticello of Georgetown ⟨⟩

This hotel gets a lot of repeat business from both corporate and leisure travelers, who appreciate the intimacy of a small hotel, including personalized service from a staff who greets you by name and protects your privacy. It's also a favorite choice for families celebrating weddings or graduations (both Georgetown and George Washington universities are close by); they sometimes book several suites, or maybe a whole floor. A major renovation in 2000 gutted the whole building and created a more upscale setting (this used to be the Georgetown Dutch Inn). Rooms now bring in much more light, thanks to layout and design changes, better use of windows, and the placement of French doors with frosted glass between rooms. You'll notice that the top sheet on your bed is monogrammed, the sofa in the living room folds out, and those are Hermès bath products in the new marble bathrooms. Next in the works is a total remodeling of the penthouse suites, which may still be going on when you read this.

Accommodations are medium-size one- and two-bedroom apartment-like suites. Six of the suites are studios, in which the living room and bedroom are joined, and nine of them are duplex penthouses with 1½ bathrooms. Every suite has a wet bar with a microwave and refrigerator. The duplex penthouses have full kitchens. In addition to continental breakfast in the morning, fresh fruit, coffee, and herbal tea are available in the lobby all day.

The hotel is in the heart of Georgetown, surrounded by shops and restaurants. The C&O Canal towpath, just down the block, is ideal for jogging and cycling, though you should be wary at night.

1075 Thomas Jefferson St. NW (just below M St.), Washington, DC 20007. ℭ **800/ 388-2410** or 202/337-0900. Fax 202/333-6526. www.monticellohotel.com. 47 suites. Peak-season weekdays $219–$269, off-peak weekdays $169–$189; peak-season weekends $169–$189, off-peak weekends $149–$169. Call for penthouse suite rates (renovation may affect prices). Extra person $20. Rates include continental breakfast. Children under 14 stay free in parents' room. Promotional rates and discounts may be available. AE, DC, DISC, MC, V. Parking $10. Metro: Foggy Bottom, with a 20-min. walk. Bus: 32, 34, and 36 go to all major Washington tourist attractions. **Amenities:** Free access to Monarch Hotel's extensive health club and spa; business center; in-room massage; babysitting; same-day laundry/dry cleaning except Sun; 4 rooms for guests with disabilities, 3 with roll-in showers. *In room:* A/C, TV, 2-line phone w/dataport, kitchenette with microwave, fridge, coffeemaker, hair dryer, iron.

The Latham ⍟   The Latham is at the hub of Georgetown's trendy nightlife/restaurant/shopping scene, but since its accommodations are set back from the street, none of the noise of nighttime revelers will reach your room. Charming earth-tone rooms are decorated in a French-country motif, with pine furnishings and multipaned windows; cable TVs are housed in armoires. All rooms have large desks. Some 7th- through 10th-floor rooms offer gorgeous canal views; third-floor accommodations, all two-room suites, have windows facing a hallway designed to replicate a quaint Georgetown street. Most luxurious are the two-story carriage suites with cathedral ceilings, full living rooms, and 1½ bathrooms. Fax machines/printers are in a third of the rooms; CD players with headphones are in third-floor and carriage suites. All of the suites have mini-refrigerators. A renovation completed in 2000 refurbished hallways and replaced linens, carpeting, and furnishings in guest rooms. Most of the rooms are "executive kings," which means their beds are made up with Egyptian cotton sheets, down comforters, duvets, and feather pillows, and added amenities include printer/fax machines and heated towel bars.

Michel Richard's highly acclaimed **Citronelle** ⍟⍟, one of D.C.'s best restaurants, is on the premises (p. 92). And fronting the hotel is the country-French La Madeleine.

3000 M St. NW (between 30th and Thomas Jefferson sts.), Washington, DC 20007. ⍟ **800/528-4261** or 202/726-5000. Fax 202/337-4250. www.thelatham.com. 143 units. Weekdays $195–$245 double; weekends $139–$245 double; from $345 suite. Call hotel directly for promotional rates. Extra person $20. Children under 12 stay free in parents' room. AE, DC, DISC, MC, V. Valet parking $22. Metro: Foggy Bottom, with a 20-min. walk, or take a cab. **Amenities:** Restaurant (French) with bar; small, unheated, outdoor pool; free access to Monarch Hotel's extensive health club and spa; 24-hr. concierge; business center; room service during restaurant hours; same-day laundry/dry cleaning; 2 rooms for guests with disabilities, both with roll-in showers. *In room:* A/C, TV w/pay movies and Nintendo, 2-line phone w/dataport and high-speed Internet access, hair dryer, iron, robes.

8 Woodley Park

EXPENSIVE

Omni Shoreham ⍟ *Kids*   This is Woodley Park's *other* really big hotel, though with 836 rooms, the Omni Shoreham is still 500 short of the behemoth Marriott Wardman Park. And it's all the more appealing for it, since it's not quite so overwhelming as the Marriott. Its design—wide corridors, vaulted ceilings and archways, and arrangements of pretty sofas and armchairs in the lobby and public spaces—endows the Shoreham with the air of a grand hotel.

A massive $80 million renovation completed in 2000 installed a new air-conditioning system, restructured the pool, upgraded the already excellent fitness center health spa, and restored a traditional, elegant look to guest rooms and the lobby. The spacious guest rooms remain twice the size of your average hotel room. Most of the 52 suites are junior suites, with the sitting room and bedroom combined. The hotel sits on 11 acres overlooking Rock Creek Park; park-side rooms are a little smaller but offer spectacular views.

With its 22 meeting rooms and 7 ballrooms (some of which open to terraces overlooking the park!), the hotel is popular as a meeting and convention venue. Leisure travelers appreciate the Shoreham for its large outdoor swimming pool, its proximity to the National Zoo and excellent restaurants, and the immediate access to biking, hiking, and jogging paths through Rock Creek Park. The hotel is just down the street from the Woodley Park–Zoo Metro station. You can also walk to the more hip neighborhoods of Adams-Morgan and Dupont Circle from the hotel; the stroll to Dupont Circle, taking you over the bridge that spans Rock Creek Park, is especially nice (and safe at night, too).

Built in 1930, the Shoreham has been the scene of inaugural balls for every president since FDR. Do you believe in ghosts? Ask about Room 870, the haunted suite (available for $3,000 a night).

2500 Calvert St. NW (near Connecticut Ave.), Washington, DC 20008. ℂ 800/843-6664 or 202/234-0700. Fax 202/265-7972. www.omnihotels.com. 836 units. $179–$309 double; from $350–$3,000 suite. Call the hotel directly for best rates. Extra person $20. Children under 18 stay free in parents' room. AE, DC, DISC, MC, V. Valet parking $22; self-parking $19. Metro: Woodley Park–Zoo. **Amenities:** Restaurant (continental; terrace overlooks Rock Creek Park), gourmet carryout; bar/lounge (serves light fare and has live music nightly); fitness center and spa with heated outdoor pool, separate kids' pool, and whirlpool; children's gifts; concierge; travel/sightseeing desk; business center; shops; 24-hr. room service; massage; same-day laundry/dry cleaning; 41 rooms for guests with disabilities, half with roll-in showers. *In room:* A/C, TV w/pay movies and Nintendo, 2-line phone w/dataport, hair dryer, iron, robe.

4

Where to Dine

Sightseeing works up an appetite—you can count on it. Instead of waiting for hunger to hit and then appeasing your pangs with junk food from the nearest street vendor, why not plan ahead and make restaurant stops part of your itinerary? Sure, you may have come to Washington to visit the Capitol and the Smithsonian museums, but if you leave without dining at least once at one of the city's excellent restaurants, you've missed a delicious and quintessential Washington experience. I've sampled a variety of the city's restaurants, and in this chapter, I've selected some of the best the capital has to offer.

1 Capitol Hill

For information on eating at the Capitol and other government buildings, see the box "Dining at Sightseeing Attractions," on p. 66.

EXPENSIVE

B. Smith's *Finds* TRADITIONAL SOUTHERN   This is one of the few upscale restaurants on Capitol Hill, and the only one in Union Station, and even if the restaurant isn't on your route, it's worth coming here—for the food, of course, but also to admire the restaurant's amazing interior. The dramatic dining room once served as a presidential reception room hall, and now its 30-foot-high ceilings, white marble floors, and towering Ionic columns make it a fitting place for lobbyists, senators, and other well-paid Washingtonians to discuss serious business. On weekends, the ambience lightens up and romantic couples and families dine here. Background music is always mellow (Nat King Cole, Ray Charles, Sarah Vaughan). The restaurant features live jazz on Friday and Saturday evenings and at Sunday brunch.

The restaurant's Southern cuisine and its quality seldom change. Chef James Oakley's menu offers such appetizers as jambalaya or red beans and rice studded with andouille sausage and *tasso* (spicy smoked pork). Standouts among the main dishes are the trout imperial (sautéed Virginia trout piled high with crab meat/vegetable "stuffing" and served over mesclun with rice) and something called "Swamp Thing" (seafood served over greens with a mustard sauce). A basket of minibiscuits, corn and citrus poppy-seed muffins, and sourdough rolls accompanies all dishes. For dessert, try either pecan sweet-potato pie or coconut cake. An almost all-American wine list features many by-the-glass selections.

In Union Station, 50 Massachusetts Ave. NE. ℂ **202/289-6188.** Reservations recommended. Main courses mostly $15–$30. AE, DC, DISC, MC, V. Mon–Sat 11:30am–4pm; Mon–Thurs 5–11pm; Fri–Sat 5pm–midnight; Sun 11:30am–9pm. Metro: Union Station.

Barolo ✹✹ PIEDMONTESE ITALIAN   This excellent, sophisticated Italian restaurant stands out among the pubs and inexpensive eateries that line this stretch of Pennsylvania Avenue on Capitol Hill. In fact, Barolo lies upstairs from its less costly sister restaurant, Il Radicchio; both are owned by chef/proprietor, Roberto Donna, the dynamo behind Galileo, too. (See review of Il Radicchio on p. 68, and of Galileo on p. 77). The intimate main room is paneled and has wooden floors, a working fireplace, and well-spaced tables. Encircling the upper reaches of the room is a charming, narrow balcony set with tables for two; look out the window and you'll just be able to glimpse the Capitol. You can also expect to stumble across Washington notables, since the private room is a popular fundraising spot at both lunch and dinner.

Though the menu changes daily, you can expect Piedmontese cuisine that may include a white endive salad with balsamic vinaigrette and basil dressing; saffron pappardelle with sautéed lobster, asparagus, roasted garlic, and fresh basil; or roasted filet of red snapper over sweet potato, rosemary, black olives, and fresh basil. The pastas are always good. The wine list is entirely Italian, focusing on Piedmont wines, with emphasis on those produced from the Barolo grape.

223 Pennsylvania Ave. SE. ℂ **202/547-5011.** Reservations recommended. Lunch main courses $15–$17.50; dinner main courses $15–$23. AE, DC, DISC, MC, V. Mon–Fri 11:30am–2:30pm; Mon–Thurs 5:30–10pm; Fri–Sat 5:30–10:30pm. Metro: Capitol South.

Bistro Bis ✹✹ FRENCH BISTRO   The chic Hotel George is the home of this excellent French restaurant, whose owner-chef, Jeff Buben, and his wife, Sallie, also run Vidalia (p. 80). You can sit at tables in the bar area (which always seem loud, even when it's not that crowded), on the balcony overlooking the bar, or at leather banquettes in the main dining room, where you can watch Buben and staff at work in the glass-fronted kitchen. (In warm weather,

Downtown & Capitol Hill Dining

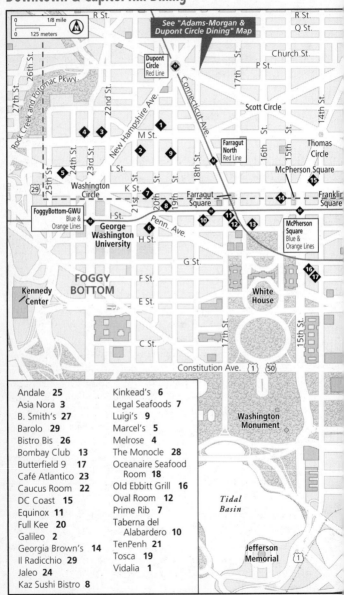

See "Adams-Morgan & Dupont Circle Dining" Map

Dupont Circle
Red Line

Farragut North
Red Line

Scott Circle

Thomas Circle

McPherson Square

Washington Circle

Farragut Square

Franklin Square

FoggyBottom-GWU
Blue & Orange Lines

George Washington University

McPherson Square
Blue & Orange Lines

FOGGY BOTTOM

Kennedy Center

White House

Constitution Ave.

Washington Monument

Tidal Basin

Jefferson Memorial

Andale **25**	Kinkead's **6**
Asia Nora **3**	Legal Seafoods **7**
B. Smith's **27**	Luigi's **9**
Barolo **29**	Marcel's **5**
Bistro Bis **26**	Melrose **4**
Bombay Club **13**	The Monocle **28**
Butterfield 9 **17**	Oceanaire Seafood
Café Atlantico **23**	Room **18**
Caucus Room **22**	Old Ebbitt Grill **16**
DC Coast **15**	Oval Room **12**
Equinox **11**	Prime Rib **7**
Full Kee **20**	Taberna del
Galileo **2**	Alabardero **10**
Georgia Brown's **14**	TenPenh **21**
Il Radicchio **29**	Tosca **19**
Jaleo **24**	Vidalia **1**
Kaz Sushi Bistro **8**	

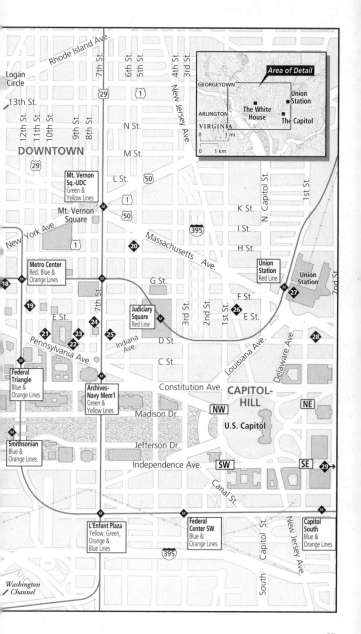

Rhode Island Ave.

Logan
Circle

13th St.

DOWNTOWN

(29)

7th St.
6th St.
5th St.
4th St.
3rd St.

(29)

(1)

New Jersey Ave.

12th St.
11th St.
10th St.
9th St.
8th St.

N St.

M St.

**Mt. Vernon
Sq.-UDC**
Green &
Yellow Lines

L St.

(1)

(50)

Mt. Vernon
Square

New York Ave.

(1)

Massachusetts Ave.

(50)

(395)

K St.

I St.

H St.

N. Capitol St.

1st St.

20

18

Metro Center
Red, Blue &
Orange Lines

19

E St.

21

22

23

24

7th St.

25

G St.

3rd St.

2nd St.

1st St.

**Judiciary
Square**
Red Line

Indiana
Ave.

Pennsylvania Ave.

D St.

**Union
Station**
Red Line

F St.

26

E St.

Louisiana Ave.

**Union
Station**

27

2nd St.

28

Delaware Ave.

C St.

**Federal
Triangle**
Blue &
Orange Lines

**Archives-
Navy Mem'l**
Green &
Yellow Lines

Constitution Ave.

Madison Dr.

**CAPITOL-
HILL**

NW

NE

U.S. Capitol

Smithsonian
Blue &
Orange Lines

Jefferson Dr.

Independence Ave.

SW

SE

29→

Canal St.

L'Enfant Plaza
Yellow, Green,
Orange &
Blue Lines

(395)

**Federal
Center SW**
Blue &
Orange Lines

South Capitol St.

New Jersey Ave.

**Capitol
South**
Blue &
Orange Lines

*Washington
Channel*

Area of Detail

GEORGETOWN

Union
Station

ARLINGTON

The White
House

The Capitol

VIRGINIA

0   1 mi

0   1 km

Dining at Sightseeing Attractions

Most eateries at sightseeing attractions are overpriced and too crowded, even if they are convenient. But a few places stand out, for their admirable cuisine, noteworthy setting, or both.

Prior to September 11, 2001, three restaurants within the Capitol building itself were open to the public at lunchtime, with certain conditions. As I write this, the Capitol Guide Service tells me that the **House of Representatives Restaurant** (also called the "Members' Dining Room") in Room H118, at the South end of the Capitol (© **202/ 225-6300**), the **Senate Dining Room** (© **202/224-2350**), and the **Refectory,** first floor, Room S112, Senate side of the Capitol (© **202/224-4870**), remain closed to the public. I mention them here on the chance that they may have reopened by the time you read this; if they have, and you would like to dine at one of them, be sure to call and find out the specific dress code and other requirements.

You are always welcome (after you've gone through security, of course) in the eateries located in the Capitol office buildings across the street from the Capitol. You'll be surrounded by Hill staffers, who head to places like the immense, full-service **Rayburn House Office Building Cafeteria** (© **202/225-7109**), which is in the basement of the building, at First Street and Independence Avenue SW. Adjoining the cafeteria is a carryout that sells pizza and sandwiches. At the **Longworth Building Cafeteria,** Independence Avenue and South Capitol Street SE (© **202/ 225-4410**), you can grab a bite from a fairly nice food court. By far the best deal for visitors is the **Dirksen Senate Office**

there's a sidewalk cafe.) The menu covers French classics like bouillabaisse, pistou, steak *frites* (fries), as well as Buben's own take on grilled salmon (with a fricassee of oysters and leeks on brioche), pan-seared red snapper, and seared scallops with tomatoes, garlic, olives, and an eggplant custard. Some items, such as steak au poivre, appear on both the lunch and dinner menus, but are considerably cheaper at lunch. The restaurant has been popular from the day it opened, with hungry movers and shakers intermingling with ordinary folk

Building South Buffet Room, First and C streets NE (℡ 202/ 224-4249). For just $10.95 per adult, $7.95 per child under 10, you can choose from a buffet that includes a carving station and eight other hot entrees; the price covers a non-alcoholic drink and dessert, too. The dining room gets crowded, but accepts reservations for parties of six or more.

In the same neighborhood, two institutions offering great deals and views (of famous sights or people) at week-day lunch are the **Library of Congress's** Cafeteria and its more formal Montpelier Room (℡ 202/707-8300 or 707-7512 for both), where the lunch options always cost under $10 per person; and the **Supreme Court's** Cafeteria (℡ 202/ 479-3246), where you'll likely spy a justice or two enjoying the midday meal.

Among museum restaurants, the ones that shine are the **Corcoran Gallery of Art's** Café des Artistes (℡ 202/639-1786); the six-story Atrium Cafe in the **National Museum of Natural History** (℡ 202/357-2700); the **National Gallery of Art's** Sculpture Garden Pavilion Café (℡ 202/289-3360) and Garden Café (℡ 202/216-2480); and the **Phillips Collection's** snug Café (℡ 202/387-2151).

Finally, the **Kennedy Center's** three restaurants, the Roof Terrace Restaurant and the Hors d'Oeuvrerie (℡ 202/416-8555, for both), offer theater-goers convenient, gourmet dining in glamorous settings. The Roof Terrace and the KC Café are especially dramatic, since immense windows provide panoramic views of the Potomac River and Washington landmarks.

who just love good food. The wine list is mostly French and American.

15 E St. NW. ℡ 202/661-2700. Reservations recommended. Breakfast $6.75–$12; lunch main courses $15–$22; dinner main courses $18.50–$28.50 AE, DC, DISC, MC, V. Daily 7–10am, 11:30am–2:30pm, and 5:30–10:30pm. Metro: Union Station.

The Monocle ⭐ *Finds* AMERICAN   A Capitol Hill institution, the Monocle has been around since 1960. This is a men-in-suits place, where the litter of briefcases resting against the too-close-together tables can make for treacherous navigating. But you might want to take a look at whose briefcase it is you're stumbling over, for its proximity to both the Supreme Court and the Capitol guarantees that the Monocle is the haunt of Supreme Court justices and members of Congress. At lunch you'll want to order either the hamburger, which is excellent, the tasty federal salad (field greens and tomatoes tossed with balsamic vinaigrette), the penne pasta with tomato-basil sauce and olives, or the white-bean soup, whenever it's on the menu. At dinner, consider the baked oysters or the pork-rib chop with pommery mustard sauce. Don't bother with the crab cakes. Service is old-style, all-male.

107 D St. NE. ⓒ **202/546-4488.** Reservations recommended. Lunch main courses $7.50–$17.95; dinner main courses $13.75–$28.50. AE, DC, MC, V. Mon–Fri 11:30am–midnight. Closed 2 weeks preceding Labor Day. Metro: Union Station.

INEXPENSIVE

Il Radicchio *Value* ITALIAN   What a great idea: Order a replenishable bowl of spaghetti for the table at a set price of $6.50, and each of you chooses your own sauce from a long list, at prices that range from $1.50 to $4. Most are standards, like the puttanesca with black olives, capers, garlic, anchovies, and tomato. My favorite is the radicchio, sausage, red wine, and tomato sauce. It's a great deal.

The kitchen prepares daily specials, like a sautéed fresh trout with sautéed green beans, and garlic and tomato sauce, as well as sandwiches, and an assortment of 14 wood-baked pizzas, with a choice of 26 toppings.

Ingredients are fresh and flavorful, the service quick and solicitous. The restaurant gets a lot of overworked and underpaid Hill staffers, who appreciate Il Radicchio's heartening food, and its low prices. See review of Barolo, above, if you are more interested in fine Italian dining.

223 Pennsylvania Ave. SE. ⓒ **202/547-5114.** Reservations not accepted. Main courses $5.50–$15.95. AE, DC, DISC, MC, V. Mon–Thurs 11:30am–10pm; Fri–Sat 11:30am–11pm; Sun 5–10pm. Metro: Capitol South.

2 Downtown, East of 16th Street NW

VERY EXPENSIVE

Butterfield 9 𝒜𝒜 NEW AMERICAN   In spring 2001, less than a year after opening, Butterfield 9 was chosen by *Condé Nast Traveler* magazine as one of the top 100 new restaurants *in the world*. It continues to win kudos. My husband and I have been pleased with our meals. Specifically, we like an appetizer called the "foie gras pancake," which is warmed goose liver within a pastry; as well as fried calamari, which is not the deep-fried ringlets you might expect, but a breaded slice of squid that has been stuffed with chorizo; and entrees, such as the pan-seared filet mignon, the horseradish-crusted Chilean sea bass with leek puree, and a pan-roasted rockfish served with lump crab-meat hash. Executive chef Martin Saylor changes his menu four times a year.

The highlight of Butterfield 9's classy decor is a series of large, stylized black-and-white prints of handsome men and women dressed in 1930s, '40s, and '50s fashions. Butterfield 9 is the latest venture of restaurateur Amarjeet (Umbi) Singh, owner of New Heights (p. 97). A bar menu of about nine items priced from $8 to $13 is available all day, featuring items like the soup of the day, a cheese plate with fresh fruit, and a sliced bison sandwich, crab cake, and gnocchi.

600 14th St. NW. © 202/BU9-8810. Reservations recommended. Lunch main courses $18–$22; dinner main courses $18–$33. AE, DC, DISC, MC, V. Mon–Fri 11:30am–2:30pm; Sun–Thurs 5:30–10pm; Fri–Sat 5:30–11pm. Metro: Metro Center.

The Caucus Room STEAK Washington's powerful people like steakhouses, and that's a fact. Since the Caucus Room is owned by a bipartisan bunch of heavy-hitting politicos and entrepreneurs (Democratic fundraiser and Clinton bud Terry McAuliffe and former Republican National Committee chairman Haley Barbour, to name but 2 of the 70 investors), the Caucus Room was almost a guaranteed success even before it opened in August 2000. At lunch and dinner, it's a true Washington scene, with all that that entails: a sprinkling of congressmen and -women, television newscasters, and corporate VIPs throughout the main dining room; lots of backslapping and shaking of hands; and private meetings taking place behind closed doors (the restaurant has a number of private dining rooms).

But I'm here to tell you, the food is good. Haley's chopped salad of diced bell peppers, blue cheese, and mustard vinaigrette is a hit. The porterhouse steak is juicy, and the rack of lamb, which bears a crust of goat cheese and fresh basil, is thoroughly delicious. The restaurant also is known for certain non-meat entrees, such as the crab cakes (the pass/fail test for a D.C. restaurant) and the timbale of lobster and crab, which layers romaine, diced yellow tomato and avocado, and corn, with lobster and crab meat placed on top, drizzled with a tequila-lime vinaigrette. Even side dishes, like the creamed spinach and the horseradish-spiked mashed potatoes, are winners.

When you've finished all that, you can lean back against the leather banquettes and discreetly search for famous faces while you enjoy dessert. I polished off a big slice of coconut cake, but I hear the pecan pie is pretty good, too.

401 9th St. NW (at D St.). ℂ 202/393-0777. Reservations recommended. Lunch items $10–$25; dinner main courses $24–$59; pretheater 25% discount (5:30–6:30); AE, DISC, MC, V. Mon–Fri 11:30am–2:30pm; Mon–Sat 5:30–10:30pm. Metro: Navy/Archives or Gallery Place.

EXPENSIVE

Andale 𝒢 MEXICAN   During a visit to the Yucatan peninsula in 2001, chef Allison Swope was so taken with the cuisine of Oaxaca, Mexico, that upon her return to Washington she set about transforming her "robust American" restaurant, The Mark, into the inventive Mexican Andale (*andale* means "let's go!"). The menu features dishes that combine authentic regional Mexican cuisine with fresh and often non-traditional ingredients: sushi grade tuna marinated with achiote, garlic, Mexican oregano, and sour orange juice; *pato al mole Negro oaxaqueno,* which is roasted duck served over Mexican red rice with a nut-based sauce that includes dried chiles, garlic, tomatillos, chocolate, and cinnamon. The slow-roasted leg of lamb, which has been rubbed with a paste of red chiles, garlic, and oregano, is a standout. Not to miss: the smoky, spicy salsa picante appetizer and the Mexican-style doughnuts with dipping chocolate for dessert. The bar offers 35 brands of tequila and concocts an excellent margarita.

Avoid being shown to the windowless back room, opting instead for seating in either the storefront window for optimum people-watching (Andale is in the middle of downtown), or in the main dining room, where Mexican artwork now hangs. Great deal: Every Monday after 5pm, you can order a bottle of wine or champagne for half price with the order of an entree.

401 7th St. NW. ℂ 202/783-3133. Reservations recommended. Lunch main courses $8–$14; dinner main courses $14–$22. AE, DC, DISC, MC, V. Mon–Sat 11:30am–3pm; Mon 5–9pm; Tues–Thurs 5–10pm; Fri–Sat 5–11pm; Mon–Fri bar stays open but no food is served, 3–5pm. Metro: Gallery Place or Archives/Navy Memorial.

Café Atlantico 𝒢𝒢 *Finds* SOUTH AMERICAN   This place rocks all week long, but especially on weekend nights, it's a favorite hot spot in Washington's still-burgeoning downtown. The colorful three-tiered restaurant throbs with Latin, calypso, and reggae music, and everyone is having a fiesta—including, it seems, the waiters. If the place is packed, try to snag a seat at the second-level bar, where you can watch the genial bartender mix the potent drinks for which Café Atlantico is famous: the *caipirinha,* made of limes, sugar, and *cachacha* (sugar-cane liqueur); the *mojito,* a rum and crushed mint cocktail; or the passion-fruit cocktail, a concoction of passion-fruit juice, ginger, and jalapeño mixed with mandarin orange–flavored vodka. But take a gander at the remarkable, award-winning wine list, too, whose 150 selections are mostly from South America, with many bottles priced under $30.

Seated at the bar or table, you'll watch as your waiter makes fresh guacamole right before your eyes. As for the main dishes, you can't get a more elaborate meal for the price. The ceviche, duck confit quesadilla with roasted red onions, Ecuadorian seared scallops, and Argentine rib eye are standouts (though the menu may change, you'll almost always find these on the menu), and tropical side dishes and pungent sauces produce a burst of color on the plate. Feel free to ask your friendly waiter for guidance.

405 8th St. NW. ✆ **202/393-0812.** Reservations recommended. Lunch main courses $9–$13; dinner main courses $18–$24; pretheater menu $22 (5–6:30pm); Latino dim sum $19.95 all you can eat (Sat 11:30am–1:30pm). AE, DC, DISC, MC, V. Mon–Fri 11:30am–2:30pm; Sun brunch 11:30am–3pm; Sun–Thurs 5–10pm; Fri–Sat 5–11pm. The bar stays open late on weekends. Metro: Archives–Navy Memorial and Gallery Place/MCI Center.

DC Coast ✿ AMERICAN

The dining room is sensational: two stories high, with glass-walled balcony, immense oval mirrors hanging over the bar, and a full-bodied stone mermaid poised to greet you at the entrance. Gather at the bar first to feel a part of the loud and trendy scene; while you're there, why not nosh on something from the bar menu, perhaps the Chinese lacquered duck and scallions or maybe a luscious lobster spring roll? This continues as one of the city's most popular restaurants, so call way ahead to book a reservation. Chef Jeff Tunks returned in 1998 from stints in Texas, California, and New Orleans, and some of the dishes Washingtonians remember from his years at the River Club have returned with him. His Chinese-style smoked lobster with crispy fried spinach is the most famous, and deservedly so—it's still tasty. Other entrees to recommend include the pan-seared sea scallops with gnocchi, crabmeat, Smithfield ham, and truffled veal jus, and the fish filet encrusted with portobello paste and served with truffled potatoes and porcini broth. Seafood is a big part of the menu, but there are a handful of meat dishes, too.

1401 K St. NW. ✆ **202/216-5988.** Reservations recommended. Lunch main courses $12–$18; dinner main courses $16–$29; light fare $6–$11. AE, DC, DISC,

MC, V. Mon–Fri 11:30am–2:30pm; Mon–Thurs 5:30–10:30pm; Fri–Sat 5:30–11pm
(light fare weekdays 2:30–5:30pm). Metro: McPherson Square.

Georgia Brown's ⍟ SOUTHERN   In Washington restaurants,
seldom do you find such a racially diverse crowd. The harmony may
stem from the waiters, whose obvious rapport results in gracious
service, and certainly extends from the open kitchen, where the chef
directs his multicultural staff. But in this large, handsome room,
whose arched windows overlook McPherson Square, the food may
capture all of your attention. A plate of corn bread and biscuits
arrives, to be slathered with butter that's been whipped with diced
peaches and honey. The menu is heavily Southern, with the emphasis on the Low Country cooking of South Carolina and Savannah:
collards, grits, and lots of seafood, especially shrimp dishes. The
Charleston *perlau* is a stew-like mix of duck, spicy sausage, jumbo
shrimp, and rice, topped with toasted crumbs and scallions. It has
bite but isn't terribly spicy. For something totally decadent, try the
buttermilk batter-fried chicken. Georgia Brown's is famous for its
Sunday brunch, lively with the sounds of jazz and conversation, and
luscious with the tastes of country sausage, omelets made to order,
creamy grits, and many other dishes.

950 15th St. NW. ✆ **202/393-4499.** Reservations recommended. Lunch main
courses $7–$20; dinner main courses $12–$23; Sun jazz brunch $22.95. AE, DC, DISC,
MC, V. Mon–Thurs 11:30am–10:30pm; Fri 11:30am–11:30pm; Sat 5:30–11:30pm;
Sun 11:30am–4:30pm (brunch 10:30am–2:30pm) and 5:30–10:30pm. Metro:
McPherson Square.

Oceanaire Seafood Room ⍟ SEAFOOD   The Oceanaire is a
good spot for a lively party, with its red-leather booths, Art Deco-
ish decor, long bar, and festive atmosphere. It would be hard to get
romantic or serious about business here—there's just too much to
distract you, like the sight of mile-high desserts en route to another
table. Oceanaire serves big portions of everything (including cocktails, another reason to bring a bunch of friends here). Two of the
best items on the menu are the crab cakes, which are almost all lump
crab meat, and the fisherman's platter, a fresh, fried selection of oysters, scallops, shrimp, and other seafood, with hot matchstick fries
alongside it all. The dozen varieties of oysters are fresh and plump,
but if you want to start with a salad, consider the Caesar. The
desserts turn out to look more enticing than they taste; the cherry
brown Betty is probably the best of the bunch.

1201 F St. NW. ✆ **202/347-2277.** Reservations recommended. Lunch main courses
$16–$25; dinner main courses $18–$35. AE, DISC, MC, V. Mon–Thurs
11:30am–10pm; Fri 11:30am–11pm; Sat 5–11pm; Sun 5–9pm. Metro: Metro Center.

TenPenh 🕿🕿 ASIAN FUSION   We'd heard that the service was excellent here, and this proved to be true: Our waiter actually split a glass of wine for me and my friend, when we both wanted a little more, but not an entire additional glass. And then our waiter checked out someone we thought was Rob Lowe in the bar, reporting back to us, alas, that it was not he. Anyway, what should bring you here is not just great service, but a warm atmosphere and stellar food. This is one of those restaurants that has a separate, loungy, hard-to-leave bar, but the dining room itself is inviting, with soft lighting, comfortable booths, and an open kitchen. In this, his second restaurant (DC Coast is his other), Jeff Tunks presents translations of dishes he's discovered in travels throughout Asia: smoked salmon and crisp wonton napoleon (which actually had too much salmon); halibut dusted with ground macadamia nuts and Japanese bread crumbs; whole deep-fried flounder; wok-seared calamari; and dumplings filled with chopped shrimp and water chestnuts. We finished with a trio of crème brûlée, the best of which was the coffee-crème.

1001 Pennsylvania Ave. NW (at 10th St.). 🕿 **202/393-4500.** Reservations recommended. Lunch main courses $11.95–$16.95; dinner main courses $13.95–$23.95. AE, DISC, MC, V. Mon–Fri 11:30am–2:30pm; Mon–Thurs 5:30–10:30pm; Fri–Sat 5:30–11pm. Metro: Archives–Navy Memorial.

Tosca 🕿🕿 NORTHERN ITALIAN   Washington probably has more Italian restaurants than any other kind of ethnic eatery, yet this central part of downtown has almost no Italian fare. In fact, when it opened in spring 2001, Tosca's was the only fine *ristorante italiano* between Capitol Hill and the western edge of downtown, a range of at least 20 blocks. (Since then, the new, less formal, Filomonde joined the neighborhood.) Tosca's interior design of pale pastels in the thick carpeting and heavy drapes creates a hushed atmosphere, a suitable foil to the rich food.

The menu, meanwhile, emphasizes the cooking of chef Cesare Lanfranconi's native Lake Como region of Italy. A good example of a traditional pasta dish is the "scapinasch," a ravioli of aged ricotta and raisins (or sometimes it's made with amaretto cookies) with butter and sage sauce. Lanfranconi's take on a veal filet is to marinate and grill the meat, serving it with braised cabbage and veal roasted-porcini mushroom sauce. Tosca has something for everyone, including simply grilled fish accompanied by organic vegetables for the health conscious, tiramisu and apple fritters for those with a sweet tooth. No wonder the restaurant is always full. Remarkably, even

Kids Family-Friendly Restaurants

Baby-boomer parents (and I am one) are so insistent upon taking their children with them everywhere that sometimes it seems all restaurants are forced to be family friendly, even if you wish certain ones were not. Hotel restaurants, no matter how refined, usually welcome children, since they may be guests of the hotel. The cafeterias at tourist attractions (see the box "Dining At Sightseeing Attractions" on p. 66) are always a safe bet, since they cater to the multitudes. Inexpensive ethnic restaurants tend to be pretty welcoming to kids, too. Aside from those general suggestions, I recommend the following:

Austin Grill   Another easygoing, good-service joint, with great background music. Kids will probably want to order from their own menu here, and their drinks arrive in unspillable plastic cups with tops and straws.

Legal Sea Foods *(p. 81)*   Believe it or not, this seafood restaurant has won awards for its kids' menu. It features the usual macaroni and cheese and hot dogs, but also kids' portions of steamed lobster; fried popcorn shrimp; a small fisherman's platter of shrimp, scallops, and clams; and other

when there's a crowd, Tosca doesn't get too noisy—the restaurant's designers kept the acoustics in mind.

1112 F St. NW. © 202/367-1990. Reservations recommended. Lunch main courses $12–$18; dinner main courses $15–$26. AE, DC, MC, V. Mon–Fri 11:30am–2:30pm; Sun–Thurs 5:30–10:30pm; Fri–Sat 5:30–11pm. Metro: Metro Center.

MODERATE

Jaleo ⊗ *Finds* SPANISH   In theater season, Jaleo's dining room fills and empties each evening according to the performance schedule of the Shakespeare Theater, right next door. Lunchtime always draws a crowd from nearby office buildings and the Hill. This restaurant, which opened in 1993, may be credited with initiating the tapas craze in Washington. The menu lists about 55 tapas, including a very simple but not-to-be-missed grilled bread layered with a paste of fresh tomatoes and topped with anchovies; savory warm goat cheese served with toast points; a skewer of grilled chorizo sausage atop garlic mashed potatoes; and a delicious mushroom tart served with roasted items, each of which comes with fresh fruit and a choice of baked potato, mashed potatoes, or french fries. Prices range from $3.95 for the hot dog to $15.95 for the 1-pound lobster.

Luigi's *(p. 81)*   Introduce your kids to pre-Domino's pizza. Luigi's, which has been around since 1943, serves the real thing: big, thick, ungreasy pizza, with fresh toppings. The restaurant also offers a full slate of pastas, sized and priced for children, everything from a $4.25 spaghetti and tomato sauce to a $4.95 lasagna. You sit at tables covered in red-checked cloths that have probably withstood countless spilled drinks and splotches of tomato sauce in their time. The restaurant gets noisy, so chances are that any loud ones in your party will blend right in.

Old Glory Barbecue *(p. 96)*   A loud, laid-back place where the waiters are friendly without being patronizing. Go early, since the restaurant becomes more of a bar as the evening progresses. There is a children's menu, but you may not need it—the barbecue, burgers, muffins, fries, and desserts are so good that everyone can order from the main menu.

red-pepper sauce. Paella is among the few heartier entrees (it feeds 4). Spanish wines, sangrias, and sherries are available by the glass. Finish with a rum-and-butter soaked apple charlotte in bread pastry or a plate of Spanish cheeses. The casual-chic interior focuses on a large mural of a flamenco dancer inspired by John Singer Sargent's painting *Jaleo*. On Wednesday at 8 and 9pm, flamenco dancers perform.

Jaleo recently opened a second and very pretty restaurant in the suburbs, at 7271 Woodmont Ave., Bethesda, Maryland (© **301/ 913-0003**). Though this new branch is within walking distance of my house, I prefer the ambience of the original D.C. location.

480 7th St. NW (at E St.). © 202/628-7949. Reservations accepted until 6:30pm. Lunch main courses $7.50–$10.75; dinner main courses $10.50–$28; tapas $3.95–$7.95. AE, DC, DISC, MC, V. Sun–Mon 11:30am–10pm; Tues–Thurs 11:30am–11:30pm; Fri–Sat 11:30pm–midnight. Metro: Archives or Gallery Place.

Old Ebbitt Grill AMERICAN   You won't find this place listed among the city's best culinary establishments, but you can bet it's included in every tour book. It's an institution. Located 2 blocks from the White House, this is the city's oldest saloon, founded in 1856. Among its artifacts are animal trophies bagged by Teddy Roosevelt, and Alexander Hamilton's wooden bears—one with a secret compartment in which it's said he hid whiskey bottles from his wife. The Old Ebbitt is attractive, with Persian rugs strewn on beautiful oak and marble floors, beveled mirrors, flickering gaslights, etched-glass panels, and paintings of Washington scenes. The long, dark mahogany Old Bar area emphasizes the men's saloon ambience.

Tourists and office people fill the Ebbitt during the day, flirting singles take it over at night. You'll always have to wait for a table if you don't reserve ahead. The waiters are friendly and professional in a programmed sort of way; service could be faster. Menus change daily but always include certain favorites: burgers, trout Parmesan (Virginia trout dipped in egg batter and Parmesan cheese, deep-fried), crab cakes, and oysters (there's an oyster bar). The tastiest dishes are usually the seasonal ones, whose fresh ingredients make the difference.

675 15th St. NW (between F and G sts.). ℂ **202/347-4801.** Reservations recommended. Breakfast $6.95–$9.95; brunch $5.95–$13.95; lunch main courses $6.95–$13.95 (as much as $24.95 when crab cakes are on the menu); dinner main courses $13.95–$20.95 (again, up to $24.95 for crab cakes); burgers and sandwiches $6.95–$10.95; raw bar $8.95–$18.50. AE, DC, DISC, MC, V. Mon–Thurs 7:30am–2am; Fri 7:30am–3am; Sat 8:30am–3am; Sun 9:30am–2am (kitchen closes at 1am nightly). Raw bar open until midnight daily. Metro: McPherson Square or Metro Center.

INEXPENSIVE

Full Kee ℛ CHINESE   Washington's Chinatown restaurants tend to look a little sketchy and Full Kee is no exception. Full Kee's two rooms are brightly lit and crammed with Chinese-speaking customers sitting on metal-legged chairs at plain rectangular tables. There's no such thing as a no-smoking section. A cook works in the small open kitchen at the front of the room, hanging roasted pig's parts on hooks and wrapping dumplings. Still, it has the best food in Chinatown.

Chefs from some of Washington's best restaurants sometimes congregate here after hours, and here's their advice: Ask the waitress for translations of the seasonal specials written (in Chinese) on the wall. If you don't hear them mentioned, be sure to ask about two selections I can personally vouch for: the jumbo breaded oyster casserole with ginger and scallions, and the whole steamed fish. If you love dumplings, you must order the Hong Kong–style shrimp dumpling broth: You get either eight shrimp dumplings or four if you order the broth with noodles. Bring your own wine or beer if you'd like to have a drink, since Full Kee does not serve any alcohol.

509 H St. NW. ✆ 202/371-2233. Reservations accepted. Lunch main courses $4.25–$9; dinner main courses $6.95–$17. No credit cards. Sun–Thurs 11am–1am; Fri–Sat 11am–3am. Metro: Gallery Place/Chinatown.

3 Downtown, 16th Street NW & West
VERY EXPENSIVE

Galileo ✰✰✰ PIEDMONTESE ITALIAN   Food critics mention Galileo as one of the best Italian restaurants in the country and Roberto Donna as one of the nation's best chefs. The likable Donna opened the white-walled grottolike Galileo in 1984; since then, he has opened several other restaurants in the area, including Il Radicchio (p. 68) and Barolo (p. 63), both on Capitol Hill. He's also written a cookbook, and has established himself as an integral part of Washington culture.

Donna cures his own ham for salami and prosciutto, and his sausages, pastas, mozzarella, marmalades, and breads are all made in-house. Galileo features the cuisine of Donna's native Piedmont region, an area in northern Italy influenced by neighboring France and Switzerland—think truffles, hazelnuts, porcini mushrooms, and veal. The atmosphere is relaxed; some diners are dressed in jeans, others in suits. Waiters can be supercilious, though.

You have many options. You can order a la carte, or choose either of two different fixed-price menus, at $60 or $80. Typical entrees include a risotto with black truffles, whole roasted baby pig stuffed with sausage and porcini mushrooms, a house-made saffron pasta with ragout of veal, or a roasted black sea bass served with sesame sauce. Finish with a traditional tiramisu, or, better yet, the milk chocolate passion fruit torte with a crème brûlée center. The cellar boasts more than 900 vintages of Italian wine (40% Piedmontese).

But wait—there's more. For the ultimate dining experience, book a seat at the table in Donna's **Laboratorio del Galileo** ✰✰✰, a private dining area and kitchen enclosed by glass, where Donna prepares the 10- to 12-course tasting menu ($98 weekdays, $110 weekends) and entertains you and 29 other lucky diners. There is also a terrace for warm-weather dining.

1110 21st St. NW. ✆ 202/293-7191. Reservations recommended. Lunch main courses $12–$19; dinner main courses $24–$35. AE, DC, DISC, MC, V. Mon–Fri

11:30am–2pm and 5:30–10pm; Sat 5:30–10:30pm; Sun 5:30–10pm. Metro: Foggy Bottom.

The Prime Rib ✿ STEAK/SEAFOOD   The Prime Rib has plenty of competition now, but it makes no difference. Beef lovers still consider this The Place. It's got a definite men's club feel about it, with brass-trimmed black walls, leopard-skin carpeting, and comfortable black-leather chairs and banquettes. Waiters are in black tie, and a pianist at the baby grand plays show tunes and Irving Berlin classics.

The meat is from the best grain-fed steers and has been aged for 4 to 5 weeks. Steaks and cuts of roast beef are thick, tender, and juicy. In case you had any doubt, The Prime Rib's prime rib is the best item on the menu, juicy and thick, top-quality meat. For less carnivorous diners, there are about a dozen seafood entrees, including an excellent crab imperial. Mashed potatoes are done right, as are the fried potato skins, but I recommend the hot cottage fries.

2020 K St. NW. ✆ **202/466-8811.** Reservations recommended. Jacket and tie required for men. Lunch main courses $11–$20; dinner main courses $20–$35. AE, DC, MC, V. Mon–Thurs 11:30am–3pm and 5–11pm; Fri 11:30am–3pm and 5–11:30pm; Sat 5–11:30pm. Metro: Farragut West.

Taberna del Alabardero ✿✿ *Finds* SPANISH   Dress up to visit this truly elegant restaurant, where you receive royal treatment from the Spanish staff, which is quite used to attending to the real thing (Spain's King Juan Carlos and Queen Sofia and their children regularly dine here when in Washington). In 1999, the Spanish ministry of agriculture named Taberna the best Spanish restaurant in the United States.

Newly refurbished, the dining room remains ornate, with green leather covering booths and stools, satin stretched across chairs, and gilded cherubs placed at ceiling corners. Order a plate of tapas to start: lightly fried calamari, shrimp in garlic and olive oil, thin smoky ham, and marinated mushrooms. Although the a la carte menu changes with the seasons, four paellas (the menu says each feeds 2, but you can ask for a single serving) are always available. The lobster and seafood paella served on saffron rice is rich and flavorful. (Ask to have the lobster shelled; otherwise, you do the cracking.) Another signature dish is the stuffed squid sauced in its own ink. The wine list features 250 Spanish wines.

This is the only Taberna del Alabardero outside of Spain, where there are seven locations. All are owned and operated by Father Luis de Lezama, who opened his first tavern outside the palace gates in Madrid in 1974, as a place to train delinquent boys for employment.

1776 I St. NW (entrance on 18th St. NW). (C) **202/429-2200.** Reservations recommended. Jacket and tie for men suggested. Lunch main courses $17.25–$20.75; dinner main courses $19–$32; tapas $7.75–$12. AE, DC, DISC, MC, V. Mon–Fri 11:30am–2:30pm and 5:30–10:30pm; Sat 5:30–11pm. Metro: Farragut West.

EXPENSIVE

Equinox ✷✷ NEW AMERICAN Everyone seems to love Equinox. It's not splashy in any way, just a pretty, comfortable restaurant that serves creatively delicious American food. Even if you aren't vegetarian, you'll eat all your vegetables here, because as much care is taken with these garnishes as with the entree itself. And every entree comes with a garnish or two, like the leek fondue or the forest mushrooms with applewood bacon, or the cherry tomatoes with Indian corn sauce. You can order additional side dishes; consider the macaroni and cheese: Vermont cheddar, Parmesan, and black truffle reduction. The home runs, of course, are the entrees: the crab cakes, which are made with lump crab mixed with capers, brioche bread crumbs, mayonnaise, and lemon-butter sauce; or perhaps the pork chop with Calvados sauce and braised kale. For love of vegetables, Equinox always offers a vegetable entree, such as the wide spinach noodles with caramelized salsify, baby carrots, and roasted garlic cream. Equinox has two tasting menus, a $60 five-course dinner available most nights, and the $35 three-course tasting menu served only on Sunday evenings.

818 Connecticut Ave. NW. (C) **202/331-8118.** Reservations recommended. Lunch main courses $15–$24; dinner main courses $19–$29. AE, DC, DISC, MC, V. Mon–Fri 11:30am–2pm, Mon–Thurs 5:30–10pm; Fri–Sat 5:30–10:30pm; Sun 5–9pm. Metro: Farragut West.

Oval Room at Lafayette Square ✷✷ NEW AMERICAN The Oval Room is a local favorite, another winner for owner Ashok Bajaj, who also owns the Bombay Club (p. 80), across the street, and several other restaurants around town. Everyone talks about how nicely the renovation turned out, but since I never saw the original look, all I can tell you is that the Oval Room's new decor and layout do make for a congenial atmosphere. It is a handsome restaurant, with contemporary art hanging on its lettuce-colored walls. But it isn't stuffy, no doubt because the bar area separating the restaurant into two distinct rooms sends cheerful sounds in either direction. The quality of the food has always been top-notch: I've liked the napoleon of jumbo lump crab with cracked spices, and the roasted New York strip steak with oven roasted potatoes, grilled asparagus, and béarnaise sauce. In case you haven't figured it out, the Oval Room is a short walk from the White House.

800 Connecticut Ave. NW, at Lafayette Square. © **202/463-8700.** Reservations recommended. Lunch main courses $12–$18; dinner main courses $17.50–$25.50. AE, DISC, MC, V. Mon–Fri 11:30am–3pm; Mon–Thurs 5:30–10pm; Fri–Sat 5:30–10:30pm. Metro: Farragut West.

Vidalia ✹✹ REGIONAL AMERICAN/SOUTHERN If you're hesitant to dine at a restaurant that's down a flight of steps from the street, your doubts will vanish as soon as you enter Vidalia's tiered dining room. There's a party going on down here. In fact, Vidalia is so popular, you may have to wait a short time in the narrow bar, even if you arrive on time for your reservation. But the bar is fun, too, and gives you a jump start on getting into the mood of the place.

Executive chef Peter Smith adds Asian and French accents to owner/chef Jeff Buben's regional Southern cuisine. The menu changes frequently, but recommended constants include crisp East Coast lump crab cakes and a fried grits cake with taso ham. Venture from the regular items and you may delight in a timbale of roasted onion and foie gras, sautéed sea scallops with udon cake, or monkfish on a creamy saffron risotto. A signature entree is the scrumptious sautéed shrimp on a mound of creamed grits and caramelized onions in a thyme-and-shrimp cream sauce. Corn bread and biscuits with apple butter are served at every meal. Vidalia is known for its lemon chess pie, which tastes like pure sugar; I prefer the pecan pie. A carefully chosen wine list highlights American vintages.

1990 M St. NW. © **202/659-1990.** Reservations recommended. Lunch main courses $6.75–$18.75; dinner main courses $19–$29. AE, DC, DISC, MC, V. Mon–Fri 11:30am–2:30pm; Mon–Thurs 5:30–10pm; Fri–Sat 5:30–10:30pm; Sun 5–9pm (closed Sun July 4–Labor Day). Metro: Dupont Circle.

MODERATE

Bombay Club ✹ *Finds* INDIAN This used to be a favorite stop for the Clintons, but perhaps the menu is too exotic for the current president—no word yet of Bush sightings here. (The White House is just across Lafayette Park.) But I would encourage the Bushes to come by, especially since the Bombay Club dishes present an easy introduction to Indian food for the uninitiated, and are sensitive to varying tolerances for spiciness.

The Indian menu ranges from fiery green chile chicken ("not for the fainthearted," the menu warns) to the delicately prepared lobster malabar, a personal favorite. Tandoori dishes, like the chicken marinated in a yogurt, ginger, and garlic dressing, are specialties, as is the vegetarian fare—try the black lentils cooked overnight on a slow fire. Patrons are as fond of the service as the cuisine: Waiters seem straight out of *Jewel in the Crown,* attending to your every whim. This is one place where you can linger over a meal as long as you like. The Bombay Club is known for its vegetarian offerings (at least 9 items are on the menu) and for its Sunday champagne brunch, which offers a buffet of fresh juices, fresh baked breads, and assorted Indian dishes. Slow-moving ceiling fans and wicker furniture accentuate the colonial British ambience.

815 Connecticut Ave. NW. ✆ 202/659-3727. Reservations recommended. Main courses $7.50–$18.95; Sun brunch $18.50. AE, DC, MC, V. Mon–Fri and Sun brunch 11:30am–2:30pm; Mon–Thurs 6–10:30pm; Fri–Sat 6–11pm; Sun 5:30–9pm. Metro: Farragut West.

Legal Sea Foods 🏃 (Kids) SEAFOOD   This famous family run Boston-based seafood empire, whose motto is "If it's not fresh, it's not Legal," made its Washington debut in 1995. The softly lit dining room is plush, with terrazzo marble floors and rich cherry-wood paneling. Sporting events, especially Boston games, are aired on a TV over the handsome marble bar/raw bar, and you can usually pick up a copy of the *Boston Globe* near the entrance. As for the food, not only is everything fresh, but it's all from certified-safe waters.

Legal's buttery-rich clam chowder is a classic. Other worthy appetizers include garlicky golden-brown farm-raised mussels au gratin and fluffy pan-fried Maryland lump crab cakes served with a green salad and apple slices. You can have one of eight or so varieties of fresh fish grilled or opt for one of Legal's specialty dishes, like the Portuguese fisherman's stew, in which cod, mussels, clams, and chorizo are prepared in a saffron-tomato broth. Top it off with a slice of Boston cream pie. Wine lovers will be happy to know that Legal's wine list has received recognition from *Wine Spectator* magazine; parents will be glad that Legal's award-winning kid's menu offers not just macaroni and cheese, but steamed lobster, popcorn shrimp, and other items, each of which comes with fresh fruit and a choice of baked potato, mashed potatoes, or french fries. At lunch, oyster po' boys and the lobster roll are real treats.

You'll find another Legal Sea Foods in the new terminal at National Airport (✆ 703/413-9810); a third location is at 704 Seventh St. NW (✆ 202/347-0007), across from the MCI Center.

2020 K St. NW. ✆ 202/496-1111. Reservations recommended, especially at lunch. Lunch main courses $8–$15; sandwiches $9–$17; dinner main courses $12–$30. AE, DC, DISC, MC, V. Mon–Thurs 11am–10pm; Fri 11am–10:30pm; Sat 4–10:30pm. Metro: Farragut North or Farragut West.

INEXPENSIVE

Famous Luigi's Pizzeria Restaurant (Kids) ITALIAN   Before there was Domino's or Pizza Hut or Papa John's, there was Luigi's.

Make that *way* before—Luigi's opened in 1943. People who grew up in Washington consider Luigi's an essential part of their childhood. So I took my daughters here one weekday several summers ago, and sure enough, it's remained a favorite place ever since. (They often ask to be taken here on their birthdays.) Whether you go at lunch or dinner, you can expect to be among a sea of office folks. At night, the restaurant's atmosphere changes a little, as office workers come in groups to unwind, have a drink, or get a bite; but this isn't a bar, so it doesn't get rowdy. The menu is long, listing all kinds of pastas, sandwiches, grilled dishes, and pizzas. Come here for a little local color, and to please everyone in the family. Luigi's children's menu is really children's portions of Luigi specialties: spaghetti with tomato sauce, cheese ravioli, lasagna, penne with cream sauce, plain cheese pizza, and cheese manicotti, for less than $5 each.

1132 19th St. NW (between L and M sts.). ✆ **202/331-7574.** Main courses $4.25–$14.95. AE, DC, DISC, MC, V. Mon–Sat 11am–midnight; Sun noon–midnight. Metro: Dupont Circle or Farragut North.

4 U Street Corridor

INEXPENSIVE

Ben's Chili Bowl *(Finds* AMERICAN Ben's is a veritable institution, a mom-and-pop place, where everything looks, tastes, and probably even costs the same as when the restaurant opened in 1958. The most expensive item on the menu is the turkey sub, for $6.10. Formica counters, red bar stools, and a jukebox that plays Motown and reggae tunes—that's Ben's. Ben's continues as a gathering place for black Washington and visitors like Bill Cosby, who's a longtime customer (a chili dog is named after him). Everyone's welcome, though, even the late-nighters who come streaming out of nearby nightclubs at 2 or 3 in the morning on the weekend. Of course, the chili, cheese fries, and half-smokes are great, but so are breakfast items. Try the salmon cakes, grits, scrapple, or blueberry pancakes.

1213 U St. NW. ✆ **202/667-0909.** Reservations not accepted. Main courses $2.48–$6.11. No credit cards. Mon–Thurs 6am–2am; Fri–Sat 6am–4am; Sun noon–8pm. Metro: U St.–Cardozo.

5 Adams-Morgan

EXPENSIVE

Cashion's Eat Place ✦✦ *(Finds* AMERICAN Cashion's has all the pleasures of a neighborhood restaurant—easy, warm, comfortable—combined with cuisine that is out of this world. Owner/chef Ann Cashion continues to rack up culinary awards as easily as she pleases

Adams-Morgan & Dupont Circle Dining

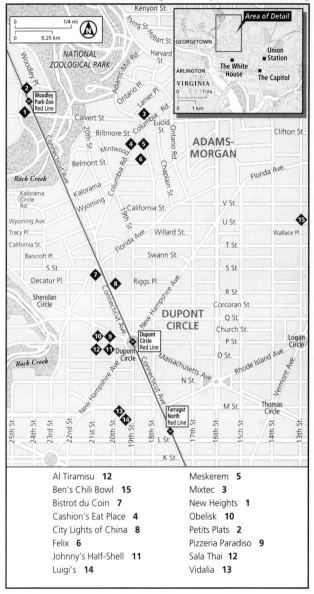

Al Tiramisu **12**	Meskerem **5**
Ben's Chili Bowl **15**	Mixtec **3**
Bistrot du Coin **7**	New Heights **1**
Cashion's Eat Place **4**	Obelisk **10**
City Lights of China **8**	Petits Plats **2**
Felix **6**	Pizzeria Paradiso **9**
Johnny's Half-Shell **11**	Sala Thai **12**
Luigi's **14**	Vidalia **13**

her patrons. Her menu changes daily, always featuring about eight entrees, split between seafood and meat: fritto misto of whole jumbo shrimp and black sea bass filet, served with onion rings and house-made tartar sauce, or fried sweetbreads on a bed of sautéed spinach, and so on. The side dishes that accompany each entree, such as lemon cannelloni bean purée or radish and sprout salad, are worth as much attention. Chocolate cinnamon mousse, lime tartalette, and other desserts are worth saving room for. Sunday brunch is popular, too; you can choose from breakfast fare (challah French toast, spinach and Gruyère omelets) or heartier items (grilled rainbow trout, croque monsieurs).

The charming dining room curves around a slightly raised bar. In warm weather, the glass-fronted Cashion's opens invitingly to the sidewalk, where you can also dine. Tables at the back offer a view of the small kitchen, where Cashion and her staff work away. In winter, ask for a table away from the front door, which lets in a blast of cold air with each new arrival.

1819 Columbia Rd. NW (between 18th St. and Mintwood Place). (*€* **202/797-1819.** Reservations recommended. Brunch $7–$17; dinner main courses $17–$26. MC, V. Tues 5:30–10pm; Wed–Sat 5:30–11pm; Sun 11:30am–2:30pm and 5:30–10pm.

Felix Restaurant and Lounge *(Moments* AMERICAN   Fans of Sarah Jessica Parker, martinis, good food, and live music will all be happy at Felix's. Sunday nights mean viewings of *Sex and the City;* the rest of the week, there's a different live music group every night (jazz Mon and Tues, Sinatra standards Wed, rhythm and soul Thurs, funk rock Fri and Sat). And every night presents a menu of martinis and delicious dinner options: herb-crusted sea bass with French lentils and raspberry coulis, pan-roasted rib-eye steak, or fresh yellowfin tuna pan-seared and served with sticky rice, snow peas, and wasabi cream sauce. Felix is famous for its Bananas Foster, which is always available; caramelized bananas are topped with vanilla-bean gelato, hot fudge, chopped walnuts, and whipped cream. Felix's offspring, the Spy Lounge, shares its entrance with the restaurant.

2406 18th St. NW. (*€* **202/483-3549.** Reservations recommended. Main courses $17–$27. AE, DC, DISC, MC, V. Nightly 5:30pm–3am.

INEXPENSIVE

Meskerem ETHIOPIAN   Washington has a number of Ethiopian restaurants, but this is probably the best. It's certainly the most attractive; the three-level high-ceilinged dining room (sunny by day, candlelit at night) has an oval skylight girded by a painted sunburst and walls hung with African art and musical instruments. On the mezzanine level, you sit at *messobs* (basket tables) on low, carved Ethiopian chairs or upholstered leather poufs. Ethiopian music enhances the ambience.

Diners share large platters of food, which they scoop up with a sourdough crepe-like pancake called *injera* (no silverware here). Items listed as *watt* are hot and spicy; *alitchas* are milder and more delicately flavored. You might also share an entree—perhaps *yegeb kay watt* (succulent lamb in thick, hot *berbere* sauce)—along with a platter of five vegetarian dishes served with tomato and potato salads. Some combination platters comprise an array of beef, chicken, lamb, and vegetables. There's a full bar; the wine list includes Ethiopian wine and beer.

2434 18th St. NW (between Columbia and Belmont rds.). ℂ 202/462-4100. Reservations recommended. Lunch main courses $7.95–$9.95; dinner main courses $9.95–$11.95. AE, DC, MC, V. Daily noon–midnight.

Mixtec ⍟*Value* REGIONAL MEXICAN   This cheerful Adams-Morgan spot attracts a clientele of neighborhood folks, D.C. chefs, and Hispanics from all over, all of whom appreciate the delicious authenticity of the regional Mexican cuisine. The kitchen is open, the dining room colorfully decorated, and the Mexican music lively.

Two items are served here that you can't find at any of the many other Southwestern eateries in the capital: the authentic *menudo,* a stew of tripe and calf's feet (granted, not for everyone); and *tortas,* which are a kind of Mexican sub, layered with grilled pork, chiles, guacamole, and salsa. You will also find delicious small dishes called *antojitos* ("little whims"), in the $2.50 to $4.95 range, which include *queso fundido* (a bubbling hot dish of broiled Chihuahua cheese topped with shredded spicy chorizo sausage flavored with jalapeños and cilantro); and the *enrollados mexicanos,* large flour tortillas wrapped around a variety of fillings, including grilled chicken, beef, vegetables, and salmon. The freshly prepared guacamole is excellent. Choose from 30 kinds of tequila, tequila-mixed drinks, Mexican beers, and fresh fruit juices.

1792 Columbia Rd. (just off 18th St.). ℂ 202/332-1011. Main courses $3.95–$11.95. MC, V. Sun–Thurs 8:30am–10pm, Fri–Sat 8:30am–11pm.

6 Dupont Circle
VERY EXPENSIVE
Obelisk ⍟⍟⍟ ITALIAN   Obelisk is the most consistently excellent restaurant in the city. Service and food are simply the best. In

this pleasantly spare room that seats only 36, the walls are decorated with 19th-century French botanical prints and Italian lithographs. Here, owner/chef Peter Pastan presents his small fixed-price menus of sophisticated Italian cuisine, using the freshest possible ingredients. Each night diners are offered two or three choices for each of five courses. Dinner might begin with mushroom crostini, followed by Tuscan bean soup, and then an artfully arranged dish of pan-cooked cod with fried asparagus and green sauce, or soft-shell crab upon a bed of white beans, or beef filet topped with anchovy paste. Dessert is a choice of cheese or baked specialties, like pear spice cake. Breads and desserts are all baked in-house and are divine. Pastan's carefully crafted wine list represents varied regions of Italy, as well as California vintages. The fixed-price menu is a deal, but the cost of wine and coffees can easily double the price per person.

2029 P St. NW. (near 21st St.) ✆ 202/872-1180. Reservations recommended. Fixed-price 5-course dinner $55 Tues–Thurs, $58 Fri–Sat. DC, MC, V. Tues–Sat 6–10pm. Metro: Dupont Circle.

EXPENSIVE

Al Tiramisu ✷✷ *Finds* ITALIAN I called last minute for a reservation and the staff was kind enough to squeeze in four of us (*squeeze* being the operative word, as the tables are a little snug in this narrow but intimate restaurant). But the charming servers have time to chat a little without keeping you waiting. It was refreshing to have our waiter, without any discussion, hand the wine list to me, rather than to one of the men at the table. Make sure you give the menu due consideration; this is one place where the mainstays are just as good (and certainly cheaper) than the daily specials. Al Tiramisu is known for its grilled fish and for its black and white truffles, a favorite item of certain Kennedy clan members. Also exceptional are the grilled squid, house-made spinach-ricotta ravioli with butter and sage sauce, and the osso buco. This is a place to come if you need cheering up. Ebullient chef/owner Luigi Diotaiuti makes his presence known sometimes. In 2002, Luigi directed a staff of 15 Italian chefs serving food to the Italian athletes, media, and dignitaries at the Salt Lake City Winter Olympics.

2014 P St. NW. ✆ 202/467-4466. Reservations required. Lunch main courses $6–$17; dinner main courses $14–$20. AE, DC, MC, V. Mon–Fri noon–2:30pm; Mon–Sat 5:30–10:30pm; Sun 5–9:30pm. Metro: Dupont Circle.

Johnny's Half Shell ✷ *Finds* SEAFOOD Whenever a friend visits from out of town and I haven't gotten around to making a restaurant reservation, we usually end up at Johnny's. It's easy, fun, and comfortable; it's open continuously from lunch through the afternoon to closing, and it takes no reservations, so you can usually walk right in and get something fresh from the sea (though weekend nights after 8:30pm, you'll probably have at least a 20-min. wait); and it feels like a hometown restaurant, a rare thing in a city whose residents tend to originate from many other hometowns. Johnny's owners, Ann Cashion and John Fulchino, own another very popular restaurant, Cashion's Eat Place (p. 82) in Adams-Morgan. The restaurant is small, with a decor that features an aquarium behind the long bar, booths along one paneled wall, a tile floor, and a partly open kitchen. The professional yet friendly waiters seem to be enjoying themselves.

Everything on the menu looks good, from the farm-raised chicken with old-fashioned Eastern Shore slippery dumplings, garden peas, and button mushrooms, to the crab meat imperial with a salad of *haricots verts* (young green beans), tomatoes, and shallots. I recently opted for the delicious fried oyster po'boy sandwich, while my friend Sue went for the Maryland crab cakes with coleslaw and french fries; we both devoured every morsel. If the sautéed soft-shell crabs with Old Bay and basil beurre blanc and corn pudding are on the menu, get them. My daughter Cait likes the barbecued shrimp appetizer with Asiago cheese grits. Oysters and Wellfleet clams on the half shell are always available, of course. The short wine list includes a few selections by the glass; there are four beers on tap. Desserts are simple but perfect, including homemade ice cream, a choice of hazelnut, almond, pecan or chocolate tart, and chocolate angel food cake with caramel sauce.

2002 P St. NW. ✆ **202/296-2021.** Reservations not accepted. Lunch main courses $5.95–$19.95; dinner main courses $11.95–$21.95. AE, MC, V. Mon–Thurs 11:30am–10:30pm; Fri–Sat 11:30am–11pm. Metro: Dupont Circle.

MODERATE

Bistrot du Coin ✪ FRENCH   When Michel Richard, acclaimed chef of Michel Richard Citronelle (p. 92), is homesick, he visits this restaurant, because he thinks it feels like France. I think so, too. The wooden facade that draws your attention from the street, the way the whole glass front of the dining room opens right to the sidewalk, the zinc bar, the moody waiters—everything speaks of a Paris cafe, most of all the food.

I keep hearing that the mussels are the thing to order, either curried and creamed, or hiding in a thick gratin of leeks, but so far I have chosen other dishes and been pleased. The cassoulet is delicious, and not too hearty; the *tartine baltique* turned out to be an open-faced sandwich with smoked salmon, tamara onions, capers, and olive oil, and I slurped down every bite. The steak *frites* are just what you'd hope for, tasty and comforting. The menu presents a very limited number of wines, along with a list of 16 aperitifs. I chose the licorice-flavored Ricard, which is similar to pastis.

1738 Connecticut Ave. NW (near Florida Ave.). © 202/234-6969. Main courses $12.75–$26.50. AE, DISC, MC, V. Sun 11am–11pm; Mon–Wed 11:30am–11pm; Thurs–Sat 11:30am–1am. Metro: Dupont Circle.

City Lights of China CHINESE   One of Washington's best Chinese restaurants outside of Chinatown, City Lights is a favorite of White House workaholics, whatever administration, who frequently order takeout from here. If you are staying at a nearby hotel, you might consider ordering food to go, as well; takeout prices are cheaper for some items. Some of the most popular dishes include crisp fried Cornish hen prepared in a cinnamon-soy marinade and served with a tasty dipping sauce, Chinese eggplant in garlic sauce, stir-fried spinach, crisp fried shredded beef, and Peking duck. The setting, a three-tiered dining room with much of the seating in comfortable leather booths and banquettes, is unpretentious. Neat white-linen tablecloths, cloth flower arrangements in lighted niches, and green neon track lighting complete the picture. There's a full bar.

1731 Connecticut Ave. NW (between R and S sts.). © 202/265-6688. Reservations recommended. Lunch main courses $6.95–$23.95 (most are about $8.95); dinner main courses $9.95–$25.95 (most are about $12.95). AE, DC, DISC, MC, V. Mon–Fri 11:30am–11pm; Sat noon–11pm; Sun noon–10:30pm; dinner from 3pm daily. Metro: Dupont Circle.

INEXPENSIVE

Pizzeria Paradiso ✦ ITALIAN   Peter Pastan, master chef/owner of Obelisk (located right next door and reviewed just above), owns this classy, often crowded, 16-table pizzeria. An oak-burning oven at one end of the charming room produces exceptionally doughy but light pizza crusts. As you wait, you can munch on mixed olives and gaze up at the ceiling painted to suggest blue sky peeking through ancient stone walls. Pizzas range from the plain Paradiso, which offers chunks of tomatoes covered in melted mozzarella, to the robust Siciliano, a blend of nine ingredients including eggplant and red onion. Or you can choose your own toppings from a list of 29. As popular as the pizzas are the *panini* (sandwiches) of homemade focaccia stuffed with marinated roasted lamb and vegetables and other fillings, and the salads, such as tuna and white bean. Good desserts, but a limited wine list.

2029 P St. NW. ☎ **202/223-1245.** Reservations not accepted. Pizzas $7.95–$16.25; sandwiches and salads $3.95–$6.95. DC, MC, V. Mon–Thurs 11:30am–11pm; Fri–Sat 11:30am–midnight; Sun noon–10pm. Metro: Dupont Circle.

Sala Thai THAI   At lunch, you'll see a lot of diners sitting alone and reading newspapers, happy to escape the office. At dinner, the restaurant is filled with groups and couples, plus the occasional family. Among the 53 items to recommend on the menu are no. 41, *nua kra ting tone,* which is spicy beef with onion, garlic, and parsley sauce ("not found at any other Thai restaurant in Washington," said my Thai waitress, sporting multicolored streaks in her hair), and, no. 26, *ka prow,* which is an even spicier dish of either beef, chicken, or pork sautéed with basil leaves and chile. The restaurant lies downstairs from the street; with no windows to watch what's happening on P Street, you're really here for the food, which is excellent and cheap. Even conventional pad thai doesn't disappoint. Pay attention if your waiter cautions you about the level of spiciness of a dish you order—for some dishes (like no. 38, stir-fried sliced pork in red curry sauce with peppers), you'll need an asbestos tongue.

2016 P St. NW. ☎ **202/872-1144.** Reservations accepted for 5 or more. Lunch main courses $6.25–$9; dinner main courses $7.25–$13. AE, DC, DISC, MC, V. Mon–Fri 11:30am–3pm; Mon 4–10:30pm; Tues–Thurs 4–11pm; Fri 4–11:30pm; Sat noon–11:30pm; Sun 4–10:30pm. Metro: Dupont Circle.

7 Foggy Bottom / West End

VERY EXPENSIVE

Marcel's ⭐⭐ FRENCH   When you walk through the front door, look straight ahead into the exhibition kitchen—chances are you'll be staring directly into the eyes of owner/chef Robert Wiedmaier. He is firmly at the helm here, creating French dishes that include nods to his Belgian training: pan-seared halibut with a ragout of spinach and potatoes in a Ghent mustard essence; boneless quail stuffed with duck confit, with cherry-thyme sauce; and, for dessert, seasonal tarts such as spring pear tart with raspberry coulis. The French sommelier is expert.

Marcel's, named after Wiedmaier's young son, occupies the space that once was home to the restaurant Provence, and Wiedmaier has kept that restaurant's country French décor, including panels of rough-hewn stone framed by rustic shutters and antique hutches displaying Provençal pottery. Stone walls and floors don't do much to buffer all the bustle, however, so you can expect to have a very noisy time of it. To the right of the exhibition kitchen is a spacious bar area. Marcel's offers seating on the patio, right on Pennsylvania Avenue, in warm weather, and live jazz nightly year-round.

2401 Pennsylvania Ave. NW. ✆ **202/296-1166.** Reservations recommended. Dinner main courses $26–$39; pretheater dinner 5:30–7pm (including round-trip limo to/from Kennedy Center) $42. AE, MC, V. Mon–Thurs 5:30–10:30pm; Fri–Sat 5:30–11pm; Sun 5–10pm. Metro: Foggy Bottom.

Melrose 🎯🎯 AMERICAN   Situated in an upscale hotel, this pretty restaurant offers fine cuisine presented with friendly flourishes. In nice weather, dine outdoors on the beautifully landscaped, sunken terrace whose greenery and towering fountain protect you from traffic noises. The glass-walled dining room overlooks the terrace and is decorated in accents of marble and brass, with more greenery and grand bouquets of fresh flowers.

Brian McBride is the beguiling executive chef who sometimes emerges from the kitchen to find out how you like the angel-hair pasta with mascarpone and lobster, or his sautéed Dover sole with garlic and salsify, or his pan-seared veal chop with herb butter and black truffle sauce. McBride is known for his use of seafood, which makes up at least half of the entrees and nearly all of the appetizers. Specialties of the house include shrimp ravioli with sweet corn, black pepper, tomato, and lemongrass beurre blanc, and Melrose crab cakes with grilled vegetables in a rémoulade sauce. Desserts, like the raspberry crème brûlée or the chocolate bread pudding with chocolate sorbet, are excellent. The wine list offers 30 wines by the glass. Sunday night, the restaurant dispenses with corkage fees; feel free to bring your own bottle. Friday and Saturday nights from 7 to 11pm, a quartet plays jazz, swing, and big-band tunes; lots of people get up and dance.

In the Park Hyatt Hotel, 1201 24th St. NW (at M St.). ✆ **202/419-6755.** Reservations recommended. Breakfast $9–$18.50; lunch main courses $17–$32; dinner main courses $24–$36; pretheater dinner $35; Sun brunch $50 ($53 with champagne); light fare daily 2:30–5:30pm. AE, DC, DISC, MC, V. Mon–Fri 6:30–10am; Sat–Sun 7–10am; daily 11am–2:30pm and 5:30–10:30pm. Metro: Foggy Bottom.

EXPENSIVE

Asia Nora 🎯 ASIAN FUSION   This is Nora's Asian offshoot, and it's just as organic as the original, but with an Asian bent. Literally. Everything's set at a slant here: the tables, the bar, the banquette at the back on the first floor, and the triangular cutaway balcony on the second. Museum-quality artifacts from Asia—batik carvings, Japanese helmets, and Chinese puppets—decorate the

---

Value Pretheater Dinners = Great Deals

Pretheater dinners get you great value for eating early evening: a three-course dinner for just a little bit more than the cost of a typical entree.

At one end of the spectrum is **Marcel's** ★★ (p. 89), whose $42 fixed-price includes a starter, an entree (like pan-seared Norwegian salmon), and a dessert of crème brûlée or chocolate terrine. Marcel's offers this menu Monday through Saturday from 5:30 to 7pm, and throws in complimentary limo service if you're headed to the Kennedy Center.

Café Atlantico's ★★ (p. 70) pretheater tasting menu allows you three courses for $26 with a glass of wine, $22 without; sample dishes are salmon ceviche as a first course, soft-shell crab with a Veracruz sauce for the main course, and rice-pudding mousse to finish.

Other restaurants in this chapter that offer a pretheater menu are **The Caucus Room** ★★ (p. 69), **1789** ★★ (p. 93), and **Melrose** ★★ (p. 90).

---

gold-flecked jade walls. It's intimate and exotic, a charged combination. Try sitting at the bar first, on the most comfortable bar stools in town. If you like good bourbons and single-malt scotches, you're in luck.

Waiters dressed in black-satin pajamas serve Asian fusion cuisine, all prepared with organic ingredients, including a salad of baby Asian greens with clementine-sesame vinaigrette, a starter of shu mai dumplings with tender beef short ribs, and a main dish of crispy wild rockfish with rice noodles, prawns, and basil. The menu changes monthly. The desserts here are not to be missed; try the warm chocolate five spice cake with coconut sorbet.

2213 M St. NW. ✆ **202/797-4860.** Reservations recommended. Main courses $20–$28. AE, DISC, MC, V. Mon–Thurs 5:30–10pm; Fri–Sat 5:30–10:30pm. Closed at end of Aug/beginning of Sept. Metro: Dupont Circle or Foggy Bottom.

Kinkead's ★★★ AMERICAN/SEAFOOD · When a restaurant has been as roundly praised as Kinkead's, you start to think no place can be *that* good—but Kinkead's really is. An appetizer like grilled squid with creamy polenta and tomato fondue leaves you with a permanent longing for squid. The signature dish, pepita-crusted salmon with shrimp, crab, and chiles, provides a nice hot crunch before melting in your mouth. Vegetables you may normally disdain—sweet potatoes, for instance—taste delicious here.

Award-winning chef/owner Bob Kinkead is the star at this three-tier, 220-seat restaurant. He wears a headset and orchestrates his kitchen staff in full view of the upstairs dining room, where booths and tables neatly fill the nooks and alcoves of the town house. At street level is a scattering of tables overlooking the restaurant's lower level, the more casual bar and cafe, where a jazz group or pianist performs every evening. *Beware:* If the waiter tries to seat you in the "atrium," you'll be stuck at a table mall-side just outside the doors of the restaurant—yuck.

Kinkead's menu (which changes daily for lunch and again for dinner) features primarily seafood, but always includes at least one meat and one poultry entree. The wine list comprises more than 300 selections. You can't go wrong with the desserts either, like the chocolate dacquoise with cappuccino sauce. If you're hungry but not ravenous in the late afternoon, stop in for some delicious light fare: fish and chips, lobster roll, soups, and salads.

2000 Pennsylvania Ave. NW. ✆ 202/296-7700. Reservations recommended. Lunch main courses $13–$21; dinner main courses $21–$29; light fare daily 2:30–5:30pm $5–$22. AE, DC, DISC, MC, V. Daily 11:30am–10:30pm. Metro: Foggy Bottom.

MODERATE

Kaz Sushi Bistro JAPANESE   Amiable chef/owner Kazuhiro ("Kaz") Okochi opened his own place after having worked at Sushi-Ko for many years. This is said to be the best place for sushi in the Washington area, and aficionados vie for one of the six chairs at the bar to watch Kaz and his staff do their thing, preparing salmon roe, sea urchin, tuna, and many other fish for sushi. Besides sushi, Kaz is known for his napoleon of sea trout and wonton skins, his broiled scallops, and for his bento boxes, offering exquisite tastings of pan-seared salmon, spicy broiled mussels, and the like. This is also the place to come for premium sakes.

1915 I St. NW. ✆ 202/530-5500. Reservations recommended. Sushi a la carte $3.25–$6; lunch main courses $9.25–$16.50; dinner main courses $12.95–$22.50. AE, DC, DISC, MC, V. Mon–Fri 11:30am–2pm; Mon–Sat 6–10pm. Metro: Farragut West.

8 Georgetown

VERY EXPENSIVE

Michel Richard Citronelle ✺✺✺ INNOVATIVE FRENCH   If Citronelle's ebullient chef/owner Michel Richard is in the kitchen (and you know when he is, since the dining room views the open kitchen), diners in the know decline the menu and ask simply for whatever it is Richard wants to make. Whether you go that route, or choose from the fixed-price or tasting menus, you're in for a (very expensive) treat. Emerging from the bustling kitchen are appetizers like the fricassee of escargots, sweetbreads, porcinis, and crunchy pistachios, and entrees like the crispy lentil-coated salmon or venison with mushrooms, butternut squash, and celery sauce. But each presentation is a work of art, with swirls of colorful sauce surrounding the main event.

Citronelle's decor is also breathtaking and includes a wall that changes colors, a state-of-the-art wine cellar (a glass-enclosed room that encircles the dining room, displaying its 8,000 bottles and a collection of 18th- and 19th-century corkscrews), and a Provençal color scheme of mellow yellow and raspberry red.

The dessert of choice: Michel Richard's richly layered chocolate "bar" with sauce noisette. Citronelle's extensive wine list offers 20 premium by-the-glass selections, but with all those bottles staring out at you from the wine cellar, you may want to spring for one.

In the Latham Hotel, 3000 M St. NW. (✆) 202/625-2150. Reservations required. Jacket required, tie optional for men at dinner. Breakfast $4–$14; lunch main courses $16–$25; fixed-price dinner $70 or $82; tasting menus $95 or $115. AE, DC, MC, V. Daily 6:30–10:30am; Mon–Fri noon–2pm; Sun–Thurs 6:30–9:30pm; Fri 6:30–10pm; Sat 6–10:30pm.

1789 ☞☞ AMERICAN In my brown corduroy skirt and tan wool sweater, I felt I'd dressed too casually, when I dined here recently. The staff never made me feel uncomfortable, it was a quick look around the room that did it, for fellow female diners (of all ages) were dressed in lacey tops, short flouncy dresses, and fancy long skirts.

So put on your best duds for the 1789. The formal but cozy restaurant is housed in a Federal town house near Georgetown University. The best of the five intimate dining rooms is the John Carroll Room, where the walls are hung with Currier and Ives prints and old city maps, a log fire blazes in the hearth, and a gorgeous flower arrangement tops a hunting-themed oak sideboard. Throughout, silk-shaded brass oil lamps provide romantic lighting.

Noted chef Ris Lacoste varies her menus seasonally. Appetizers might include macadamia-crusted grilled shrimp or grilled quail with barley and mushrooms. Typical entrees range from osso buco with risotto Milanese, to Nantucket Bay scallops in a creamy broth of ginger-lime coconut milk with mushrooms and curried mango rice, to roast rack of Colorado lamb with creamy feta potatoes au gratin in red-pepper-purée–infused Merlot sauce. Finish with the decadent hot fudge sundae.

The pretheater menu offered nightly through 6:45pm includes appetizer, entree, dessert, and coffee for $29.

1226 36th St. NW (at Prospect St.). ℂ 202/965-1789. Reservations recommended. Jacket required for men. Main courses $18–$36; fixed-price pretheater menu $29. AE, DC, DISC, MC, V. Mon–Thurs 6–10pm; Fri 6–11pm; Sat 5:30–11pm; Sun 5:30–10pm.

EXPENSIVE

Café Milano 🥢 ITALIAN   The beautiful people factor rises exponentially here as the night wears on. Café Milano has long been a magnet for Washington's famous and attractive, and their visitors. But this restaurant/nightclub/bar also serves very good food. Salads are big, pasta servings are small, and fish and meat entrees are just the right size. We had the endive, radicchio, and arugula salad topped with thin sheets of Parmesan cheese; a panzanella salad of tomatoes, potatoes, red onion, celery, and cucumber basking in basil and olive oil; cappellacci pockets of spinach and ricotta in cream sauce; sautéed sea bass on a bed of vegetables with lemon chive sauce; and the Santa Babila pizza, which has tomatoes, fresh mozzarella, oregano, and basil on a light pizza crust. All were delicious. At Café Milano, it's the nonsmokers who are relegated to the back room, while the smoking section takes over the main part of the restaurant and bar, which opens through the glass front to the sidewalk cafe. A bevy of good-humored waiters takes care of you.

3251 Prospect St. NW (between Wisconsin Ave. and Potomac St.). ℂ 202/333-6183. Reservations recommended. Lunch main courses $9.50–$19; dinner main courses $14.50–$39. Sun–Wed 11:30am–11pm (bar menu served until midnight); Thurs–Sat 11:30am–midnight (bar menu served until 1am).

Mendocino Grille and Wine Bar 🥢 AMERICAN   As its name suggests, you should come here to enjoy West Coast wine, along with contemporary American cuisine and a California-causal ambience. Of the 150-or-so bottles on the wine list, all are highly rated West Coast selections, 95% of them from California. Waiters are knowledgeable about these, so don't hesitate to ask questions. California-casual doesn't mean cheap, though: Bottles range from $20 to $600, although most are about $50. The restaurant offers 23 wines by the glass, in different sizes, the better for tastings.

The menu highlights grilled seafood, with offerings like mustard spiced yellowfin tuna presented on orzo with English peas and artichokes, and nori-seared Chilean sea bass with potato-ginger pot stickers. Nonseafood choices include free-range chicken served with scallion mashed potatoes and grilled vegetables, and grilled tenderloin of beef.

Rough-textured slate walls alternate with painted patches of Big Sur sky to suggest a West Coast winery in California's wine-growing region. The wall sconces resemble rectangles of sea glass and the dangling light fixtures look like turned-over wineglasses. It's a very pleasant place.

2917 M St. NW. *C* **202/333-2912.** Reservations recommended. Lunch main courses $6.75–$18.75; dinner main courses $17–$29; prix fixe: lunch $20, dinner $33. AE, DC, DISC, MC, V. Mon–Sat 11:30am–3pm; Sun–Thurs 5:30–10pm; Fri–Sat 5:30–11pm.

MODERATE

Bistrot Lepic *FRENCH*   Tiny Bistrot Lepic is the real thing—a charming French restaurant that seems plucked right off a Parisian side street. The atmosphere is bustling and cheery, and you hear a lot of French spoken—not just by the waiters, but also by customers. The Bistrot is a neighborhood place, and you'll often see diners waving hellos across the room to each other, or even leaving their table to visit with those at another. In its 8 years, the restaurant has made some changes to accommodate its popularity, most recently turning the upstairs into a tapas bar and lounge; this means that if you arrive early for your reservation, you now have a place to wait (in the past, one had to hover hungry-eyed at the door).

This is traditional French cooking, updated. The seasonal menu offers such entrees as grilled rainbow trout with carrot sauce, beef medallions with polenta and shiitake mushroom sauce, and sautéed sea scallops with ginger broccoli mousse. We opted for specials: rare tuna served on fennel with citrus vinaigrette, and grouper with a mildly spicy lobster sauce upon a bed of spinach.

The modest French wine list offers a fairly good range. The house red wine, Le Pic Saint Loup, is a nice complement to most menu choices and is less than $20 a bottle.

1736 Wisconsin Ave. NW (near S St.). *C* **202/333-0111.** Reservations recommended. Lunch main courses $9–$14.95; dinner main courses $14–$19. AE, DC, DISC, MC, V. Tues–Sun 11:30am–2:30pm and 5:30–10:30pm.

Clyde's of Georgetown AMERICAN   Clyde's has been a favorite watering hole for an eclectic mix of Washingtonians since 1963. You'll see university students, Capitol Hill types, affluent professionals, Washington Redskins, romantic duos, and well-heeled ladies who lunch. A 1996 renovation transformed Clyde's from a saloon to a theme park, whose dining areas include a cherry-paneled front room with oil paintings of sport scenes, and an atrium with vintage model planes dangling from the glass ceiling and a 16th-century French limestone chimney piece in the large fireplace.

Clyde's is known for its burgers, chili, and crab-cake sandwiches. Appetizers are a safe bet, and Clyde's take on the classic Niçoise (chilled grilled salmon with greens, oven-roasted roma tomatoes, green beans, and grilled new potatoes in a tasty vinaigrette) is also recommended. Sunday brunch is a tradition, and some brunch items are available on Saturday, too. The menu is reassuringly familiar—steak and eggs, omelets, waffles—with variations thrown in for good measure. Among bar selections are about 10 draft beers.

Note: You can park in the underground Georgetown Park garage for only $1 per hour for first 2 hours. Just show your meal receipt and ask the mall concierge to validate your parking ticket.

3236 M St. NW. ℂ 202/333-9180. Reservations recommended. Lunch/brunch $7.95–$14.95; dinner main courses $10.95–$23.95 (most under $12); burgers and sandwiches (except for crab-cake sandwich) under $10 all day. AE, DC, DISC, MC, V. Mon–Thurs 11:30am–2am; Fri 11:30am–3am; Sat 10am–3am; Sun 9:30am–9pm; Sun brunch 9am–4pm.

Miss Saigon VIETNAMESE   This is a charming restaurant, with tables scattered amid a "forest" of tropical foliage, and twinkly lights strewn upon the fronds of the potted palms and ferns.

The food here is delicious and authentic, though the service can be a trifle slow when the restaurant is busy. To begin, there is the crispy calamari, or the shrimp and pork-stuffed garden rolls. House specialties include steamed flounder, caramel salmon, and "shaking beef" (cubes of tender Vietnamese steak, marinated in wine, garlic, butter, and soy sauce, then sautéed with onions and potatoes and served with rice and salad). There's a full bar. Desserts range from bananas *flambé au rhum* to ice cream with Godiva liqueur. Not to be missed is drip-pot coffee, brewed table side and served iced over sweetened condensed milk.

3057 M St. NW. ℂ 202/333-5545. Reservations recommended, especially weekend nights. Lunch main courses $4.50–$8.95; dinner main courses $8.95–$22.95. AE, DC, MC, V. Mon–Fri 11:30am–10:30pm (lunch menu served until 3pm); Sat–Sun noon–11pm (dinner menu served all day).

Old Glory Barbecue *(Kids)* BARBECUE   Raised wooden booths flank one side of the restaurant; an imposing, old-fashioned dark-wood bar with saddle-seat stools extends down the other. Taped swing music during the day, more mainstream music into the night, plays in the background. Old Glory boasts the city's "largest selection of single-barrel and boutique bourbons" and a new rooftop deck with outdoor seating and views of Georgetown.

After 9pm or so, the two-story restaurant becomes packed with the hard-drinkin' young and restless. In early evening, though, Old Glory is prime for anyone—singles, families, or an older crowd—although it's almost always noisy. Come for the messy, tangy, delicious spare ribs; hickory-smoked chicken; tender, smoked beef brisket; or marinated, wood-fired shrimp. Six sauces are on the table, the spiciest being the vinegar-based East Carolina and Lexington. My Southern-raised husband favored the Savannah version, which reminded him of that city's famous Johnny Harris barbecue sauce. The complimentary corn muffins and biscuits; side dishes of collard greens, succotash, and potato salad; and desserts like apple crisp and coconut cherry cobbler all hit the spot.

3139 M St. NW. ✆ **202/337-3406.** Reservations accepted for 6 or more Sun–Thurs, reservations not accepted Fri–Sat. Main courses $7.95–$21.95; Sun brunch buffet $13.95, $5.95 for children 11 and under. AE, DC, DISC, MC, V. Sun 11am–2am; Mon–Thurs 11:30am–2am; Fri–Sat 11:30am–3am; Sun brunch 11am–3pm.

9 Woodley Park

EXPENSIVE

New Heights ✛ AMERICAN/INTERNATIONAL   This attractive second-floor dining room has a bank of windows looking out over Rock Creek Park, and walls hung with the colorful works of local artists. New Heights attracts a casually upscale clientele, which fills the room every night. An Indian influence will always be found in at least one or two items on the menu, to please the palate of owner Amarjeet (Umbi) Singh, as well as those of his patrons. My husband and I have dined at New Heights a lot over the years, our constancy outlasting a number of fine chefs, who seem to come and go here rather quickly. Once again, New Heights has a new chef in the kitchen, and I hope Arthur Rivaldo stays. Our recent dinner here was our best ever: seared diver scallops with creamer potatoes, spinach, and puttanesca sauce for me, and a half-seared coriander ahi tuna with sushi rice, langoustine, seaweed salad, and wasabi-tobiko aioli for Jim. Our appetizers were decadent, too: a rich lobster soup and a duckling foie gras on apple galette. In the past, I've found New Heights's innovative cuisine too adventurous, but these dishes I can handle. Sunday brunch is heavenly, too: brioche French toast, soup of puréed chestnut with foie gras, and the like.

2317 Calvert St. NW (near Connecticut Ave.). ℭ **202/234-4110.** Reservations recommended. Brunch $8.95–$17.50; dinner main courses $17.50–$28. AE, DC, DISC, MC, V. Sun–Thurs 5:30–10pm; Fri–Sat 5:30–11pm; Sun brunch 11am–2:30pm. Metro: Woodley Park–Zoo.

Petits Plats ⍟ FRENCH   Petits Plats is another French bistro, and a very pretty one, ensconced in a town house that's situated directly across from the Woodley Park Metro entrance and the Marriott Wardman Park Hotel. You can sit at the sidewalk cafe, on the porch above, or in the front room, back room, or upstairs rooms of the town house. Watching the passersby on busy Connecticut Avenue is a major amusement. Bistro fare includes shrimp bisque with crab meat; five different mussels dishes, like the mussels in a mustard, cream, and white wine sauce (each comes with french fries); Provençal-styled shrimp on an artichoke-bottom dish; Belgian endive salad with apples, walnuts, and Roquefort; and roasted rack of lamb with potatoes au gratin. The reasonably priced Petits Plats becomes even more so Tuesday through Friday at lunch, when a two-course set menu is available for $13.95; daily at early dinner, 5:30 to 7pm, when a three-course set menu is available for $18.95; and at Saturday and Sunday brunch, when $15.95 gets you a choice of entree (from eggs Benedict to steak *frites*), a house salad, and all the champagne you like. Since it opened in spring 2000, Petits Plats has gained a loyal following.

2653 Connecticut Ave. NW. ℭ **202/518-0018.** Reservations recommended. Lunch main courses $10.95–$14.95; dinner main courses $14.95–$21.95. AE, MC, V. Tues–Sun 11:30am–2:30pm and 5:30–10 or 10:30pm. Metro: Woodley Park–Zoo.

5

Exploring Washington, D.C.

Crammed into Washington's compact 67 square miles are hundreds, yes, hundreds of attractions. You are not going to be able to explore all of them. You need a strategy.

So here's what you do: Read this chapter, and refer to the map on p. 108 to pick which neighborhood holds most of your top choices. Decide which of these you most want to visit. Look at attractions located near your top choices and decide whether you might want to tour these, as well. Think about how much time you have and what you can fit into the allotted time. Most of my descriptions within this chapter roughly estimate the amount of time you should allow for touring each place. Now write it down. Voila—you've got your strategy.

1 The Three Houses of Government

Three of the most visited sights in Washington have always been the buildings housing the executive, legislative, and judicial branches of the U.S. government. All three, the Capitol, the White House, and the Supreme Court, are stunning and offer fascinating lessons in American history and government. Nevertheless, it's possible in the wake of the terrorist acts of September 11, 2001, that you will not be able to tour one or more of these sites while you are here, or that touring restrictions may prevent you from seeing all that you'd like. I'm thinking positive, though, and hoping that during your visit to the capital, general public tours are operating normally at the Capitol, White House, and Supreme Court. And if they are, here is some information that will help you as you go.

The Capitol $\overset{\star\star\star}{\text{\tiny \textcircled{}}}$ Allow at least an hour for touring here, longer if you plan to attend a session of Congress. Remember to allow time for waiting in line, too.

Very Important Note: In mid-2002, construction started on a comprehensive, underground Capitol Visitor Center, with completion scheduled for 2005. Since the Capitol Visitor Center is being created directly beneath the plaza where people traditionally line up

Call Ahead

If there were only one piece of advice I could give to a visitor, it would be to call ahead to the places you plan to tour, to make sure they're open. I don't mean in advance of your trip (although that can't hurt)—I mean on each day of touring, before you set out. Many of Washington's government buildings, museums, memorials, and monuments are open to the general public nearly all the time—except when they are not.

Because buildings like the Capitol, the Supreme Court, and the White House are "offices" as well as tourist destinations, the business of the day always poses the potential for closing one of those sites, or at least sections, to sightseers. (The White House is probably most vulnerable to this situation.) This caveat is even more important in the wake of the terrorist attack on the Pentagon; there may be changes in touring procedures and what's open to the public.

for tours on the east side of the Capitol, touring procedures have changed. The best thing to do is to call ahead (② **202/225-6827**) to find out the new procedures in place for the time you are visiting, and whether the construction work will temporarily close parts of the building you wish to visit.

At this time, I can tell you that self-guided tours and "VIP" tours (tours reserved in advance by individuals through their congressional offices) have been suspended, for the foreseeable future. The only way now to tour the Capitol Building is in groups of 40. The tours are free and last about 30 minutes.

You have two options: If you are part of an organized bunch, say a school class on a field trip, you may arrange a tour in advance, putting together groups of no more than 40 each, by contacting your congressional office at least one month ahead, and following the procedures that office outlines for you. If you are on your own, or with family or friends, you will want to get to the Capitol early, by 7:30am, to stand in line for one of only 540 timed tickets the Capitol distributes daily, starting at 8:15am. It's a first-come, first-served system, with only one ticket given to each person, and each

The White House Area

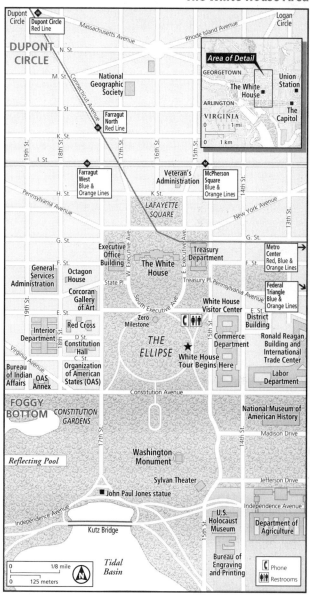

Dupont Circle

Dupont Circle
Red Line

Massachusetts Avenue

Logan Circle

Rhode Island Avenue

DUPONT CIRCLE

N. St.

National Geographic Society

M. St.

Farragut North
Red Line

L. St.

Connecticut Avenue

19th St.
18th St.
17th St.
16th St.
15th St.

K. St.

I. St.

Area of Detail

GEORGETOWN

The White House

ARLINGTON

Union Station

VIRGINIA

The Capitol

0   1 mi

0   1 km

Farragut West
Blue & Orange Lines

Veteran's Administration

McPherson Square
Blue & Orange Lines

Pennsylvania Avenue

H. St.

K St.

New York Avenue

14th St.
13th St.

LAFAYETTE SQUARE

G. St.

G. St.

Executive Office Building

The White House

Treasury Department

Metro Center
Red, Blue & Orange Lines

General Services Administration

Octagon House

F. St.

Treasury Pl.

F. St.

Pennsylvania Avenue

Federal Triangle
Blue & Orange Lines

Corcoran Gallery of Art

State Pl.

White House Visitor Center

E. St.

District Building

Interior Department

Red Cross

South Executive Ave.

Zero Milestone

E. St.

Commerce Department

Ronald Reagan Building and International Trade Center

19th St.
18th St.

D St.

Constitution Hall

C. St.

THE ELLIPSE

White House Tour Begins Here

15th St.

14th St.

Bureau of Indian Affairs

OAS Annex

Organization of American States (OAS)

Labor Department

Virginia Avenue

Constitution Avenue

FOGGY BOTTOM

CONSTITUTION GARDENS

National Museum of American History

Madison Drive

Reflecting Pool

17th St.

Washington Monument

Sylvan Theater

Jefferson Drive

14th St.

John Paul Jones statue

Independence Avenue

Independence Avenue

Kutz Bridge

15th St.

U.S. Holocaust Museum

Department of Agriculture

0   1/8 mile

0   125 meters

Tidal Basin

Bureau of Engraving and Printing

Phone

Restrooms

person, including children of any age, must have a ticket. The good news is that once you receive your ticket, you are free to go somewhere nearby to get a bite to eat, or to sightsee, while you wait for your turn to tour the Capitol. The bad news is that all of you, even 1-year-old baby Louie, have to rise early and get to the Capitol by about 7:30am, and then stand in line for another hour or more, to be sure of touring the Capitol that day. Still, I think this is an improvement over the old touring procedure, which required everyone to stay in the queue until you entered the Capitol—if you left the line, you lost your place. Again, I emphasize that you must call on the morning of your planned visit to the recorded information line ✆ **202/225-6827,** to find out exactly where you should go and what you should do, to obtain your ticket.

Now, if you wish to visit either or both the House and Senate galleries, you follow a different procedure. These galleries are always open to visitors, when the galleries are **in session** 👍👍👍, but you must have a pass to visit each gallery on weekdays until 6pm. (Families, take note that children under 6 are not allowed in the Senate gallery.) After 6pm weekdays and on Saturday and Sunday, however, you may enter either gallery without a pass and watch the session to its conclusion. Once obtained, the passes are good through the remainder of the Congress. To obtain visitor passes in advance, contact your representative for a House gallery pass, or your senator for a Senate gallery pass; District of Columbia and Puerto Rico residents should contact their delegate to Congress. If you don't receive visitor passes in the mail (not every senator or representative sends them), they're obtainable at your senator's office on the Constitution Avenue side of the building or your representative's or delegate's office on the Independence Avenue side. (Visitors who are not citizens can obtain a gallery pass by presenting a passport at the Senate or House appointments desk, located on the first floor of the Capitol.) Call the Capitol switchboard at ✆ **202/224-3121** to contact the office of your senator or congressperson. Your congressional office will issue you a pass and direct you to the House or Senate Gallery line outside the Capitol, for entry into the Capitol. If you're there after 6pm weekdays, or on a Saturday or Sunday, when a gallery is in session, simply ask a Capitol Guide or police officer to direct you to the right entrance.

You'll know the House and/or the Senate is in session if you see flags flying over their respective wings of the Capitol (House: south side, Senate: north side), or you can check the weekday "Today in

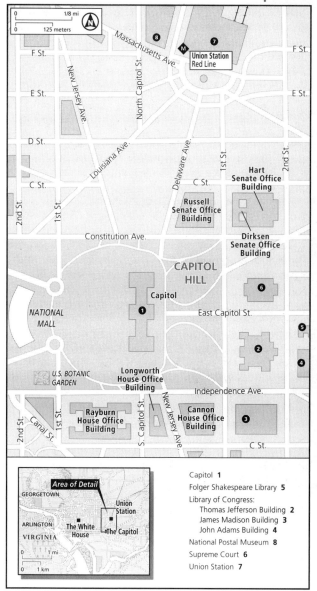

Capitol **1**

Folger Shakespeare Library **5**

Library of Congress:
   Thomas Jefferson Building **2**
   James Madison Building **3**
   John Adams Building **4**

National Postal Museum **8**

Supreme Court **6**

Union Station **7**

Congress" column in the *Washington Post* for details on times of the House and Senate sessions and committee hearings. This column also tells you which sessions are open to the public, allowing you to pick one that interests you.

At the east end of the Mall, entrance on E. Capitol St. and 1st St. NW. ℂ **202/ 225-6827.** www.aoc.gov, www.house.gov, www.senate.gov. Free admission. Year-round 9am–4:30pm Mon–Sat, with first tour starting at 9:30am and last tour starting at 3:30pm. Closed for tours Sun and Jan 1, Thanksgiving, and Dec 25. Parking at Union Station or on neighborhood streets. Metro: Union Station or Capitol South.

The Supreme Court of the United States 🐘🐘   The highest tribunal in the nation, the Supreme Court is charged with deciding whether actions of Congress, the president, the states, and lower courts are in accord with the Constitution, and with applying the Constitution's enduring principles to novel situations and a changing country. The Supreme Court's chief justice and eight associate justices have the power of judicial review—that is, authority to invalidate legislation or executive action that conflicts with the Constitution. Out of the 7,000 or so cases submitted to it each year, the Supreme Court hears only about 100 cases, many of which deal with issues vital to the nation. The Court's rulings are final, reversible only by another Supreme Court decision, or in some cases, an Act of Congress or a constitutional amendment.

Until 1935, the Supreme Court met in the Capitol. Architect Cass Gilbert designed the stately Corinthian marble palace that houses the Court today. The building was considered rather grandiose by early residents: One justice remarked that he and his colleagues ought to enter such pompous precincts on elephants.

If you're in town when the Court is in session, try to **see a case being argued** 🐘🐘🐘 (call ℂ **202/479-3211** for details). The Court meets Monday through Wednesday from 10am to noon, and, on occasion, from 1 to 2pm, starting the first Monday in October through late April, alternating in approximately 2-week intervals between "sittings" to hear cases and deliver opinions and "recesses" for consideration of Court business and writing opinions. From mid-May to late June, you can attend brief sessions (about 15 min.) at 10am on Monday, when the justices release orders and opinions. You can find out what cases are on the docket by checking the *Washington Post*'s "Supreme Court Calendar." Arrive at least an hour early—even earlier for highly publicized cases—to line up for seats, about 150 of which are allotted to the general public.

Call the Supreme Court information line to find out days and times that court arguments will take place. You may view these on a first-come, first-served basis, choosing between the 3-minute line, which ushers visitors in and out of the court every 3 minutes, starting at 10am in the morning and at 1pm in the afternoon; or the "regular" line, which admits visitors who wish to stay for the entire argument, starting at 9:30am and 12:30pm (you should try to arrive about 90 min. ahead of time to snag a spot).

When the Court is not in session, you can tour the building and attend a **free lecture** in the courtroom about Court procedure and the building's architecture. Lectures are given every hour on the half-hour from 9:30am to 3:30pm.

One 1st St. NE (between E. Capitol St. and Maryland Ave. NE). ℂ 202/479-3000. www.supremecourtus.gov. Free admission. Mon–Fri 9am–4:30pm. Closed all federal holidays. Metro: Capitol South or Union Station.

The White House   It's amazing when you think about it:
This house has served as a residence, office, reception site, and world embassy for every U.S. president since John Adams. The White House is the only private residence of a head of state that has opened its doors to the public for tours, free of charge. It was Thomas Jefferson who started this practice, which is stopped only during wartime; the administration considers that we are currently fighting a war on terrorism and, therefore, the White House, at this writing, remains closed for public tours. The White House is open for tours by certain groups, however: school groups (students in grades 4–12, who are enrolled in the same school or school district) and organized veterans groups. **If you are hoping to arrange a White House tour for your student or veterans group, you must submit a request to your senator or congressperson's office.** For those who have arranged such tours, and in the hope that general public tours have resumed by the time you read this, I provide the following information. To find out the latest White House tour information, call ℂ **202/456-7041.**

White House tours take place mornings only, Tuesday through Saturday. There are no public restrooms or telephones in the White House, and picture-taking and videotaping are prohibited.

Note: Even if you have successfully reserved a White House tour for your group, you should still call ℂ **202/456-7041** before setting out in the morning; in case the White House is closed on short notice because of unforeseen events. If this should happen to you, you should make a point of walking by the White House anyway, since its exterior is still pretty awesome. Stroll past it on Pennsylvania Avenue, down 17th Street, and along the backside and South Lawn, on E Street.

1600 Pennsylvania Ave. NW (visitor entrance gate at E St. and E. Executive Ave.). ℭ **202/456-7041** or 202/208-1631. www.whitehouse.gov. Free admission. Tours only for school and veterans groups, which have arranged the tour through their congressional offices. Metro: McPherson Square.

The White House Visitor Center 🦊 Even—especially—if you are not able to tour the White House, you should stop here. The Visitor Center opened in 1995 to provide extensive interpretive data about the White House (as well as other Washington tourist attractions) and to serve as a ticket-distribution center (though that function is suspended indefinitely). It is run under the auspices of the National Park Service and the staff is particularly well informed. Try to catch the 30-minute video about the White House, *Within These Walls,* which provides interior views of the presidential precincts (it runs continuously throughout the day). Before you leave the Visitor Center, pick up a copy of the National Park Service's brochure on the White House, which tells you a little about what you'll see in the eight or so rooms you tour and a bit about the history of the White House. The White House Historic Association runs a small shop here.

1450 Pennsylvania Ave. NW (in the Dept. of Commerce Building, between 14th and 15th sts.). ℭ **202/208-1631,** or 202/456-7041 for recorded information. Free admission. Daily 7:30am–4pm. Closed Jan 1, Thanksgiving, and Dec 25. Metro: Federal Triangle.

2 The Major Memorials

Washington Monument 🦊🦊🦊 *(Kids)* The idea of a tribute to George Washington first arose 16 years before his death, at the Continental Congress of 1783. But the new nation had more pressing problems and funds were not readily available. It wasn't until the early 1830s, with the 100th anniversary of Washington's birth approaching, that any action was taken.

Visiting the Washington Monument: The Washington Monument is the world's tallest freestanding work of masonry. It stands at the very center of Washington, D.C., landmarks, and the 360° views from the top are spectacular. Due east are the Capitol and Smithsonian buildings; due north is the White House; due west is the Lincoln Memorial (with Arlington National Cemetery beyond); and due south is the Jefferson Memorial, overlooking the Tidal Basin and the Potomac River. It's like being at the center of a compass, and it provides a marvelous orientation to the city.

Climbing the 897 steps is not allowed, but the large elevator whisks visitors to the top in just 70 seconds. If you're dying to see more of the interior, **"Walk Down" tours** are given, every Saturday at 10am and 2pm. To be sure of a spot on this tour, you need to call the National Park Reservation Service (✆ **800/967-2283**) and reserve a ticket for the "Walk Down" tour; the tour itself is free, but you'll pay $1.50 per ticket plus a 50¢ service charge per transaction. For details, call before you go or ask a ranger on duty. On this tour you'll learn more about the building of the monument and get to see the 193 carved stones inserted into the interior walls. The stones are gifts from foreign countries, all 50 states, organizations, and individuals. The most expensive stone was given by the state of Alaska in 1982—it's pure jade and worth millions. There are stones from Siam (now Thailand), the Cherokee Nation, and the Sons of Temperance. Allow half an hour here, plus time spent waiting in line.

   Ticket Information: Although admission to the Washington Monument is free, you'll still have to get a ticket. The ticket booth is located at the bottom of the hill from the monument, on 15th Street NW between Independence and Constitution avenues. It's open daily from 8am to 4:30pm. Tickets are usually gone by 9:30am, so plan to get there by 7:30 or 8am, especially in peak season, if you really want to ascend to the top of the monument. The tickets grant admission at half-hour intervals between the stated hours, on the same day you visit. If you want to save yourself the trouble and get them in advance, call the National Park Reservation Service (✆ **800/967-2283**) or go online at http://reservations.nps. gov; you'll pay $1.50 per ticket plus a 50¢ service charge per transaction.

Directly south of the White House (at 15th St. and Constitution Ave. NW). ✆ **202/ 426-6841.** Free admission. Daily 9am–5pm. Last elevators depart 15 min. before closing (arrive earlier). Closed Dec 25, open until noon July 4. Metro: Smithsonian, then a 10-min. walk.

Lincoln Memorial ★★★ (Kids)   This beautiful and moving testament to the nation's greatest president attracts millions of visitors annually. Like its fellow presidential memorials, this one was a long time in the making. Although it was planned as early as 1867—2 years after Lincoln's death—it was not until 1912 that Henry Bacon's design was completed, and the memorial itself was dedicated in 1922.

   The neoclassical temple-like structure, similar in architectural design to the Parthenon in Greece, has 36 fluted Doric columns representing the states of the Union at the time of Lincoln's death, plus two at the entrance. On the attic parapet are 48 festoons symbolizing

Washington, D.C., Attractions

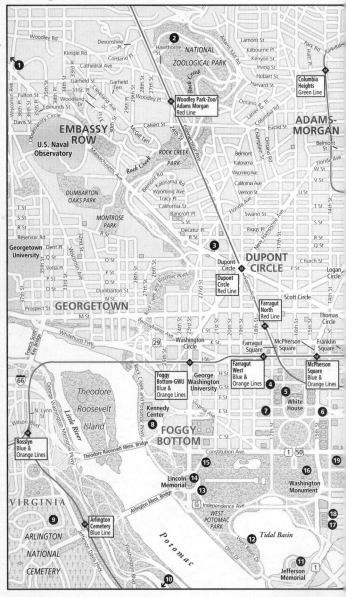

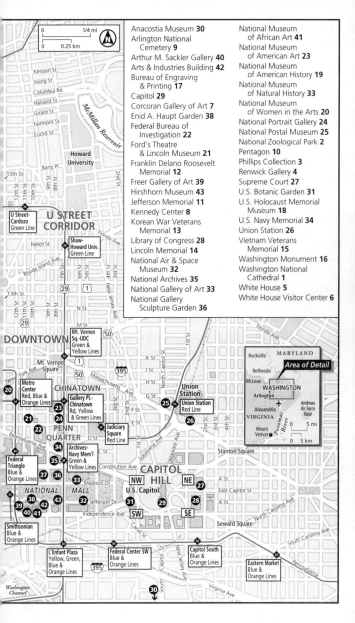

Anacostia Museum **30**
Arlington National Cemetery **9**
Arthur M. Sackler Gallery **40**
Arts & Industries Building **42**
Bureau of Engraving & Printing **17**
Capitol **29**
Corcoran Gallery of Art **7**
Enid A. Haupt Garden **38**
Federal Bureau of Investigation **22**
Ford's Theatre & Lincoln Museum **21**
Franklin Delano Roosevelt Memorial **12**
Freer Gallery of Art **39**
Hirshhorn Museum **43**
Jefferson Memorial **11**
Kennedy Center **8**
Korean War Veterans Memorial **13**
Library of Congress **28**
Lincoln Memorial **14**
National Air & Space Museum **32**
National Archives **35**
National Gallery of Art **33**
National Gallery Sculpture Garden **36**

National Museum of African Art **41**
National Museum of American Art **23**
National Museum of American History **19**
National Museum of Natural History **33**
National Museum of Women in the Arts **20**
National Portrait Gallery **24**
National Postal Museum **25**
National Zoological Park **2**
Pentagon **10**
Phillips Collection **3**
Renwick Gallery **4**
Supreme Court **27**
U.S. Botanic Garden **31**
U.S. Holocaust Memorial Museum **18**
U.S. Navy Memorial **34**
Union Station **26**
Vietnam Veterans Memorial **15**
Washington Monument **16**
Washington National Cathedral **1**
White House **5**
White House Visitor Center **6**

the number of states in 1922, when the monument was erected. Hawaii and Alaska are noted in an inscription on the terrace. Due east is the Reflecting Pool, lined with American elms and stretching 2,000 feet toward the Washington Monument and the Capitol beyond.

The memorial chamber has limestone walls inscribed with the Gettysburg Address and Lincoln's Second Inaugural Address. Most powerful, however, is Daniel Chester French's 19-foot-high seated statue of Lincoln, which disappears from your sightline as you get close to the base of the memorial, then emerges slowly into view as you ascend the stairs.

An information booth, a small museum, and a bookstore are on the premises. Rangers present 20- to 30-minute programs as time permits throughout the day. Limited free **parking** is available along Constitution Avenue and south along Ohio Drive. Twenty to thirty minutes is sufficient time for viewing this memorial.

Directly west of the Mall in Potomac Park (at 23rd St. NW, between Constitution and Independence aves.). © 202/426-6842. Free admission. Daily 8am–11:45pm. Closed Dec 25. Metro: Foggy Bottom, then a 30-min. walk.

Korean War Veterans Memorial ✿

This privately funded memorial, founded in 1995, honors those who served in Korea, a 3-year conflict (1950–53) that produced almost as many casualties as Vietnam. It consists of a circular "Pool of Remembrance" in a grove of trees and a triangular "Field of Service," highlighted by lifelike statues of 19 infantrymen, who appear to be trudging across fields. In addition, a 164-foot-long black-granite wall depicts the array of combat and support troops that served in Korea (nurses, chaplains, airmen, gunners, mechanics, cooks, and others); a raised granite curb lists the 22 nations that contributed to the U.N.'s effort there; and a commemorative area honors KIAs, MIAs, and POWs. Allow 15 minutes for viewing. Limited parking is available along Ohio Drive.

Just across from the Lincoln Memorial (east of French Dr., between 21st and 23rd sts. NW). © 202/426-6841. Free admission. Rangers on duty daily 8am–11:45pm except Dec 25. Ranger-led interpretive programs are given throughout the day. Metro: Foggy Bottom.

Vietnam Veterans Memorial ✿✿

The Vietnam Veterans Memorial is possibly the most poignant sight in Washington: two long, black-granite walls in the shape of a V, each inscribed with the names of the men and women who gave their lives, or remain missing, in the longest war in American history. Even if no one close to you died in Vietnam, it's wrenching to watch visitors grimly studying the directories to find out where their loved ones are listed, or rubbing pencil on paper held against a name etched into the wall. The walls list close to 60,000 people, many of whom died very young.

Just across from the Lincoln Memorial (east of Henry Bacon Dr. between 21st and 22nd sts. NW). ✆ **202/426-6841.** Free admission. Rangers on duty daily 8am–11:45pm except Dec 25. Ranger-led programs are given throughout the day. Metro: Foggy Bottom.

Franklin Delano Roosevelt Memorial ✮✮✮   The FDR Memorial has proven to be one of the most popular of the presidential memorials since it opened on May 2, 1997. Its popularity has to do as much with its design as the man it honors. This is a 7½-acre outdoor memorial that lies beneath a wide-open sky. It stretches out, rather than rising up, across the stone-paved floor. Granite walls define the four "galleries," each representing a different term in FDR's presidency from 1933 to 1945. Architect Lawrence Halprin's design includes waterfalls, sculptures (by Leonard Baskin, John Benson, Neil Estern, Robert Graham, Thomas Hardy, and George Segal), and Roosevelt's own words carved into the stone.

In West Potomac Park, about midway between the Lincoln and Jefferson memorials, on the west shore of the Tidal Basin. ✆ **202/426-6841.** Free admission. Ranger staff on duty daily 8am–11:45pm. Closed Dec 25. Free parking along W. Basin and Ohio drs. Metro: Smithsonian, with a 30-min. walk; or take the Tourmobile.

Jefferson Memorial ✮✮   The site for the Jefferson Memorial was of extraordinary importance. The Capitol, the White House, and the Mall were already located in accordance with architect Pierre L'Enfant's master plan for the city, but there was no spot for such a project that would maintain L'Enfant's symmetry. So the memorial was built on land reclaimed from the Potomac River, now known as the Tidal Basin. Franklin Delano Roosevelt, who laid the cornerstone in 1939, had all the trees between the Jefferson Memorial and the White House cut down so that he could see the memorial every morning.

The memorial is a columned rotunda in the style of the Pantheon in Rome, whose classical architecture Jefferson himself introduced to this country (he designed his home, Monticello, and the earliest University of Virginia buildings in Charlottesville). On the Tidal Basin side, the sculptural group above the entrance depicts Jefferson with Benjamin Franklin, John Adams, Roger Sherman, and Robert Livingston, all of whom worked on drafting the Declaration of Independence. The domed interior of the memorial contains the 19-foot bronze statue of Jefferson standing on a 6-foot pedestal of black Minnesota granite.

Tips **Parking Near the Mall**

Don't drive. Use the Metro. If you're hell-bent on driving on a weekday, set out early to nab one of the Independence or Constitution avenues spots that become legal at 9:30am, when rush hour ends. Arrive about 9:15am and just sit in your car until 9:30am (to avoid getting a ticket), then hop out and stoke the meter. So many people do this that if you arrive at 9:30am or later, you'll find most of the street parking spots gone.

Rangers present 20- to 30-minute programs throughout the day as time permits. Twenty to thirty minutes is sufficient time to spend here.

South of the Washington Monument on Ohio Dr. SW (at the south shore of the Tidal Basin). ✆ **202/426-6841**. Free admission. Daily 8am–11:45pm. Closed Dec 25. Metro: Smithsonian, with a 20- to 30-min. walk; or take the Tourmobile.

3 The Smithsonian Museums

The Smithsonian's collection of nearly 141 million objects spans the entire world and all of its history, its peoples and animals (past and present), and our attempts to probe into the future. The sprawling institution comprises 14 museums (the opening of the National Museum of the American Indian in 2004 will bring that number to 15, with 10 of them on the Mall; see the map "The Mall" on p. 113), as well as the National Zoological Park in Washington, D.C. (there are 2 additional museums in New York City). Still, the Smithsonian's collection is so vast that its museums display only about 1% or 2% of the collection's holdings at any given time. Its holdings, in every area of human interest, range from a 3.5-billion-year-old fossil to part of a 1902 Horn and Hardart Automat. Thousands of scientific expeditions sponsored by the Smithsonian have pushed into remote frontiers in the deserts, mountains, polar regions, and jungles.

To find out information about any of the Smithsonian museums, you call the same number: ✆ **202/357-2700** or TTY 202/357-1729. The information specialists who answer are very professional and always helpful. The Smithsonian museums also share the same website, **www.si.edu**, which will help get you to their individual home pages.

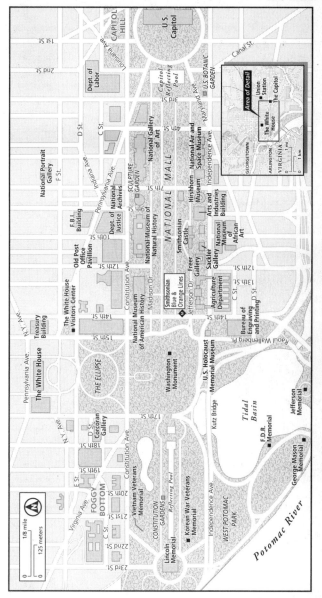

Smithsonian Information Center (the "Castle")   Make this your first stop. Built in 1855, this Norman-style red-sandstone building, popularly known as the "Castle," is the oldest building on the Mall, yet it holds the impressively high-tech and comprehensive Smithsonian Information Center.

The main information area here is the Great Hall, where a 24-minute video overview of the institution runs throughout the day in two theaters. There are two large schematic models of the Mall (as well as a 3rd in Braille), and two large electronic maps of Washington allow visitors to locate nearly 100 popular attractions and Metro and Tourmobile stops. Interactive videos, some at children's heights, offer extensive information about the Smithsonian and other capital attractions and transportation (the menus seem infinite).

1000 Jefferson Dr. SW. ☎ **202/357-2700** or TTY 202/357-1729. Daily 9am–5:30pm, info desk 9am–4pm. Closed Dec 25. Metro: Smithsonian.

Anacostia Museum and Center for African-American History and Culture   This museum is inconveniently located, but that's because it was initially created in 1967 as a neighborhood museum (which makes it unique among the Smithsonian branches). It's devoted to the African-American experience, focusing on Washington, D.C., and the Upper South. The permanent collection includes about 7,000 items, ranging from videotapes of African-American church services to art, sheet music, historic documents, textiles, glassware, and anthropological objects. In addition, the Anacostia produces a number of shows each year and offers a comprehensive schedule of free educational programs and activities in conjunction with exhibit themes. Allow about an hour here.

1901 Fort Place SE (off Martin Luther King Jr. Ave.). ☎ **202/357-2700**. www.si. edu/anacostia. Free admission. Daily 10am–5pm. Closed Dec 25. Metro: Anacostia, head to the exit marked "Local," then take a W2 or W3 bus directly to the museum.

Arthur M. Sackler Gallery 🐾   Asian art is the focus of this museum and the neighboring Freer (together, they form the

---

Tips **Information, Please**

If you want to know what's happening at any of the Smithsonian museums, just get on the phone. **Dial-a-Museum** (☎ **202/357-2020,** or 202/633-9126 for Spanish), a recorded information line, lists daily activities and special events. For other information, call ☎ 202/357-2700.

National Museum of Asian Art in the United States). The Sackler opened in 1987, thanks to a gift from Arthur M. Sackler of 1,000 priceless works. Since then, the museum has received 11th- to 19th-century Persian and Indian paintings, manuscripts, calligraphies, miniatures, and bookbindings from the collection of Henri Vever.

The Sackler's permanent collection displays Khmer ceramics; ancient Chinese jades, bronzes, paintings, and lacquerware; 20th-century Japanese ceramics and works on paper; ancient Near Eastern works in silver, gold, bronze, and clay; and stone and bronze sculptures from South and Southeast Asia. Supplementing the permanent collection are traveling exhibitions from major cultural institutions in Asia, Europe, and the United States. In the past, these have included such wide-ranging areas as 15th-century Persian art and culture, contemporary Japanese woodblock prints and ceramics, photographs of Asia, and art highlighting personal devotion in India. A visit here is an education in Asian decorative arts, but also in antiquities.

1050 Independence Ave. SW. ℭ 202/357-2700. www.asia.si.edu. Free admission. Daily 10am–5:30pm; in summer, museum often stays open Thurs until 8pm, but call to confirm. Closed Dec 25. Metro: Smithsonian.

Arts and Industries Building (Kids) Completed in 1881 as the first U.S. National Museum, this redbrick and sandstone structure was the scene of President Garfield's Inaugural Ball. (It looks quite similar to the Castle, so don't be confused; from the Mall, the Arts and Industries Building is the one on the left.) From 1976 through the mid-1990s, it housed exhibits from the 1876 U.S. International Exposition in Philadelphia—a celebration of America's centennial that featured the latest advances in technology. Some of these Victorian tools, products, art, and other objects are on permanent display. The building displays rotating exhibits, such as one offered in 2002: "Corridos sin Fronteras: A New World Ballad Tradition," which used photographs, recordings, and other memorabilia to explore the history of the ballad in North and South America since 1980.

Singers, dancers, puppeteers, and mimes perform in the **Discovery Theater** (open all year except Aug, with performances weekdays and on selected Sat). Call ℭ **202/357-1500** for show times and ticket information; admission of about $5 is charged.

Don't miss the charming Victorian-motif shop on the first floor. Weather permitting, a 19th-century **carousel** operates across the street, on the Mall.

900 Jefferson Dr. SW (on the south side of the Mall). ☏ 202/357-2700. www.si.
edu/ai. Free admission. Daily 10am–5:30pm. Closed Dec 25. Metro: Smithsonian.

Freer Gallery of Art ✪   Charles Lang Freer, a collector of Asian
and American art from the 19th and early 20th centuries, gave the
nation 9,000 of these works for his namesake gallery's opening in
1923. Freer's original interest was American art, but his good friend
James McNeill Whistler encouraged him to collect Asian works as
well. Eventually the latter became predominant. Freer's gift included
funds to construct a museum and an endowment to add to the
Asian collection only, which now numbers more than 28,000
objects. It includes Chinese and Japanese sculpture, lacquer, metalwork, and ceramics; early Christian illuminated manuscripts;
Iranian manuscripts, metalwork, and miniatures; ancient Near
Eastern metalware; and South Asian sculpture and paintings.

The Freer is mostly about Asian art, but it also displays some of
the more than 1,200 American works (the world's largest collection)
by **Whistler.** In 2003, the Freer marks the centenary of Whistler's
death by staging two exhibits back to back. On view January 19 to
June 15, 2003, are 18 pastels of Venetian scenes, executed by
Whistler between September 1879 to November 1880. From June
15 to November 3, the museum re-creates a show that Whistler
himself designed for a London art gallery in 1884, displaying at least
50 of his paintings. Most remarkable and always on view is the
famous **Peacock Room.** Originally a dining room designed for the
London mansion of F. R. Leyland, the Peacock Room displayed a
Whistler painting called *The Princess from the Land of Porcelain.* But
after his painting was installed, Whistler was dissatisfied with the
room as a setting for his work. When Leyland was away from home,
Whistler painted over the very expensive leather interior and embel-
lished it with paintings of golden peacock feathers. Not surprisingly,
a rift ensued between Whistler and Leyland. After Leyland's death,
Freer purchased the room, painting and all, and had it shipped to
his home in Detroit. It is now permanently installed here. Other
American painters represented in the collections are Thomas
Wilmer Dewing, Dwight William Tryon, Abbott Henderson
Thayer, John Singer Sargent, and Childe Hassam. All in all, you
could spend a happy 1 to 2 hours here.

On the south side of the Mall (at Jefferson Dr. and 12th St. SW). ☏ 202/357-2700.
www.asia.si.edu. Free admission. Daily 10am–5:30pm; in summer, gallery often
stays open Thurs until 8pm, but call to confirm. Closed Dec 25. Metro: Smithsonian
(Mall or Independence Ave. exit).

Hirshhorn Museum and Sculpture Garden *✿*   This museum of modern and contemporary art is named after Latvian-born Joseph H. Hirshhorn, who, in 1966, donated his vast art collection—more than 4,000 drawings and paintings and some 2,000 pieces of sculpture—to the United States "as a small repayment for what this nation has done for me and others like me who arrived here as immigrants." At his death in 1981, Hirshhorn bequeathed an additional 5,500 artworks to the museum, and numerous other donors have greatly expanded his legacy.

Constructed 14 feet above ground on sculptured supports, the doughnut-shaped concrete-and-granite building shelters a verdant plaza courtyard where sculpture is displayed. The light and airy interior follows a simple circular route that makes it easy to see every exhibit without getting lost in a honeycomb of galleries. Natural light from floor-to-ceiling windows makes the inner galleries the perfect venue for viewing sculpture—second only, perhaps, to the beautiful tree-shaded sunken **Sculpture Garden** *✿* across the street (don't miss it). Paintings and drawings are installed in the outer galleries, along with intermittent sculpture groupings.

A rotating show of about 600 pieces is on view at all times. The collection features just about every well-known 20th-century artist and touches on most of the major trends in Western art since the late 19th century, with particular emphasis on our contemporary period. Among the best-known pieces are Rodin's *The Burghers of Calais* (in the Sculpture Garden), Hopper's *First Row Orchestra,* de Kooning's *Two Women in the Country,* and Warhol's *Marilyn Monroe's Lips.*

On the south side of the Mall (at Independence Ave. and 7th St. SW). *✆* **202/ 357-2700.** http://hirshhorn.si.edu. Free admission. Museum daily 10am–5:30pm; in summer museum often stays open Thurs until 8pm, but call to confirm. Sculpture Garden daily 7:30am–dusk. Closed Dec 25. Metro: L'Enfant Plaza (Smithsonian Museums/Maryland Ave. exit).

National Air and Space Museum *✿✿* *Kids*   This museum chronicles the story of the mastery of flight, from Kitty Hawk to outer space. It holds the largest collection of historic aircraft and spacecraft in the world—so many, in fact, that the museum is able to display only about 20% of its artifacts at any one time. To supplement its space, the National Air and Space Museum is opening an extension facility, the Steven F. Udvar-Hazy Center, at Dulles Airport, to display many more. The center, which is scheduled to open in late 2003, will also serve as the Air and Space Museum's primary restoration facility. In the meantime, you should plan to spend several hours at the main Air and Space museum on the Mall.

During the tourist season and on holidays, arrive before 10am to make a beeline for the film ticket line when the doors open. The not-to-be-missed **IMAX films** 𝄞 shown here are immensely popular, and tickets to most shows sell out quickly. You can purchase tickets up to 2 weeks in advance, but they are available only at the Lockheed Martin IMAX Theater box office on the first floor. Two or more films play each day, most with aeronautical or space-exploration themes; *To Fly* and *Space Station 3D* are two that should continue into 2003. Tickets cost $7.50 for adults, $6 for ages 2 to 12 and 55 or older; they're free for children under 2. You can also see IMAX films most evenings after the museum's closing; call for details (📞 **202/357-1686**).

You'll also need tickets to attend a show at the **Albert Einstein Planetarium** 𝄞, which creates "an astronomical adventure" as projectors display blended space imagery upon a 70-foot diameter dome, making you feel as if you're traveling in 3-D dimension through the cosmos. The planetarium's main feature, called "Infinity Express, A 20-Minute Tour of the Universe," gives you the sensation that you are zooming through the solar system, as it explores such questions as "how big is the universe?" and "where does it end?" Tickets are $7.50 for adults, $6 for ages 2 to 12 and 55 or older; you can buy an IMAX film and planetarium combo ticket for $12 per adult, $9 per child.

How Things Fly, a gallery that opened in 1996 to celebrate the museum's 20th anniversary, includes wind and smoke tunnels, a boardable Cessna 150 airplane, and dozens of interactive exhibits that demonstrate principles of flight, aerodynamics, and propulsion. All the aircraft, by the way, are originals.

Kids love the walk-through **Skylab orbital workshop** on the first floor. Other galleries here highlight the solar system, U.S. manned space flights, sea-air operations, and aviation during both world wars. An important exhibit is **Beyond the Limits: Flight Enters the Computer Age,** illustrating the primary applications of computer technology to aerospace. A wonderful exhibit that opened in September 2001 is **Explore the Universe,** which presents the major discoveries that have shaped the current scientific view of the universe; it illustrates how the universe is taking shape, and probes the mysteries that remain. In 2002, the museum added a set of six, two-seat **Flight Simulators** to its first floor galleries (the Udvar-Hazy

Center has another 9), allowing visitors to climb aboard and use a joystick to pilot an aircraft. For 3 minutes you truly feel as if you are in the cockpit and airborne, maneuvering your craft up, down, and upside-down on a wild adventure, thanks to virtual reality images and high-tech sounds. You must pay $6.50 to enjoy the ride and measure at least 48 inches to do it alone; children under 48 inches must measure at least 42 inches and be accompanied by an adult.

On the south side of the Mall (between 4th and 7th sts. SW), with entrances on Jefferson Dr. or Independence Ave. ℂ **202/357-2700,** or 202/357-1686 for IMAX ticket information. www.nasm.edu. Free admission. Daily 10am–5:30pm. The museum often opens at 9am in summer, but call to confirm. Free 1½-hr. highlight tours daily at 10:15am and 1pm. Closed Dec 25. Metro: L'Enfant Plaza (Smithsonian Museums/Maryland Ave. exit) or Smithsonian.

National Museum of African Art 𝒢   Founded in 1964, and part of the Smithsonian since 1979, the National Museum of African Art moved to the Mall in 1987 to share a subterranean space with the Sackler Gallery (see above) and the Ripley Center. Its aboveground domed pavilions reflect the arch motif of the neighboring Freer.

The museum collects and exhibits ancient and contemporary art from the entire African continent, but its permanent collection of more than 7,000 objects (shown in rotating exhibits) highlights the traditional arts of the vast sub-Saharan region. Most of the collection dates from the 19th and 20th centuries. Also among the museum's holdings are the *Eliot Elisofon Photographic Archives,* comprising 300,000 photographic prints and transparencies and 120,000 feet of film on African arts and culture. Permanent exhibits include *The Ancient West African City of Benin, a.d. 1300–1897; The Ancient Nubian City of Kerma, 2500–1500 b.c.* (ceramics, jewelry, and ivory animals); *The Art of the Personal Object* (everyday items such as chairs, headrests, snuffboxes, bowls, and baskets); and *Images of Power and Identity.*

950 Independence Ave. SW. ℂ **202/357-4600.** www.si.edu/nmafa. Free admission. Daily 10am–5:30pm. Closed Dec 25. Metro: Smithsonian.

National Museum of American History 𝒢𝒢𝒢 *Kids*   This museum and its neighbor, the National Museum of Natural History, are the behemoths of the Smithsonian, each filled to the gills with artifacts. American History deals with "everyday life in the American past" and the external forces that have helped to shape our national character. Its massive contents range from General Washington's Revolutionary War tent to Archie Bunker's chair.

Start at the top, that is, the third floor, where **The American Presidency** exhibit explores the power and meaning of the presidency by studying those who have held the position. (There's a gift shop just for this exhibit on this floor.) Also on this floor, don't miss the first American flag to be called Old Glory (1824).

If you have an interest in ship models, uniforms, weapons, and other military artifacts; the experiences of GIs in World War II (and the postwar world); the wartime internment of Japanese Americans; money, medals, textiles, printing and graphic arts, or ceramics, check out third-floor exhibits on those subjects. Otherwise, head downstairs to the second floor.

Here, don't miss the intriguing opportunity to see the huge **original Star-Spangled Banner** ✰✰✰, whose 30-by-34-foot expanse has just been painstakingly conserved by expert textile conservators. This is the very flag that inspired Francis Scott Key to write the poem that became the U.S. national anthem in 1814. Though its 3-year conservation was completed in 2002, the flag remains on view and outstretched, flat, behind glass, in its specially designed conservation lab.

One of the most popular exhibits on the second floor is **First Ladies: Political Role and Public Image,** which displays the first ladies' gowns (look for that of our current first lady, Laura Welch Bush, in the American Presidency exhibit), and tells you a bit about each of these women. Infinitely more interesting, I think, is the neighboring exhibit, **From Parlor to Politics: Women and Reform in America, 1890–1925,** which chronicles the changing roles of women as they've moved from domestic to political and professional pursuits. Following that, find the exhibit called **Within These Walls . . .** which interprets the rich history of America by tracing the lives of the people who lived in this 200-year-old house, transplanted from Ipswich, MA. If this personal approach to history appeals to you, continue on to **Field to Factory,** which tells the story of African-American migration from the South between 1915 and 1940.

Finally, you're ready to hit the first floor, where some exhibits explore the development of farm machinery, power machinery, timekeeping, phonographs, and typewriters. Longtime exhibits continue: **Material World** displays artifacts from the 1700s to the 1980s, everything from a spinning wheel to a jukebox. You can have your mail stamped "Smithsonian Station" at a post office that had been located in Headsville, West Virginia, from 1861 to 1971, when it was brought, lock, stock, and barrel, to the museum. Best of all is the **Palm Court Ice Cream Parlor,** where you can stop and have an ice cream; the Palm Court includes the interior of Georgetown's Stohlman's Confectionery Shop as it appeared around 1900, and part of an actual 1902 Horn and Hardart Automat.

Many changes are afoot at the American History museum. It's possible that by the time you read this, part, or even all, of the museum will be closed for renovations. For the most up-to-date information, call ✆ **202/357-2700** or check out the museum's website, www.americanhistory.si.edu.

On the north side of the Mall (between 12th and 14th sts. NW), with entrances on Constitution Ave. and Madison Dr. ✆ 202/357-2700. www.americanhistory. si.edu. Free admission. Daily 10am–5:30pm. Closed Dec 25. Metro: Smithsonian or Federal Triangle.

National Museum of Natural History ★★ *Kids* Children refer to this Smithsonian showcase as "the dinosaur museum," since there's a dinosaur hall, or sometimes "the elephant museum," since a huge African bush elephant is the first amazing thing you see if you enter the museum from the Mall. Whatever you call it, the National Museum of Natural History is the largest of its kind in the world, and one of the most visited museums in Washington. It contains more than 124 million artifacts and specimens, everything from Ice Age mammoths to the legendary Hope Diamond. The same warning applies here as at the National Museum of American History: You're going to suffer artifact overload, so take a reasoned approach to sightseeing.

If you have children in your crew, you might want to make your first stop the first-floor **Discovery Room,** which is filled with creative hands-on exhibits "for children of all ages." Call ahead or inquire at the information desk about hours. Also popular among little kids is the second floor's **O. Orkin Insect Zoo** ★, where they enjoy looking at tarantulas, centipedes, and the like, and crawling through a model of an African termite mound. The Natural History, like its sister Smithsonian museums, is struggling to overhaul and modernize its exhibits, some of which are quite dated in appearance, if not in the facts presented. So a renovation of the gems and minerals hall has made the **Janet Annenberg Hooker Hall of Geology, Gems, and Minerals** ★★ worth a stop. You can learn all you want about earth science, from volcanology to the importance of mining in our daily lives. Interactive computers, animated graphics, and a multimedia presentation of the "big picture" story of the earth are some of the things that have moved the exhibit and the museum a bit further into the 21st century.

Other Rotunda-level displays include the **fossil collection,** which traces evolution back billions of years and includes a 3.5-billion-year-old stromatolite (blue-green algae clump) fossil—one of the earliest signs of life on Earth—and a 70-million-year-old dinosaur egg. **Life in the Ancient Seas** features a 100-foot-long mural depicting primitive whales, a life-size walk-around diorama of a 230-million-year-old coral reef, and more than 2,000 fossils that chronicle the evolution of marine life. The **Dinosaur Hall** displays giant skeletons of creatures that dominated the earth for 140 million years before their extinction about 65 million years ago. Suspended from the ceiling over Dinosaur Hall are replicas of ancient birds, including a life-size model of the pterosaur, which had a 40-foot wingspan. Also residing above this hall is the jaw of an ancient shark, the *Carcharodon megalodon,* which lived in the oceans 5 million years ago. A monstrous 40-foot-long predator, with teeth 5 to 6 inches long, it could have consumed a Volkswagen Bug in one gulp! In an effort to update this exhibit, the museum in 2001 did mount a digital triceratops (that is, a computerized rendering of that dinosaur); you can manipulate the image to learn more about it.

Don't miss the **Discovery Center,** funded by the Discovery Channel, featuring the Johnson **IMAX theater** with a six-story-high screen for 2-D and 3-D movies (*T-Rex: Back to the Cretaceous* and *Galapagos* were among those shown in 2002), a six-story Atrium Cafe with a food court, and expanded museum shops. In spring 2002, the museum opened the small **Fossil Café,** located within the dinosaur exhibit on the first floor. In this 50-seat cafe, the tables' clear plastic tops are actually fossil cases that present fossilized plants and insects for your inspection as you munch away on smoked turkey sandwiches, goat cheese quiche, and the like.

The theater box office is on the first floor of the museum; purchase tickets as early as possible, or at least 30 minutes before the screening. The box office is open daily from 9:45am through the last show. Films are shown continuously throughout the day. Ticket prices are $7.50 for adults and $6 for children (2–12) and seniors 55 or older. On Friday nights from 6 to 10pm, the theater stages live jazz nights, starring excellent local musicians

On the north side of the Mall (at 10th St. and Constitution Ave. NW), with entrances on Madison Dr. and Constitution Ave. (℡ **202/357-2700,** or 202/633-7400 for information about IMAX films. www.mnh.si.edu. Free admission. Daily 10am–5:30pm. In summer the museum often stays open until 8pm, but call to confirm. Closed Dec 25. Free highlight tours Mon–Thurs 10:30am and 1:30pm, Fri 10:30am. Metro: Smithsonian or Federal Triangle.

National Postal Museum ✪   This museum is, somewhat surprisingly, a hit, a pleasant hour spent for the whole family. Bring your address book and you can send postcards to the folks back home through an interactive exhibit that issues a cool postcard and stamps it. That's just one feature that makes this museum visitor-friendly. Many of its exhibits involve easy-to-understand activities, like postal-themed video games.

The museum documents America's postal history from 1673 (about 170 years before the advent of stamps, envelopes, and mailboxes) to the present. (Did you know that a dog sled was used to carry mail in Alaska until 1963, when it was replaced by an airplane?) In the central gallery, titled **Moving the Mail,** three planes that carried mail in the early decades of the 20th century are suspended from a 90-foot atrium ceiling. Here, too, are a railway mail car, an 1851 mail/passenger coach, a Ford Model-A mail truck, and a replica of an airmail beacon tower. In **Binding the Nation,** historic correspondence illustrates how mail kept families together in the developing nation. Several exhibits deal with the famed Pony Express, a service that lasted less than 2 years but was romanticized to legendary proportions by Buffalo Bill and others. In the Civil War section you'll learn about Henry "Box" Brown, a slave who had himself "mailed" from Richmond to a Pennsylvania abolitionist in 1856.

The Art of Cards and Letters gallery displays rotating exhibits of personal (sometimes wrenching, always interesting) correspondence taken from different periods in history, as well as greeting cards and postcards. And an 800-square-foot gallery, called **Artistic License: The Duck Stamp Story,** focuses on federal duck stamps (first issued in 1934 to license waterfowl hunters), with displays on the hobby of duck hunting and the ecology of American water birds. In addition, the museum houses a vast research library for philatelic researchers and scholars, a stamp store, and a museum shop. Inquire about free walk-in tours at the information desk.

Opened in 1993, this most recent addition to the Smithsonian complex occupies the lower level of the palatial beaux arts quarters of the City Post Office Building, which was designed by architect Daniel Burnham and is situated next to Union Station.

2 Massachusetts Ave. NE (at 1st St.). ✆ **202/633-9360.** www.si.edu/postal. Free admission. Daily 10am–5:30pm. Closed Dec 25. Metro: Union Station.

National Zoological Park 🐾🐾 *Kids* Established in 1889, the National Zoo is home to some 500 species, many of them rare and/or endangered. A leader in the care, breeding, and exhibition of animals, it occupies 163 beautifully landscaped and wooded acres and is one of the country's most delightful zoos. You'll see cheetahs, zebras, camels, elephants, tapirs, antelopes, brown pelicans, kangaroos, hippos, rhinos, giraffes, apes, and, of course, lions, tigers, and bears (oh my).

Pointers: Enter the zoo at the Connecticut Avenue entrance; you'll be right by the Education Building, where you can pick up a map and find out about feeding times and any special activities. Note that from this main entrance, you're headed downhill; the return uphill walk can prove trying if you have young children and/or it's a hot day. But the zoo rents strollers, and snack bars and ice-cream kiosks are scattered throughout the park.

Adjacent to Rock Creek Park, main entrance in the 3000 block of Connecticut Ave. NW. 📞 **202/673-4800** (recording), or 202/673-4717. www.si.edu/natzoo. Free admission. Daily May to mid-Sept (weather permitting): grounds 6am–8pm, animal buildings 10am–6pm. Daily mid-Sept to May: grounds 6am–6pm, animal buildings 10am–4:30pm. Closed Dec 25. Metro: Woodley Park–Zoo or Cleveland Park.

Renwick Gallery of the Smithsonian American Art Museum 🐾 *Finds* A department of the Smithsonian American Art Museum (though located nowhere near it), the Renwick is a showcase for American creativity in crafts, housed in a historic mid-1800s landmark building of the French Second Empire style. The original home of the Corcoran Gallery, it was saved from demolition by First Lady Jacqueline Kennedy in 1963, when she recommended that it be renovated as part of the Lafayette Square restoration. In 1965, it became part of the Smithsonian and was renamed for its architect, James W. Renwick, who also designed the Smithsonian Castle.

Although the setting—especially the magnificent Victorian Grand Salon with its wainscoted plum walls and 38-foot skylight ceiling—evokes another era, the museum's contents are mostly contemporary. On view on the first floor are temporary exhibits of American crafts and decorative arts. On the second floor, the museum's rich and diverse displays boast changing crafts exhibits and contemporary works from the museum's permanent collection, such as Larry Fuente's *Game Fish,* or Wendell Castle's *Ghost Clock.* The **Grand Salon** on the second floor, styled in 19th-century opulence, is newly refurbished and currently displays 170 paintings and sculptures from the American Art Museum, which is closed for renovation. The great thing about this room, besides its fine art and grand design, is its cushiony, velvety banquettes, perfect resting stops for the weary sightseer. Tour the gallery for about an hour, rest for a minute, then go on to your next destination.

The Renwick offers a comprehensive schedule of crafts demonstrations, lectures, and films. Inquire at the information desk. And check out the museum shop near the entrance for books on crafts, design, and decorative arts, as well as craft items, many of them for children. *Note:* It is the main branch of the Smithsonian American Art Museum that is closed for renovation, not this offshoot.

Pennsylvania Ave. and 17th St. NW. ℭ **202/357-2700.** www.nmaa.si.edu. Free admission. Daily 10am–5:30pm. Closed Dec 25. Metro: Farragut West or Farragut North.

4 Elsewhere on the Mall

National Archives   The Rotunda of the National Archives closed for renovation on July 5, 2001, and will reopen in the summer or fall of 2003. Until then, you won't be able to look at the nation's three most important documents—the Declaration of Independence, the Constitution of the United States, and the Bill of Rights—as well as the 1297 version of the Magna Carta. You will, however, be able to use the National Archives center for genealogical research—this is where Alex Haley began his work on *Roots.*

This federal institution is charged with sifting through the accumulated papers of a nation's official life—billions of pieces a year— and determining what to save and what to destroy. The Archives' vast accumulation of census figures, military records, naturalization papers, immigrant passenger lists, federal documents, passport applications, ship manifests, maps, charts, photographs, and motion picture film (and that's not the half of it) spans 2 centuries. And it's all available for the perusal of anyone age 16 or over (call for details). If you're interested, visit the building, entering on Pennsylvania Avenue, and head to the fourth floor, where a staff member can advise you about the time and effort that will be involved, and, if you decide to pursue it, exactly how to proceed.

The National Archives building itself is worth an admiring glance. The neoclassical structure, designed by John Russell Pope (also the architect of the National Gallery of Art and the Jefferson Memorial) in the 1930s, is an impressive example of the beaux arts style. Seventy-two columns create a Corinthian colonnade on each of the four facades. Great bronze doors mark the Constitution Avenue entrance, and allegorical sculpture centered on *The Recorder of the Archives* adorns the pediment. On either side of the steps are male and female figures symbolizing guardianship and heritage, respectively. *Guardians of the Portals* at the Pennsylvania Avenue entrance represent the past and the future, and the theme of the pediment is destiny.

Constitution Ave. NW (between 7th and 9th sts.; enter on Pennsylvania Ave.). ℭ **202/501-5000** for general information, or 202/501-5400 for research information. www.nara.gov. Free admission. Call for research hours. Closed Dec 25. Metro: Archives–Navy Memorial.

National Gallery of Art ★★★   Most people don't realize it, but the National Gallery of Art is not part of the Smithsonian complex. Housing one of the world's foremost collections of Western painting, sculpture, and graphic arts, spanning from the Middle Ages through the 20th century, the National Gallery has a dual personality. The original West Building, designed by John Russell Pope (architect of the Jefferson Memorial and the National Archives), is a neoclassic marble masterpiece with a domed rotunda over a colonnaded fountain and high-ceilinged corridors leading to delightful garden courts. It was a gift to the nation from Andrew W. Mellon, who also contributed the nucleus of the collection, including 21 masterpieces from the Hermitage, two Raphaels among them. The ultramodern East Building, designed by I. M. Pei and opened in 1978, is composed of two adjoining triangles with glass walls and lofty tetrahedron skylights. The pink Tennessee marble from which both buildings were constructed was taken from the same quarry; it forms an architectural link between the two structures.

The West Building: On the main floor of the West Building, about 1,000 paintings are always on display. To the left (as you enter off the Mall) is the **Art Information Room,** housing the **Micro Gallery,** where those so inclined can design their own tours of the permanent collection and enhance their knowledge of art via user-friendly computers.

Continuing to the left of the rotunda are galleries of 13th-through 18th-century Italian paintings and sculpture, including what is generally considered the finest **Renaissance collection** outside Italy; here you'll see the only painting by Leonardo da Vinci housed outside Europe: *Ginevra de'Benci.* Paintings by El Greco, Ribera, and Velázquez highlight the Spanish galleries; Grünewald, Dürer, Holbein, and Cranach can be seen in the German; Van Eyck, Bosch, and Rubens in the Flemish; and Vermeer, Steen, and Rembrandt in the Dutch. To the right of the rotunda, galleries display 18th- and 19th-century French paintings (including one of the world's greatest **Impressionist collections**), paintings by Goya, works of late 18th- and 19th-century Americans—such as Cole, Stuart, Copley, Homer, Whistler, and Sargent—and of somewhat earlier British artists, such as Constable, Turner, and Gainsborough. Room decor reflects the period and country of the art shown: Travertine marble adorns the Italian gallery, and somber oak panels define the Dutch galleries.

Down a flight of stairs are prints and drawings, 15th- through 20th-century sculpture (with many pieces by Daumier, Degas, and Rodin), American naive 18th- and 19th-century paintings, Chinese porcelains, small Renaissance bronzes, 16th-century Flemish tapestries, and 18th-century decorative arts.

The **National Gallery Sculpture Garden** ⟨⟨, just across Seventh Street from the West Wing, opened to the public in May 1999. The park takes up 2 city blocks and features open lawns; a central pool with a spouting fountain (the pool turns into an ice rink in winter); an exquisite glassed-in pavilion housing a cafe; 17 sculptures by renowned artists like Roy Lichtenstein and Ellsworth Kelly (and Scott Burton, whose *Six-Part Seating* you're welcome to sit upon); and informally landscaped shrubs, trees, and plants. It continues to be a hit, especially in warm weather, when people sit on the wide rim of the pool and dangle their feet in the water while they eat their lunch. Friday evenings in summer, the gallery stages live jazz performances here.

The East Building: Hard to miss outside the building is Frank Stella's giant sculpture, newly installed at the corner of Third Street and Pennsylvania Avenue. Called "Prince of Homburg," the aluminum and fiberglass creation is more than 30 feet high, weighs 10 tons, and moves with the wind.

Inside this wing is a showcase for the museum's collection of 20th-century art, including works by Picasso, Miró, Matisse, Pollock, and Rothko; this is also the home of the art history research center. Always on display are the massive aluminum Calder mobile dangling under a seven-story skylight and an exhibit called **Small French Paintings,** which I love.

Altogether, you should allow a leisurely 2 hours to see everything here.

Note: To avoid the crowds at the National Gallery, the best time to visit is Monday morning; the worst is Sunday afternoon.

4th St. and Constitution Ave. NW, on the north side of the Mall (between 3rd and 7th sts. NW). ℂ **202/737-4215.** www.nga.gov. Free admission. Mon–Sat

10am–5pm; Sun 11am–6pm. Closed Jan 1 and Dec 25. Metro: Archives, Judiciary Square, or Smithsonian.

United States Holocaust Memorial Museum ⓕⓕ This museum remains a top draw, as it has been since it opened in 1993. If you arrive without a reserved ticket specifying an admission time, you'll have to join the line of folks seeking to get one of the 1,575 day-of-sale tickets the museum makes available each day. The museum opens its doors at 10am and the tickets are usually gone by 10:30am. Get in line early in the morning (around 8am).

The noise and bustle of so many visitors can be disconcerting, and it's certainly at odds with the experience that follows. But things settle down as you begin your tour. When you enter, you will be issued an identity card of an actual victim of the Holocaust. By 1945, 66% of those whose lives are documented on these cards were dead.

The tour begins on the fourth floor, where exhibits portray the events of 1933 to 1939, the years of the Nazi rise to power. On the third floor (documenting 1940–44), exhibits illustrate the narrowing choices of people caught up in the Nazi machine. You board a Polish freight car of the type used to transport Jews from the Warsaw ghetto to Treblinka and hear recordings of survivors telling what life in the camps was like. This part of the museum documents the details of the Nazis' "Final Solution" for the Jews.

The second floor recounts a more heartening story: It depicts how non-Jews throughout Europe, by exercising individual action and responsibility, saved Jews at great personal risk. Denmark—led by a king who swore that if any of his subjects wore a yellow star, so would he—managed to hide and save 90% of its Jews. Exhibits follow on the liberation of the camps, life in Displaced Persons camps, emigration to Israel and America, and the Nuremberg trials. A highlight at the end of the permanent exhibition is a 30-minute film called *Testimony,* in which Holocaust survivors tell their personal stories. The tour concludes in the hexagonal Hall of Remembrance, where you can meditate on what you've experienced and light a candle for the victims. The museum notes that most people take 2 to 3 hours on their first visit; many people take longer.

The museum recommends not bringing children under 11; for older children, it's advisable to prepare them for what they'll see. There's a cafeteria and museum shop on the premises.

You can see some parts of the museum without tickets. These include two special areas on the first floor and concourse: **Daniel's**

Story: Remember the Children and the **Wall of Remembrance** (Children's Tile Wall), which commemorates the 1.5 million children killed in the Holocaust, and the **Wexner Learning Center.**

100 Raoul Wallenberg Place SW (formerly 15th St. SW; near Independence Ave., just off the Mall). ✆ **202/488-0400.** www.ushmm.org. Free admission. Daily 10am–5:30pm, staying open until 8pm Tues and Thurs mid-Apr to mid-June. Closed Yom Kippur and Dec 25. Metro: Smithsonian.

5 Other Government Agencies

Bureau of Engraving and Printing *Kids*   This is where they will literally show you the money. A staff of 2,600 works around the clock churning it out at the rate of about $700 million a day. Everyone's eyes pop as they walk past rooms overflowing with new greenbacks. But although the money draws everyone in, it's not the whole story. The bureau prints many other products, including 25 billion postage stamps a year, presidential portraits, and White House invitations.

Many people line up each day to get a peek at all that moola, so arriving early, especially during the peak tourist season, is essential. Consider securing VIP tickets from your senator or congressperson; VIP tours are offered Monday through Friday at 8:15 and 8:45am, with additional 4, 4:15, 4:30 and 5pm tours added in summer, and last about 45 minutes. Write at least 3 months in advance for tickets.

Tickets for general public tours are required every day, and every person taking the tour must have a ticket. To obtain a ticket, go to the ticket booth on Raoul Wallenberg Place and show a valid photo ID. You will receive a ticket specifying a tour time for that same day, and be directed to the 14th Street entrance of the bureau. Booth hours are from 8am to 2pm all year long, and reopening in summer from 3:30 to 7pm.

The 40-minute guided tour begins with a short introductory film. Then you'll see, through large windows, the processes that go into the making of paper money: the inking, stacking of bills, cutting, and examination for defects. Most printing here is done from engraved steel plates in a process known as *intaglio,* the hardest to counterfeit, because the slightest alteration will cause a noticeable change in the portrait in use. Additional exhibits include bills no longer in use, counterfeit money, and a $100,000 bill designed for official transactions (since 1969, the largest denomination printed for the general public is $100).

14th and C sts. SW. ✆ **800/874-3188** or 202/874-2330. www.bep.treas.gov. Free admission. Mon–Fri 9am–2pm (last tour begins at 1:40pm); in summer, extended hours 5–6:40pm. Closed Dec 25–Jan 1 and federal holidays. Metro: Smithsonian (Independence Ave. exit).

Federal Bureau of Investigation *(Kids)*   More than half a million visitors (many of them kids) come here annually to learn why crime doesn't pay. Tours begin with a short videotape presentation about the priorities of the bureau. You'll see some of the weapons used by big-time gangsters such as Al Capone, John Dillinger, Bonnie and Clyde, and "Pretty Boy" Floyd; and an exhibit on counterintelligence operations. There are photographs of the 10 most-wanted fugitives (2 were recognized at this exhibit by people on the tour, and 10 have been located via the FBI-assisted TV show *America's Most Wanted*). Other exhibits deal with white-collar crime, organized crime, terrorism, drugs, and agent training. On display are more than 5,000 weapons, most of them confiscated from criminals.

You'll also visit the **Firearms Unit** (where agents determine whether a bullet was fired from a given weapon); the **Material Analysis Unit** (where the FBI can deduce the approximate make and model of a car from a tiny piece of paint); the unit where hairs and fibers are examined; and a **Forfeiture and Seizure Exhibit,** a display of jewelry, furs, and other proceeds from illegal narcotics operations. The tour ends with a bang, lots of them in fact, when an agent gives a sharpshooting demonstration and discusses the FBI's firearm policy and gun safety.

Guided congressional tours take place at 9:45 and 11:45am, and 1:45 and 3:15pm, with an additional 2:45pm tour added in summer. If you're coming between April and August, try to arrange for tickets ahead of time. At the height of this season, you could get in line at 8am and still not get in. Even if you call for advance tickets, the tour office might tell you that they won't confirm your tickets until a week before your visit. You can expect to pass through a metal detector to enter the FBI Building.

J. Edgar Hoover FBI Building, E St. NW (between 9th and 10th sts.). (℃ **202/324-3447.** www.fbi.gov. Free admission. Mon–Fri 8:45am–4:15pm. Closed Jan 1, Dec 25, and other federal holidays. Metro: Metro Center or Federal Triangle.

Library of Congress *(★)*   The question most frequently asked by visitors to the Library of Congress is: Where are the books? The answer is: on the 532 miles of shelves located throughout the library's three buildings: the **Thomas Jefferson, James Madison Memorial,** and **John Adams** buildings. Established in 1800, "for the purchase of such books as may be necessary for the use of Congress," the library today serves the nation, with holdings for the visually impaired (for whom books are recorded on cassette and/or translated into Braille), research scholars, and college students—and tourists. Its first collection of books was destroyed in 1814 when the British burned the Capitol (where the library was then housed) during the War of 1812. Thomas Jefferson then sold the institution his personal library of 6,487 books as a replacement, and this became the foundation of what would grow to become the world's largest library.

Today, the collection contains a mind-boggling 121 million items. Its buildings house more than 18 million catalogued books, 54 million manuscripts, 12 million prints and photographs, 2.5 million audio holdings (discs, tapes, talking books, and so on), more than 700,000 movies and videotapes, musical instruments from the 1700s, and the letters and papers of everyone from George Washington to Groucho Marx. The library offers a year-round program of free concerts, lectures, and poetry readings, and houses the Copyright Office.

Just as impressive as the scope of the library's holdings is its architecture. Most magnificent is the ornate Italian Renaissance–style **Thomas Jefferson Building,** which was erected between 1888 and 1897 to hold the burgeoning collection and establish America as a cultured nation with magnificent institutions equal to anything in Europe. Fifty-two painters and sculptors worked for 8 years on its interior. There are floor mosaics of Italian marble, allegorical paintings on the overhead vaults, more than 100 murals, and numerous ornamental cornucopias, ribbons, vines, and garlands within. The building's exterior has 42 granite sculptures and yards of bas-reliefs. Especially impressive are the exquisite marble **Great Hall** and the **Main Reading Room,** the latter under a 160-foot dome. Originally intended to hold the fruits of at least 150 years of collecting, the Jefferson Building was, in fact, filled up in a mere 13 years. It is now supplemented by the James Madison Memorial Building and the John Adams Building.

On permanent display in the Jefferson Building's Great Hall are several exhibits: The **American Treasures of the Library of Congress** rotates a selection of more than 200 of the rarest and most interesting items from the library's collection—like Thomas Jefferson's rough draft of the Declaration of Independence with notations by Benjamin Franklin and John Adams in the margins, and the contents of Lincoln's pockets when he was assassinated. Across the Great Hall from the American Treasures exhibit is one that showcases the **World Treasures of the Library of Congress.** Its multimedia display of books, maps, videos, and illustrations invites visitors to examine artifacts from the library's vast international collections. Tucked away in a corner of the Jefferson Building is another permanent exhibit, the **Bob Hope Gallery of American Entertainment,** which presents on a rotating basis, film clips, memorabilia, and manuscript pages from a collection that the comedian donated to the library in 2000.

1st St. SE (between Independence Ave. and E. Capitol St.). ⓒ 202/707-8000. www.loc.gov. Free admission. Madison Bldg. Mon–Fri 8:30am– 9:30pm; Sat 8:30am–6pm. Jefferson Bldg. Mon–Sat 10am–5pm. Closed federal holidays. Stop at the information desk inside the Jefferson Building's west entrance on 1st St. to obtain same-day free tickets to tour the Library. Tours of the Great Hall: Mon–Fri 10:30 and 11:30am, and 1:30, 2:30, and 3:30pm; Sat 10:30 and 11:30am, and 1:30 and 2:30pm. Metro: Capitol South.

6 More Museums

Corcoran Gallery of Art ⭑⭑ The first art museum in Washington, the Corcoran Gallery was housed from 1869 to 1896 in the redbrick and brownstone building that is now the Renwick. The collection outgrew its quarters and was transferred in 1897 to its present beaux arts building, designed by Ernest Flagg.

The collection, shown in rotating exhibits, focuses chiefly on American art. A prominent Washington banker, William Wilson Corcoran was among the first wealthy American collectors to realize the importance of encouraging and supporting this country's artists. Enhanced by further gifts and bequests, the collection comprehensively spans American art from 18th-century portraiture to 20th-century moderns like Nevelson, Warhol, and Rothko. Nineteenth-century works include Bierstadt's and Remington's imagery of the American West; Hudson River School artists; expatriates like Whistler, Sargent, and Mary Cassatt; and two giants of the late 19th century, Homer and Eakins.

The Corcoran is not exclusively an American art museum. On the first floor is the collection from the estate of Sen. William Andrews Clark, an eclectic grouping of Dutch and Flemish masters; European painters; French Impressionists; Barbizon landscapes; Delft porcelains; a Louis XVI *salon dore* transported in toto from Paris; and more. Clark's will stated that his diverse collection, which any curator would undoubtedly want to disperse among various museum departments, must be shown as a unit. He left money for a wing to house it and the new building opened in 1928. Don't miss the small walnut-paneled room known as "Clark Landing," which showcases 19th-century French Impressionist and American art; a room of exquisite Corot landscapes; another of medieval Renaissance tapestries; and numerous Daumier lithographs donated by Dr. Armand Hammer. Allow an hour for touring the collection.

500 17th St. NW (between E St. and New York Ave.). ℂ 202/639-1700. www.corcoran.org. $5 adults, $3 seniors, $1 students 13–18, $8 families, children under 12 free; admission is free all day Mon, and Thurs after 5pm. Open Wed–Mon 10am–5pm, with extended hours Thurs until 9pm. Free walk-in tours daily (except Tues) at noon, as well as at 7:30pm Thurs and at 2:30pm Sat and Sun. Closed Jan 1 and Dec 25. Metro: Farragut West or Farragut North.

Ford's Theatre and Lincoln Museum *Kids*   On April 14, 1865, President Abraham Lincoln was in the audience at Ford's Theatre, one of the most popular playhouses in Washington. Everyone was laughing at a funny line from Tom Taylor's celebrated comedy, *Our American Cousin,* when John Wilkes Booth crept into the president's box, shot the president, and leapt to the stage, shouting *"Sic semper tyrannis!"* ("Thus ever to tyrants!") With his left leg broken from the vault, Booth mounted his horse in the alley and galloped off. Doctors carried Lincoln across the street to the house of William Petersen, where the president died the next morning.

The theater was closed after Lincoln's assassination and used as an office by the War Department. In 1893, 22 clerks were killed when three floors of the building collapsed. It remained in disuse until the 1960s, when it was remodeled and restored to its appearance on the night of the tragedy. Except when rehearsals or matinees are in progress (call before you go), visitors can see the theater and trace Booth's movements on that fateful night. Free 15-minute talks on the history of the theater and the story of the assassination are given throughout the day. Be sure to visit the Lincoln Museum in the basement, where exhibits—including the Derringer pistol used by Booth and a diary in which he outlines his rationalization for the deed—focus on events surrounding Lincoln's assassination and the trial of the conspirators. Thirty minutes is plenty of time to spend here.

The theater stages productions most of the year (see p. 153).

517 10th St. NW (between E and F sts.). ℂ 202/426-6925. www.nps.gov/foth. Free admission. Daily 9am–5pm. Closed Dec 25. Metro: Metro Center.

National Museum of Women in the Arts   Sixteen years after it opened, this museum remains the only one in the world dedicated to celebrating "the contribution of women to the history of art." Founders Wilhelmina and Wallace Holladay, who donated the core of the permanent collection—more than 200 works by women from the 16th through the 20th century—became interested in women's art in the 1960s. After discovering that no women were included in H. W. Janson's *History of Art*, a standard text (which, by the way, did not address this oversight until 1986!), the Holladays began collecting art by women, and the concept of a women's art museum soon evolved.

Since its opening, the collection has grown to more than 2,700 works by more than 800 artists, including Rosa Bonheur, Frida Kahlo, Helen Frankenthaler, Barbara Hepworth, Georgia O'Keeffe, Camille Claudel, Lila Cabot Perry, Mary Cassatt, Elaine de Kooning, Käthe Kollwitz, and many other lesser-known artists from earlier centuries. You will discover here, for instance, that the famed Peale family of 19th-century portrait painters included a very talented sister, Sarah Miriam Peale. The collection is complemented by an ongoing series of changing exhibits. You should allow an hour here.

1250 New York Ave. NW (at 13th St.). ℂ 202/783-5000. www.nmwa.org. $5 adults, $3 students over 18 with ID and seniors; youth 18 and under free. Mon–Sat 10am–5pm; Sun noon–5pm. Closed Jan 1, Thanksgiving, and Dec 25. Metro: Metro Center (13th St. exit).

Phillips Collection 𝒦𝒦 Conceived as "a museum of modern art and its sources," this intimate establishment, occupying an elegant 1890s Georgian Revival mansion and a more youthful wing, houses the exquisite collection of Duncan and Marjorie Phillips, avid collectors and proselytizers of modernism. Carpeted rooms with leaded- and stained-glass windows, oak paneling, plush chairs and sofas, and fireplaces establish a comfortable, homelike setting. Today the collection includes more than 2,500 works. Among the highlights: superb Daumier, Dove, and Bonnard paintings; some splendid small Vuillards; five van Goghs; Renoir's *Luncheon of the Boating Party;* seven Cézannes; and six works by Georgia O'Keeffe. Ingres, Delacroix, Manet, El Greco, Goya, Corot, Constable, Courbet, Giorgione, and Chardin are among the "sources" or forerunners of modernism represented. Modern notables include Rothko, Hopper, Kandinsky, Matisse, Klee, Degas, Rouault, Picasso, and many others. It's a collection you'll enjoy viewing for an hour or so.

1600 21st St. NW (at Q St.). ℂ 202/387-2151. www.phillipscollection.org. Admission Sat–Sun $7.50 adults, $4 students and seniors, free for children 18 and under; contribution suggested Tues–Fri. Special exhibits may require an additional fee. Tues–Sat 10am–5pm year-round (Thurs until 8:30pm); Sun noon–7pm. Free tours Wed and Sat 2pm. Closed Jan 1, July 4, Thanksgiving, and Dec 25. Metro: Dupont Circle (Q St. exit).

7 Other Attractions

Arlington National Cemetery ☆☆   Upon arrival, head over to the **Visitor Center,** where you can view exhibits, pick up a detailed map, use the restrooms (there are no others until you get to Arlington House), and purchase a **Tourmobile ticket** ($5.25 per adult, $2.50 for children 3–11), which allows you to stop at all major sites in the cemetery and then reboard whenever you like. Service is continuous and the narrated commentary is informative; this is the only guided tour of the cemetery offered. If you've got plenty of stamina, consider doing part or all of the tour on foot. Remember as you go that this is a memorial frequented not just by tourists but by those attending burial services or visiting the graves of beloved relatives and friends who are buried here.

This shrine occupies approximately 612 acres on the high hills overlooking the capital from the west side of the Memorial Bridge. It honors many national heroes and more than 260,000 war dead, veterans, and dependents. Many graves of the famous at Arlington bear nothing more than simple markers. Five-star Gen. John J. Pershing's is one of those. Secretary of State John Foster Dulles is buried here. So are Pres. William Howard Taft and Supreme Court Justice Thurgood Marshall. Cemetery highlights include:

The Tomb of the Unknowns, containing the unidentified remains of service members from both world wars, the Korean War, and, until 1997, the Vietnam War. In 1997, the remains of the unknown soldier from Vietnam were identified as those of Air Force 1st Lt. Michael Blassie, whose A-37 was shot down in South Vietnam in 1962. Blassie's family, who had reason to believe that the body was their son's, had beseeched the Pentagon to exhume the soldier's remains and conduct DNA testing to determine if what the family suspected was true. Upon confirmation, the Blassies buried Michael in his hometown of St. Louis. The crypt honoring the dead but unidentified Vietnam War soldiers remains empty for the time being. The entire tomb is an unembellished, massive white-marble block, moving in its simplicity. A 24-hour honor guard watches over the tomb, with the changing of the guard taking place every half-hour April to September, every hour on the hour October to March, and every hour at night.

Within a 20-minute walk, all uphill, from the Visitor Center is **Arlington House** (© **703/557-0613**). From 1831 to 1861, this was the legal residence of Robert E. Lee, where he and his family lived off and on until the Civil War. Lee married the great-grand-daughter of Martha Washington, Mary Anna Randolph Custis, who inherited the estate.

Pierre Charles L'Enfant's grave was placed near Arlington House at a spot that is believed to offer the best view of Washington, the city he designed.

Below Arlington House, an 8-minute walk from the Visitor Center, is the **Gravesite of John Fitzgerald Kennedy.** John Carl Warnecke designed a low crescent wall embracing a marble terrace, inscribed with the 35th president's most famous utterance: "And so my fellow Americans, ask not what your country can do for you, ask what you can do for your country." Jacqueline Kennedy Onassis rests next to her husband, and Robert Kennedy is buried close by. The Kennedy graves attract streams of visitors. Arrive close to 8am to contemplate the site quietly; otherwise, it's mobbed. Looking north, there's a spectacular view of Washington.

In 1997, the **Women in Military Service for America Memorial** (© 800/222-2294 or 703/533-1155; www.womensmemorial.org) was added to Arlington Cemetery to honor the more than 1.8 million women who have served in the armed forces from the American Revolution to the present. The impressive new memorial lies just beyond the gated entrance to the cemetery, a 3-minute walk from the Visitor Center.

Plan to spend half a day at Arlington Cemetery and the Women in Military Service Memorial.

Just across the Memorial Bridge from the base of the Lincoln Memorial. © 703/607-8052. www.arlingtoncemetery.org or www.mdw.army.mil/cemetery.htm. Free admission. Apr–Sept daily 8am–7pm; Oct–Mar daily 8am–5pm. Metro: Arlington National Cemetery. If you come by car, parking is $1.25 an hr. for the 1st 3 hr., $2 an hr. thereafter. The cemetery is also accessible via Tourmobile.

John F. Kennedy Center for the Performing Arts ☆

Opened in 1971, the Kennedy Center is both the national performing arts center and a memorial to John F. Kennedy. Set on 17 acres overlooking the Potomac, the striking facility, designed by noted architect Edward Durell Stone, encompasses an opera house, a concert hall, two stage theaters, a theater lab, and a film theater. The best way to see the Kennedy Center is to take a free 50-minute guided tour (which takes you through some restricted areas). You can beat the crowds by writing in advance to a senator or congressperson for passes for a free VIP tour, given year-round Monday through Friday at 9:30am and 4:30pm, and at 9:30am only on Saturday. Call © 202/416-8341 for details.

Arlington National Cemetery

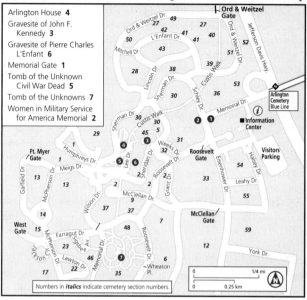

Arlington House **4**

Gravesite of John F. Kennedy **3**

Gravesite of Pierre Charles L'Enfant **6**

Memorial Gate **1**

Tomb of the Unknown Civil War Dead **5**

Tomb of the Unknowns **7**

Women in Military Service for America Memorial **2**

Numbers in *italics* indicate cemetery section numbers.

New Hampshire Ave. NW (at Rock Creek Pkwy.). © **800/444-1324,** or 202/416-8341 for information or tickets. www.kennedy-center.org. Free admission. Daily 10am–midnight. Free guided tours Mon–Fri 10am–5pm; Sat–Sun 10am–1pm. Metro: Foggy Bottom (there's a free shuttle service between the station and the center, running every 15 min. from 9:45am–midnight weekdays, 10am–midnight Sat, and noon–midnight Sun). Bus: no. 80 from Metro Center.

Washington National Cathedral ⭑   Pierre L'Enfant's 1791 plan for the capital city included "a great church for national purposes," but possibly because of early America's fear of mingling church and state, more than a century elapsed before the foundation for Washington National Cathedral was laid. Its actual name is the Cathedral Church of St. Peter and St. Paul. The church is Episcopal, but it has no local congregation and seeks to serve the entire nation as a house of prayer for all people. It has been the setting for every kind of religious observance, from Jewish to Serbian Orthodox.

A church of this magnitude—it's the sixth largest cathedral in the world, and the second largest in the U.S.—took a long time to build. Its principal (but not original) architect, Philip Hubert Frohman, worked on the project from 1921 until his death in 1972. The foundation stone was laid in 1907 using the mallet with which George Washington set the Capitol cornerstone. Construction was interrupted by both world wars and by periods of financial difficulty. The cathedral was completed with the placement of the final stone atop a pinnacle on the west front towers on September 29, 1990, 83 years (to the day) after it was begun.

English Gothic in style (with several distinctly 20th-century innovations, such as a stained-glass window commemorating the flight of *Apollo 11* and containing a piece of moon rock), the cathedral is built in the shape of a cross, complete with flying buttresses and 110 gargoyles. It is, along with the Capitol and the Washington Monument, one of the dominant structures on the Washington skyline. Its 57-acre landscaped grounds have two lovely gardens (the lawn is ideal for picnicking), four schools, a greenhouse, and two gift shops.

Over the years the cathedral has seen much history. Services to celebrate the end of world wars I and II were held here. It was the scene of President Wilson's funeral (he and his wife are buried here), as well as President Eisenhower's. Helen Keller and her companion, Anne Sullivan, were buried in the cathedral at her request. And during the Iranian crisis, a round-the-clock prayer vigil was held in the Holy Spirit Chapel throughout the hostages' captivity. When they were released, the hostages came to a service here.

The best way to explore the cathedral is to take a 30- to 45-minute **guided tour;** they leave continually from the west end of the nave. You can also walk through on your own, using a self-guiding brochure available in several languages.

Massachusetts and Wisconsin aves. NW (entrance on Wisconsin Ave.). ℂ 202/ 537-6200. www.cathedral.org/cathedral. Donation $3 adults, $2 seniors, $1 children. Cathedral daily 10am–4:30pm; May 1 to Labor Day, the nave level stays open Mon–Fri until 9pm. Gardens daily until dusk. Regular tours Mon–Sat 10–11:30am and 12:45–3:15pm; Sun 12:45–2:30pm. No tours on Palm Sunday, Easter, Thanksgiving, Dec 25, or during services. Worship services vary throughout the year, but you can count on a weekday Evensong service at 4:30pm, a weekday noon service, and an 11am service every Sun; call for other service times. Metro: Tenleytown, with a 20-min. walk. Bus: Any N bus up Massachusetts Ave. from Dupont Circle or any 30-series bus along Wisconsin Ave. This is a stop on the Old Town Trolley Tour.

8 Parks & Gardens

PARKS
POTOMAC PARK

West and East Potomac parks, their 720 riverside acres divided by the Tidal Basin, are most famous for their spring display of **cherry blossoms** and all the hoopla that goes with it. So much attention is lavished on Washington's cherry blossoms that the National Park Service devotes a home page to the subject: **www.nps.gov/nacc/cherry**. You can access this site to find out forecasts for the blooms and assorted other details. You can also call the National Park Service (© **202/485-9880**) for information. In all, there are more than 3,700 cherry trees planted along the Tidal Basin in West Potomac Park, East Potomac Park, the Washington Monument grounds, and in other pockets of the city.

To get to the Tidal Basin by car (*not* recommended in cherry-blossom season), you want to get on Independence Avenue and follow the signs posted near the Lincoln Memorial that show you where to turn to find parking and the FDR Memorial. If you're walking, you'll want to cross Independence Avenue where it intersects with West Basin Drive (there's a stoplight and crosswalk), and follow the path to the Tidal Basin. There is no convenient Metro stop near here.

West Potomac Park encompasses Constitution Gardens; the Vietnam, Korean, Lincoln, Jefferson, and FDR memorials; a small island where ducks live; and the Reflecting Pool (see "The Major Memorials," earlier in this chapter for full listings of the memorials). It has 1,628 trees bordering the Tidal Basin, some of them Akebonos with delicate pink blossoms, but most Yoshinos with white, cloudlike flower clusters. The blossoming of the cherry trees is the focal point of a 2-week-long celebration, including the lighting of the 300-year-old Japanese Stone Lantern near Kutz Bridge, presented to the city by the governor of Tokyo in 1954. (This year's Cherry Blossom Festival is scheduled to run Mar 22–Apr 7, 2003.) The trees bloom for a little less than 2 weeks beginning sometime between March 20 and April 17; April 5 is the average date. Planning your trip around the blooming of the cherry blossoms is an iffy proposition, and I wouldn't advise it. All it takes is one good rain and those cherry blossoms are gone. The cherry blossoms are not illuminated at night. See "Washington, D.C., Calendar of Events," in chapter 1, for further details on cherry-blossom events.

East Potomac Park has 1,681 cherry trees in 11 varieties. The park also has picnic grounds, tennis courts, three golf courses, a large swimming pool, and biking and hiking paths by the water.

ROCK CREEK PARK

Created in 1890, **Rock Creek Park** ⚘ (**www.nps.gov/rocr**) was purchased by Congress for its "pleasant valleys and ravines, primeval forests and open fields, its running waters, its rocks clothed with rich ferns and mosses, its repose and tranquillity, its light and shade, its ever-varying shrubbery, its beautiful and extensive views." A 1,750-acre valley within the District of Columbia, extending 12 miles from the Potomac River to the Maryland border, it's one of the biggest and finest city parks in the nation. Parts of it are still wild; it's not unusual to see a deer scurrying through the woods in more remote sections.

For full information on the wide range of park programs and activities, visit the **Rock Creek Nature Center and Planetarium,** 5200 Glover Rd. NW (© **202/895-6070**), Wednesday through Sunday from 9am to 5pm; or Park Headquarters, 3545 Williamsburg Lane NW (© **202/895-6015**), Monday through Friday from 7:45am to 4:15pm. To get to the Nature Center by public transportation, take the Metro to Friendship Heights and transfer to bus no. E2 or E3 to Military Road and Oregon Avenue/Glover Road.

GARDENS

Enid A. Haupt Garden Named for its donor, a noted supporter of horticultural projects, this stunning garden presents elaborate flower beds and borders, plant-filled turn-of-the-20th-century urns, 1870s cast-iron furnishings, and lush baskets hung from reproduction 19th-century lampposts. Although on ground level, the garden is actually a 4-acre rooftop garden above the subterranean Sackler and African Art museums. An **"Island Garden"** near the Sackler Gallery, entered via a 9-foot moon gate, has benches backed by English boxwoods under the shade of weeping cherry trees.

A **"Fountain Garden"** outside the African Art Museum provides granite seating walls shaded by hawthorn trees. Three small terraces, shaded by black sour-gum trees, are located near the Arts and Industries Building. And five majestic linden trees shade a seating area around the Downing Urn, a memorial to American landscapist Andrew Jackson Downing. Elaborate cast-iron carriage gates made according to a 19th-century design by James Renwick, flanked by four red sandstone pillars, have been installed at the Independence Avenue entrance to the garden.

10th St. and Independence Ave. SW. © **202/357-2700.** Free admission. Mid May–Aug daily 6am–8pm; Sept to mid-May daily 7am–5:45pm. Closed Dec 25. Metro: Smithsonian.

United States Botanic Garden The Botanic Garden reopened in late 2001 after a major, 5-year renovation. In its new incarnation, the grand conservatory devotes half of its space to exhibits that focus on the importance of plants to people, and half to exhibits that focus on ecology and the evolutionary biology of plants. A 93-foot-high Palm House encloses a jungle of palms, ferns, and vines, the Orchid Room holds 12,000 varieties of orchids, and the new National Garden outside the conservatory includes a First Ladies Water Garden, a formal rose garden, and a lawn terrace. You'll also find a Meditation Garden and gardens created especially with children in mind.

Also visit the garden annex across the street, **Bartholdi Park.** The park is about the size of a city block, with a stunning cast-iron classical fountain created by Frédéric Auguste Bartholdi, designer of the Statue of Liberty. Charming flower gardens bloom amid tall ornamental grasses, benches are sheltered by vine-covered bowers, and a touch and fragrance garden contains such herbs as pineapple-scented sage.

100 Maryland Ave. (at 1st St. SW at the east end of the Mall). ℰ 202/225-8333. www.usbg.gov. Free admission. Daily 10am–5pm. Metro: Federal Center SW.

The **Herb Garden,** another highlight, includes a historic rose garden (150 old-fashioned fragrant varieties) and 10 specialty gardens. Along **Fern Valley Trail** is the **Franklin Tree,** a species now extinct in the wild, discovered in 1765 by a botanist friend of Benjamin Franklin. And a magnificent sight is the arboretum's acropolis, 22 of the original U.S. Capitol columns designed by Benjamin Latrobe in a setting created by the noted English landscape artist Russell Page. The **American Friendship Garden** is a collection of ornamental grasses and perennials, with brick walkways, terraces, and a statue of Demeter, the Greek goddess of agriculture. And the **Asian Collections,** in a landscaped valley, include rare plants from China and Korea.

Magnolias and early bulbs bloom in late March or early April; azaleas, daffodils, and flowering cherry trees in mid-April; rhododendrons and peonies in May; daylilies and crape myrtles in summer. In autumn, the arboretum is ablaze in reds and oranges as the leaves change color.

Purchase tickets for the open-air **tram tour** at the ticket kiosk (located in the parking lot next to the administration building) for the day of the tour only. Extremely popular is the National Arboretum's **monthly full moon tour,** a strenuous 5-mile hike through the Arboretum grounds as you make your way by the light of the full moon. Reserve in advance (ℰ 202/245-5898). Tours ($10) take place once a month year-round and include a maximum of 30 people per tour.

3501 New York Ave. NE. © 202/245-2726. www.usna.usda.gov. Free admission. Daily 8am–5pm; bonsai collection 10am–3:30pm. 40-min. open-air tram tour Apr–Oct Sat–Sun 10:30 (may be presold to groups) and 11:30am, 1, 2, 3, and 4pm (only in peak season); $3 adults, $2 members and seniors, $1 children 4–16. Closed Dec 25. Free parking. Metro: Union Station, then take the special X6 Metro shuttle that goes directly to the Arboretum. (The shuttle runs on weekends and holiday weekdays only; on other days, take a taxi, since it's only a few dollars.)

9 Organized Tours

ON FOOT

TourDC, Walking Tours of Georgetown, Dupont Circle and Embassy Row (© 301/588-8999; www.tourdc.com) conducts 90-minute ($12) walking tours of Georgetown, telling about the neighborhood's history up to the present and taking you past the homes of notable residents.

Guided Walking Tours of Washington ⟨ (© 301/294-9514; www.dcsightseeing.com) offers 2-hour walks through the streets of Georgetown, Adams-Morgan, and other locations, guided by author/historian Anthony S. Pitch. Inquire about private tours. Rates are $10 per person, $6 for seniors and students.

BY BUS

TOURMOBILE Best-known and least expensive, **Tourmobile Sightseeing** (© 888/868-7707 or 202/554-5100; www.tourmobile. com) is a good choice if you're looking for an easy-on/easy-off tour of major sites. The comfortable red, white, and blue sightseeing trams travel to as many as 24 attractions (the company changes its schedule and number of stops, depending on whether sites are open for public tours), as far out as Arlington National Cemetery ($5.25) and even Mount Vernon ($25). Tourmobile is the only narrated sightseeing shuttle tour authorized by the National Park Service. Rates are roughly half price for children ages 3 to 11.

BY BOAT

Spirit of Washington Cruises, Pier 4 at Sixth and Water streets SW (© 866/211-3811 or 202/554-8000; www.spiritcruises.com; Metro: Waterfront), offers a variety of trips daily, including evening dinner, lunch, and brunch, and moonlight dance cruises, as well as a half-day excursion to Mount Vernon and back. Lunch and dinner cruises include a 40-minute high-energy musical revue. Prices range from $29.95 to $43.95 for a lunch excursion and from $53.95 to $82.95 for a dinner cruise, drinks not included. Call to make reservations.

The *Spirit of Washington* is a luxury climate-controlled harbor cruise ship with carpeted decks and huge panoramic windows designed for sightseeing. There are three well-stocked bars on board. Mount Vernon cruises are aboard an equally luxurious sister ship, the *Potomac Spirit.*

The **Capitol River Cruise's** *Nightingale I* and *Nightingale II* (© **800/405-5511** or 301/460-7447; www.capitolrivercruises.com) are historic 65-foot steel riverboats that can accommodate up to 90 people. The *Nightingale's* narrated jaunts depart Georgetown's Washington Harbour every hour on the hour, from 11am to 9pm, April through October. The 50-minute narrated tour travels past the monuments and memorials as you head to National Airport and back. A snack bar on board sells light refreshments, beer, wine, and sodas; you're welcome to bring your own picnic aboard. The price is $10 per adult, $5 per child ages 3 to 12. To get here, take the Metro to Foggy Bottom and then take the Georgetown Metro Connection Shuttle or walk into Georgetown, following Pennsylvania Avenue, which becomes M Street. Turn left on 31st Street NW, which dead-ends at the Washington Harbour complex.

6

Shopping

Washington-area stores are usually open daily from 10am to 5 or 6pm Monday through Saturday, with one late night (usually Thurs) when hours extend to 9pm. Sunday hours are usually from noon to 5 or 6pm. Exceptions are the malls, which are open late nightly, and antiques stores and art galleries, which tend to keep their own hours. Play it safe and call ahead if there's a store you really want to get to.

Sales tax on merchandise is 5.75% in the District, 5% in Maryland, and 4.5% in Virginia.

Most gift, arts, and crafts stores, including those at the Smithsonian museums, will handle shipping for you; clothes stores generally do not.

If you're a true bargain hunter, scope out the *Washington Post* website (**www.washingtonpost.com**) in advance of your trip for sales. Once you get to the *Post's* home page, hit "Entertainment" at the top of your screen, click on "Shopping," and then click on "Sales and Bargains," a column that's updated weekly.

ANTIQUES

Antiques-on-the-Hill A Capitol Hill institution since the 1960s, this place sells silver, furniture, glassware, jewelry, porcelain, and lamps. 701 North Carolina Ave. SE. ✆ **877/509-3772** or 202/543-1819. Metro: Eastern Market.

Brass Knob Architectural Antiques When early homes and office buildings are demolished in the name of progress, these savvy salvage merchants spirit away saleable treasures, from chandeliers to wrought-iron fencing. 2311 18th St. NW. ✆ **202/332-3370**. www.thebrass knob.com. Metro: Woodley Park or Dupont Circle. A second location across the street is called the **Brass Knob's Back Doors Warehouse**, 2329 Champlain St. NW (✆ **202/265-0587**).

cherry This is an antiques store, all right, but as its name suggests, a little offbeat. Expect affordable eclectic furnishings and decorative arts, and lots of mirrors and sconces. 2603 P St. NW. ✆ **202/342-3600**. Metro: Dupont Circle, then a 10–15 min. walk.

Susquehanna Antiques This Georgetown store specializes in American, English, and European furniture, paintings, and garden items of the late 18th and early 19th centuries. 3216 O St. NW. ℂ 202/333-1511. www.susquehannaantiques.com. Metro: Foggy Bottom, then take the Georgetown Metro Connection.

ART GALLERIES

Art galleries abound in Washington, but are especially prolific in Dupont Circle and Georgetown, and along Seventh Street downtown.

For a complete listing of local galleries, get your hands on a copy of **"Galleries,"** a monthly guide to major galleries and their shows; the guide is free at galleries and many hotel concierge desks.

DUPONT CIRCLE

For all galleries listed below, the closest Metro stop is Dupont Circle.

Affrica Authentic and traditional African masks, figures, and artifacts. The gallery's clients include major museums and private collectors from around the world. 2010 R St. NW. ℂ **202/745-7272.** www.affrica.com.

Anton Gallery Expect to find contemporary American paintings, as well as sculpture, functional ceramics, and prints. Anton represents national and international artists. 2108 R St. NW. ℂ **202/328-0828.** www.antongallery.com.

GEORGETOWN

For all galleries listed below, the closest Metro stop is Foggy Bottom, with a transfer to the Georgetown Metro Connection bus.

Addison/Ripley Fine Art This gallery represents both nationally and regionally recognized artists, from the 19th century to the present; works include paintings, sculpture, photography, and fine arts. 1670 Wisconsin Ave. NW. ℂ **202/338-5180.** www.addisonripleyfineart.com.

Govinda Gallery This place generates a lot of media coverage, since it often shows artwork created by famous names and features photographs of celebrities. In 2002, the gallery's exhibits included Doug Kirkland's photographs of Marilyn Monroe and Kate Simon's photos of Bob Marley. 1227 34th St. NW. ℂ **202/333-1180.** www.govinda gallery.com.

SEVENTH STREET ARTS CORRIDOR

To get here, take the Metro to either the Archives/Navy Memorial (Blue–Orange Line) or Gallery Place/Chinatown/MCI Center (Red–Yellow Line) stations.

406 Art Galleries   Several first-rate art galleries, some of them interlopers from Dupont Circle, occupy this historic building, with its 13-foot high ceilings and spacious rooms. The first floor of the building is a furniture store, so keep going to the next level. Look for the **David Adamson Gallery** (*©* **202/628-0257;** www.art net.com/davidadamsongallery.html), probably the largest gallery space in D.C., with two levels featuring the works of contemporary artists, like locals Kevin MacDonald and Renee Stout, and national artists KiKi Smith and William Wegman. The **Touchstone Gallery** (*©* **202/347-2787;** www.touchstonegallery.com) is a self-run co-op of 36 artists who take turns exhibiting their work.

Zenith Gallery   Across the street from the 406 Group, Zenith shows diverse works by contemporary artists, most American, about half of whom are local. You can get a good deal here, paying anywhere from $50 to $50,000 for a piece. Among the things you'll find are annual humor shows, neon exhibits, realism, abstract expressionism, and landscapes. 413 7th St. NW. *©* **202/783-2963.** www. zenithgallery.com.

BOOKS

Barnes & Noble   This wonderful three-story shop has sizable software, travel book, and children's title sections. A cafe on the second level sometimes hosts concerts. 3040 M St. NW. *©* **202/965-9880.** www.barnesandnoble.com. Metro: Foggy Bottom, then take the Georgetown Metro Connection shuttle. Other area locations include 555 12th St. NW (*©* 202/ 347-0176) and 4801 Bethesda Ave., in Bethesda, Maryland (*©* 301/986-1761).

Borders   With its overwhelming array of books, records, videos, and magazines, this outpost of the expanding chain has taken over the town. Many hardcover bestsellers are 30% off. The store often hosts local musicians. 1800 L St. NW. *©* **202/466-4999.** www.borders.com. Metro: Farragut North. Other Borders stores in the District include 5333 Wisconsin Ave. NW (*©* 202/686-8270), in upper northwest D.C.; and 600 14th St. NW (*©* 202/737-1385).

Kramerbooks & Afterwords Café *(Finds)*   The first bookstore/cafe in Washington, maybe in this country, this place has launched countless romances. It's jammed and often noisy, stages live music Wednesday through Saturday evenings, and is open all night weekends. Paperback fiction takes up most of the inventory, but they carry a little of everything. No discounts. 1517 Connecticut Ave. NW. *©* **202/387-1400;** www.kramers.com. Metro: Dupont Circle.

Olsson's Books and Records. This 30-year-old independent, quality bookstore chain has about 60,000 to 70,000 books on its shelves. Members of its helpful staff know what they're talking about and will order books they don't have in stock. Some discounts are given on books, tapes, and CDs, and their regular prices are pretty good, too. 12th and F sts. NW (© 202/347-3686, www.olssons.com). Metro: Metro Center.

Trover Shop The only general-interest bookstore on Capitol Hill, Trover specializes in its political selections and its magazines. The store discounts 30% on the *Washington Post* hardcover fiction and nonfiction bestsellers. 221 Pennsylvania Ave. SE. © 202/547-BOOK. www.trover.com. Metro: Capitol South.

CAMERAS & FILM DEVELOPING

Ritz Camera Centers Ritz sells camera equipment for the average photographer and offers 1-hour film processing. Call for other locations; there are many throughout the area. 1740 Pennsylvania Ave. NW. © 202/466-3470. www.ritzpix.com. Metro: Farragut West.

CRAFTS

A mano Owner Adam Mahr frequently forages in Europe and returns with the unique handmade, imported French and Italian ceramics, linens, and other decorative accessories that you'll covet here. 1677 Wisconsin Ave. NW. © 202/298-7200. www.amanoinc.com. Metro: Foggy Bottom, then take the Georgetown Metro Connection shuttle.

American Studio Plus This store features exquisite contemporary handcrafted American ceramics and jewelry, plus international objets d'art. 2906 M St. NW. © 202/965-3273. Metro: Foggy Bottom, then take the Georgetown Metro Connection shuttle.

Indian Craft Shop *(Finds)* The Indian Craft Shop has represented authentic Native American artisans since 1938, selling their hand-woven rugs and handcrafted baskets, jewelry, figurines, paintings, pottery, and other items. You need a photo ID to enter the building. Use the C Street entrance, which is the only one open to the public. Department of the Interior, 1849 C St. NW, Room 1023. © 202/208-4056. Weekdays and the third Saturday of each month. www.indiancraftshop.com. Metro: Farragut West or Foggy Bottom.

FARMER'S & FLEA MARKETS

Dupont Circle FreshFarm Market *(Kids)* Fresh flowers, produce, eggs, and cheeses are for sale here. The market also features kids' activities and guest appearances by chefs and owners of some of Washington's best restaurants: Bis, Vidalia, Restaurant Nora, Tosca, and 1789. Held Sundays from 9am to 1pm, April through December. On 20th St. NW, between Q St. and Massachusetts Ave., and in the adjacent Riggs Bank parking lot. © 202/331-7300. Metro: Dupont Circle, Q St. exit.

Eastern Market *Value*   This is the one everyone knows about, even if they've never been here. Located on Capitol Hill, Eastern Market is an inside/outside bazaar of stalls, where greengrocers, butchers, bakers, farmers, artists, craftspeople, florists, and other merchants sell their wares on weekends. Saturday morning is the best time to go. On Sunday, the food stalls become a flea market. Indoor market and art space stays open during the week. Tuesday through Saturday 7am to 6pm, Sunday 9am to 4pm. 225 7th St. SE, between North Carolina Ave. and C St. SE. © 202/546-2698. Metro: Eastern Market.

Georgetown Flea Market *Finds*   Grab a coffee at Starbucks across the lane and get ready to barter. The Georgetown Flea Market is frequented by all types of Washingtonians looking for a good deal—they often get it—on antiques, painted furniture, vintage clothing, and decorative garden urns. Nearly 80 vendors sell their wares here. Open year-round on Sunday from 9am to 5pm.

The school recently converted part of its parking lot into an athletic field, sending another 50 of its original 100 vendors to set up at a new location: Georgetown Flea Market at U Street, 1345 U St. NW, which is open every Saturday and Sunday from 9am to 5pm. In the Hardy Middle School parking lot bordering Wisconsin Ave., between S and T sts. NW. Metro: Foggy Bottom, then take the Georgetown Metro Connection shuttle.

MEN'S CLOTHING

Britches of Georgetowne   See where Washington men go for that straight-laced look. Britches sells moderately priced to expensive dress apparel, both designer wear and from its own label. Its sportswear selections are more extensive than in the past. 1247 Wisconsin Ave. NW. © 202/338-3330. www.britchesusa.com. Metro: Foggy Bottom, then take the Georgetown Metro Connection shuttle. Also at 1776 K St. NW (© 202/347-8994).

Brooks Brothers   Brooks sells traditional men's clothes, as well as the fine line of Peal's English shoes. This store made the news as the place where Monica Lewinsky bought a tie for President Clinton. It also sells an extensive line of women's clothes. 1201 Connecticut Ave. NW. © 202/659-4650. www.brooksbrothers.com. Metro: Dupont Circle or Farragut

North. Other locations are at Potomac Mills, at National Airport (✆ 703/417-0602), and at 5500 Wisconsin Ave., in Chevy Chase, MD (✆ 301/654-8202).

Thomas Pink   For those who like beautifully made, bright-colored shirts, this new branch of the London-based high-end establishment should please. The store also sells ties, boxer shorts, women's shirts, cufflinks, and other accessories. 1127 Connecticut Ave. NW (inside the Mayflower Hotel). ✆ 202/223-5390. www.thomaspink.com. Metro: Farragut North.

MUSIC

Tower Records   When you need a record at midnight on Christmas Eve, you go to Tower. This large, funky store, across the street from George Washington University, has a wide selection in every category—but the prices are high. 2000 Pennsylvania Ave. NW. ✆ 202/331-2400. Metro: Foggy Bottom.

POLITICAL MEMORABILIA

Political Americana   This is another great place to pick up souvenirs. The store sells political novelty items, books, bumper stickers, old campaign buttons, and historical memorabilia. At 14th St. and Pennsylvania Ave. NW (✆ 202/547-1685. www.politicalamericana.com. Metro: Metro Center.

WOMEN'S CLOTHING

Betsey Johnson   New York's flamboyant flower-child designer decorated the bubble-gum pink walls in her Georgetown shop. Her sexy, offbeat play-dress-up styles are great party and club clothes for the young and the still-skinny young at heart. 1319 Wisconsin Ave. NW. ✆ 202/338-4090. www.betseyjohnson.com. Metro: Foggy Bottom, then take the Georgetown Metro Connection shuttle.

Betsy Fisher   A walk past the store is all it takes to know it's a tad different. Its windows and racks show off whimsically feminine fashions by new American designers. 1224 Connecticut Ave. NW. ✆ 202/785-1975. www.betsyfisher.com. Metro: Dupont Circle.

Chanel Boutique   A modest selection of Chanel's signature designs, accessories, and jewelry, at immodest prices. 1455 Pennsylvania Ave. NW, in the courtyard of the Willard Inter-Continental Hotel. ✆ 202/638-5055. Metro: Metro Center.

7

Washington, D.C., After Dark

Contrary to popular belief, political theater is not the only show in town. All through the day, as government officials deliberate headline-making decisions, and members of Congress strut across the C-Span stage, Washington's cultural arts professionals are also hard at work, preparing their entertainments and diversions for Washington's hardworking and weary, and for visitors like you. No matter what happens by day, by night the show must go on—and it does, in art houses, nightclubs, bars, and theaters all over town.

So read over the listings that follow to see which forms of entertainment most appeal. For up-to-date schedules of events, from live music and theater, to children's programs and flower shows, check the Friday "Weekend" section of the *Washington Post,* or browse the *Post* online at www.washingtonpost.com. The *City Paper,* available free at restaurants, bookstores, and other places around town, is another good source.

TICKETS
TICKETplace, Washington's only discount day-of-show ticket outlet, has one location: in the Old Post Office Pavilion, 1100 Pennsylvania Ave. NW (Metro: Federal Triangle). Call © **202/ TICKETS** (842-5387), www.ticketplace.org, for information. You must purchase the tickets in person. Enter the pavilion through its South Plaza entrance, on 12th Street NW, where you must pass through metal detectors to enter the building. On the day of performance only (except Sun and Mon; see below), you can buy half-price tickets (with cash, select debit and credit cards, or traveler's checks) to performances with tickets still available at most major Washington-area theaters and concert halls, as well as for performances of the opera, ballet, and other events. TICKETplace is open Tuesday through Saturday from 11am to 6pm; half-price tickets for Sunday and Monday shows are sold on Saturday. Though tickets are half price, you have to pay a service charge of 10% of the full face value of the ticket. TICKETplace is a service of the Cultural Alliance of Washington.

Full-price tickets for most performances in town can be bought through **Ticketmaster** (℡ 202/432-SEAT; www.ticketmaster. com), if you're willing to pay a hefty service charge. Purchase tickets to Washington theatrical, musical, and other events before you leave home by going online or by calling ℡ **800/551-SEAT.** Or you can wait until you get here and visit one of Ticketmaster's 18 locations throughout the city, including the TICKETplace outlet in the Old Post Office Pavilion (see above).

Another similar ticket outlet is **Tickets.com** (formerly Protix). You can order tickets by calling ℡ **800/955-5566** or 703/218-6500, or by accessing its website at www.tickets.com.

1 The Performing Arts

THE TOP THEATERS

Arena Stage   This outpost on the unattractive Washington waterfront is worth seeking out, despite its poor location. (Dine at a downtown restaurant, then drive or take a taxi here; or you can take the Metro, but be careful walking the block or so to the theater.)

Founded by the brilliant Zelda Fichandler in 1950, the Arena Stage is home to one of the oldest acting ensembles in the nation. Several works nurtured here have moved to Broadway, and many graduates have gone on to commercial stardom, including Ned Beatty, James Earl Jones, and Jane Alexander.

Arena presents eight productions annually on two stages: the **Fichandler** (a theater-in-the-round) and the smaller, fan-shaped **Kreeger.** In addition, the Arena houses the **Old Vat,** a space used for new play readings and special productions. 1101 6th St. SW (at Maine Ave.). ℡ 202/488-3300. www.arenastage.org. Tickets $27–$50; discounts available for students, people with disabilities, groups, and seniors. Metro: Waterfront.

John F. Kennedy Center for the Performing Arts   This 30-year-old theater complex strives to be not just the hub of Washington's cultural and entertainment scene, but a performing arts theater for the nation. Don't expect cutting-edge productions, but do look here for top-rated performances by the best ballet, opera, jazz, modern dance, musical, and theater companies in the world. The best costs the most, and you are likely to pay more for a ticket here than at any other theater in D.C.—from $12 for a children's play to more than $280 for a box seat on a Saturday night at the opera, although most ticket prices run in the $50 to $60 range.

But the Kennedy Center is committed to being a theater for the people, and toward that end, it continues to stage its **free concert**

series, known as "Millennium Stage," which features daily performances by area musicians and sometimes national artists each evening at 6pm in the center's Grand Foyer. (You can check out broadcasts of the nightly performances on the Internet at www.kennedy-center.org/millennium.) During the summer, the Ken-Cen adds Millennium Stage performances every Wednesday at noon on the steps of the Library of Congress's Thomas Jefferson Building. The Friday "Weekend" section of the *Washington Post* lists the free performances scheduled for the coming week; the daily "Style" section lists nightly performances under "Free Events," in the "Guide to the Lively Arts" column. Also call about "pay what you can" performances, scheduled throughout the year on certain days, for certain shows.

The Kennedy Center is actually made up of six different national theaters: the Opera House, the Concert Hall, the Terrace Theater, the Eisenhower Theater, the Theater Lab, and the American Film Institute (AFI) theater. At the southern end of New Hampshire Ave. NW and Rock Creek Pkwy. ✆ 800/444-1324 or 202/467-4600 for tickets and information. www.kennedy-center.org. 50% discounts are offered (for most attractions) to students, seniors 65 and over, people with permanent disabilities, enlisted military personnel, and persons with fixed low incomes (call ✆ 202/416-8340 for details). Garage parking $10. Metro: Foggy Bottom (though it's a fairly short walk, there's a free shuttle between the station and the Kennedy Center, departing every 15 min. 9:45am–midnight, Mon–Sat, noon–midnight Sun). Bus: 80 from Metro Center.

National Theatre The luxurious Federal-style National Theatre is the oldest continuously operating theater in Washington (since 1835) and the third oldest in the nation. It's exciting just to see the stage on which Sarah Bernhardt, John Barrymore, Helen Hayes, and so many other notables have performed. The 1,672-seat National is the closest thing Washington has to a Broadway-style playhouse.

One thing that has never flagged at The National is its commitment to offering free public-service programs: Saturday-morning children's theater (puppets, clowns, magicians, dancers, and singers) and Monday-night showcases of local groups and performers September through May, plus free summer films. Call ✆ 202/783-3372 for details. 1321 Pennsylvania Ave. NW. ✆ 202/628-6161, or 800/447-7400 to charge tickets. www.nationaltheatre.org. Tickets $30–$75; discounts available for students, seniors, military personnel, and people with disabilities. Metro: Metro Center.

Shakespeare Theatre Try and snag tickets to a play here, for the productions are reliably outstanding. Season subscriptions claim many of the seats and the plays almost always sell out, so if you're interested in attending a play here, you'd better buy your tickets now. This internationally renowned classical ensemble company offers five plays, usually three Shakespearean and two modern classics each September-to-June season. 450 7th St. NW (between D and E sts.). © 202/547-1122. www.shakespearetheatre.org. Tickets $14.50–$64, $10 for standing-room tickets sold 1 hr. before sold-out performances; discounts available for students, seniors, and groups. Metro: Archives–Navy Memorial or MCI Center/Gallery Place.

SMALLER THEATERS

The **Source Theatre Company,** 1835 14th St. NW, between S and T streets (© **202/462-1073;** www.sourcetheatre.org), is Washington's major producer of new plays. Joy Zinoman, the artistic director of the **Studio Theatre,** 1333 P St. NW, at 14th Street (© **202/332-3300;** www.studiotheatre.org), showcases interesting contemporary plays and nurtures Washington acting talent.

In addition, I highly recommend productions staged at the **Folger Shakespeare Library,** 201 E. Capitol St. SE (© **202/ 544-7077;** www.folger.edu). Plays take place in the library's Elizabethan Theatre, which is styled after the inn-yard theater of Shakespeare's time. The theater is intimate and charming, the theater company is remarkably good, and an evening spent here guarantees an absolutely marvelous experience. The Elizabethan Theatre is also the setting for musical performances, lectures, readings, and other events.

Finally, there's **Ford's Theatre,** 511 10th St. NW, between E and F streets (© **202/347-4833;** www.fordstheatre.org), the actual theater where, on the evening of April 14, 1865, actor John Wilkes Booth shot President Lincoln. Though popular among Washingtonians for its annual holiday performance of Dickens's *A Christmas Carol,* Ford's stages generally mediocre presentations, usually intertwined with American history themes.

INDOOR ARENAS & OUTDOOR PAVILIONS

When Madonna, U2, the Rolling Stones, or the Backstreet Boys come to town, they usually play at one of the huge indoor or outdoor arenas. The 20,600-seat **MCI Center,** 601 F St. NW, where it meets Seventh Street (© **202/628-3200;** www.mcicenter.com), in the center of downtown, hosts plenty of concerts and also is Washington's premier indoor sports arena (home to the NBA Wizards, the WNBA Mystics, the NHL Capitals, and Georgetown NCAA basketball).

My favorite summer setting for music is **Wolf Trap Farm Park for the Performing Arts,** 1551 Trap Rd., Vienna, Virginia (☎ 703/255-1868; www.wolftrap.org). The country's only national park devoted to the performing arts, Wolf Trap, 30 minutes by car from downtown D.C., offers performances by the National Symphony Orchestra (it's their summer home), and has hosted Lucinda Williams, Shawn Colvin, Lyle Lovett, The Temptations, Ani DiFranco, and many others. Performances take place in the 7,000-seat Filene Center, about half of which is under the open sky. You can also buy cheaper lawn seats on the hill, which is sometimes best. If you do, arrive early (the lawn opens 90 min. before the performance) and bring a blanket and a picnic dinner—it's a tradition. Wolf Trap also hosts a number of very popular **festivals.** The park features a daylong Irish music festival in May; the Louisiana Swamp Romp Cajun Festival and a weekend of jazz and blues in June; and the International Children's Festival each September.

The **Carter Barron Amphitheater,** 16th Street and Colorado Avenue NW (☎ 202/426-0486), way out 16th Street, is in Rock Creek Park, close to the Maryland border. This is the area's smallest outdoor venue, with 4,250 seats. Summer performances include a range of gospel, blues, and classical entertainment. The shows are usually free, but tickets are required. You can always count on Shakespeare: The **Shakespeare Theatre Free For All** takes place at the Carter Barron usually for 2 weeks in June, Tuesday through Sunday evenings; the free tickets are available the day of performance only, on a first-come, first-served basis (call ☎ 202/334-4790 for details).

SMALLER AUDITORIUMS

At the 1,500-seat **Lisner Auditorium,** on the campus of George Washington University, 21st and H streets NW (☎ 202/994-1500; www.lisner.org), you always feel close to the stage. Bookings sometimes include musical groups like Siouxsie and the Banshees, comedians like "Weird Al" Yankovic, monologist Spalding Gray, and children's entertainers like Raffi, but are mostly cultural shows—everything from a Pakistani rock group to the Washington Revels' annual romp at Christmas.

The **Warner Theatre,** 1299 Pennsylvania Ave. NW, with the entrance on 13th Street, between E and F streets (☎ 202/783-4000; www.warnertheatre.com), opened in 1924 as the Earle Theatre (a movie/vaudeville palace) and was restored to its original, neoclassical-style appearance in 1992 at a cost of $10 million. It's worth coming by just to see its ornately detailed interior. The 2,000-seat auditorium offers year-round entertainment, alternating dance performances (from Baryshnikov to the Washington Ballet's *The Nutcracker*) and Broadway/off-Broadway shows (*Cabaret, Lord of the Dance, Godspell*) with headliner entertainment (Sheryl Crow, Natalie Merchant, Wynton Marsalis).

2 The Club & Music Scene

COMEDY

The Capitol Steps *(Moments* This musical political satire troupe is made up of former Congressional staffers, equal-opportunity spoofers all, who poke endless fun through song and skits at politicians on both sides of the aisle, and at government goings-on in general. Shows take place in the Amphitheater, on the concourse level of the Ronald Reagan Building and International Trade Center, at 7:30pm Friday and Saturday. 1300 Pennsylvania Ave. NW (in the Ronald Reagan Bldg.). ☎ 202/312-1555. www.capsteps.com. Tickets $31.50. Metro: Federal Triangle.

The Improv The Improv features top performers on the national comedy club circuit as well as comic plays and one-person shows. *Saturday Night Live* performers David Spade, Chris Rock, and Adam Sandler have all played here, as have comedy bigs Ellen DeGeneres, Jerry Seinfeld, and Robin Williams. Shows are about 1½ hours long and include three comics (an emcee, a feature act, and a headliner). Show times are 8:30pm Sunday through Thursday, 8 and 10:30pm on Friday and Saturday. You must be 18 to get in. 1140 Connecticut Ave. NW (between L and M sts.). ☎ 202/296-7008. www.dc improv.com. Cover $12 Sun–Thurs, $15 Fri–Sat, plus a 2-drink minimum (waived if you dine). Metro: Farragut North.

POP/ROCK/RAVE/ALTERNATIVE

Black Cat This comfortable, low-key club draws a black-clad crowd to its concert hall, which features national, international, and local indie and alternative groups. The place is made for dancing, accommodating more than 600 people. Adjoining the hall is the Red Room Bar, a large, funky, red-walled living-roomy lounge with booths, tables, a red-leather sofa, pinball machines, a pool table, and a jukebox stocked with a really eclectic collection. A college crowd collects on weekends, but you can count on seeing a 20- to 30-something bunch here most nights, including members of various bands who like to stop in for a drink. Black Cat also hosts film

---

(*Tips*   **Metro Takes You There**

Recognizing that Washingtonians are keeping later hours these days, Metro not only keeps its trains running until 2am on weekends, but has also inaugurated special shuttle service to Adams-Morgan (a late night hotspot without a Metro station).

Here's what you do: Take the Metro to the Red Line's Woodley Park–Adams-Morgan Station or to the Green Line's U St.–Cardozo Station, and hop on the no. 98 Adams-Morgan–U St. Link Shuttle, which travels through Adams-Morgan, between these two stations, after 6pm daily, except on Saturday, when service starts at 10am. The U Link Shuttle operates every 15 minutes and costs only 25¢ with a transfer from Metrorail, or $1.10 without a transfer.

---

screenings, poetry readings, and other quiet forms of entertainment in its ground floor room called "Backstage," and serves vegetarian food in its smoke-free cafe. The Red Room Bar is open until 2am Sunday through Thursday, and until 3am Friday and Saturday. Concerts take place 4 or 5 nights a week, beginning at about 8:30pm (call for details). 1811 14th St. NW (between S and T sts.). *C* **202/667-7960.** www.blackcatdc.com. Cover $5–$15 for concerts; no cover in the Red Room Bar. Metro: U St.–Cardozo.

Eighteenth Street Lounge   This place maintains its "hot" status. First you have to find it, and then you have to convince the bouncer to let you in. So here's what you need to know: Look for the mattress shop south of Dupont Circle, then look up. "ESL" (as those in the know call it) sits above the shop, and hangs only a tiny plaque at street level to advertise its existence. Wear something exotic and sexy. If you pass inspection, you may be surprised to find yourself in a restored mansion (Teddy Roosevelt once lived here) with fireplaces, high ceilings, and a deck out back. Or maybe you'll just get right out there on the hardwood floors to dance to acid jazz, hip-hop, reggae, or Latin jazz tunes spun by a deejay. 1212 18th St. NW. *C* **202/466-3922.** Cover $10–$20 Thurs–Sat; no cover Sun–Wed. Metro: Dupont Circle or Farragut North.

Metro Café   The Metro holds about 100 people in a room with a big stage, an L-shaped bar, red-velvet curtains, and tall ceilings. Acts range from live hip-hop and local rock bands to artist-specific themed dance events, with DJs spinning music by one group all night long, Depeche Mode, maybe, or Prince. The club attracts all ages, everyone in black. The Metro holds its own by featuring different entertainment every night, presenting short plays, poetry readings, improvisational comedy, as well as diverse kinds of music. Open nightly after 7pm. 1522 14th St. NW (between P and Q sts.). © 202/ 588-9118. www.metrocafe.net. Cover $5–$15. Metro: McPherson Square.

Nation   This concert/dance space has separate areas for live music, dance music, and lounging, and a three-tiered outdoor patio. This is primarily a Gen-X mecca (though some performers attract an older crowd). It's also D.C.'s largest club, accommodating about 2,000 people a night. The Pet Shop Boys and Pink are among the groups to have performed here recently. But Nation is best known for its dance parties. Friday is "Buzz" night, when those 19 and older come here to rave to deejay-spun house, trance, techno and other music. Thursday is Goth night for those addicted to psytrance and darkwave music, black leather and eyeliner. Saturday is given over to a gay dance party called "Velvet." The game room and state-of-the-art lighting/laser/sound systems are a plus. The Nation is in a pretty bad neighborhood, so make sure you have good directions to get there; the building itself is very secure. 1015 Half St. SE (at K St.). © 202/ 554-1500. www.nationdc.com. Cover $7–$30. Metro: Navy Yard.

9:30 Club   Housed in yet another converted warehouse, this major live-music venue hosts frequent record-company parties and features a wide range of top performers. You might catch Sheryl Crow, Simple Minds, The Clarks, Luna, The Tragically Hip, Lucinda Williams, or even Tony Bennett. It's only open when there's a show on, which is almost every night (but call ahead), and, obviously, the crowd (as many as 1,200) varies with the performer. The sound system is state of the art and the sight lines are excellent. There are four bars: two on the main dance-floor level, one in the upstairs VIP room (anyone is welcome here unless the room is being used for a private party), and another in the distressed-looking cellar. The 9:30 Club is a standup place, literally—there are few seats. 815 V St. NW (at Vermont Ave.). © 202/265-0930. www.930.com. Metro: U St.–Cardozo, 10th St. exit.

Polly Esther's   This is a three-dance-clubs-in-one emporium with '70s disco music (think the Village People, ABBA, the BeeGees) blaring from the sound system on the "Polly Esther's" dance floor, '80s tunes by artists like Madonna and Prince playing in the "Culture Club," and current radio hits blasting throughout

"Club Expo." Decor for each floor matches the music of that era, so, for instance, you'll see such artifacts as a John Travolta memorial and Brady Bunch memorabilia in the Polly Esther's club. Open Thursday through Saturday. 605 12th St. NW. ✆ 202/737-1970. www.polly esthers.com. Cover $7 Thurs, $8 Fri, $10 Sat. Metro: Metro Center.

JAZZ & BLUES

Blues Alley   Blues Alley, in Georgetown, has been Washington's top jazz club since 1965, featuring such artists as Nancy Wilson, McCoy Tyner, Sonny Rollins, Wynton Marsalis, Rachelle Ferrell, and Maynard Ferguson. There are usually two shows nightly at 8 and 10pm; some performers also do midnight shows on weekends. Reservations are essential (call after noon); since seating is on a first-come, first-served basis, it's best to arrive no later than 7pm and have dinner. Entrees on the steak and Creole seafood menu are in the $15 to $22 range, snacks and sandwiches are $5.25 to $10, and drinks are $5.35 to $9. The decor is classic jazz club: exposed brick walls, beamed ceiling, and small, candlelit tables. Sometimes well-known visiting musicians get up and jam with performers. 1073 Wisconsin Ave. NW (in an alley below M St.). ✆ 202/337-4141. www.bluesalley. com. Cover $16–$40, plus $7 food or drink minimum, plus $1.75 surcharge. Metro: Foggy Bottom, then take the Georgetown Metro Connection Shuttle.

Bohemian Caverns   Rising from the ashes on the very spot where jazz greats such as Duke Ellington, Billie Holiday, and so many others performed decades ago, Bohemian Caverns hopes to establish that same presence and host today's jazz stars. The club's decor is cavelike, as it was in the '20s. Musicians you might catch here include Shirley Horn, Nap Turner, and Esther Williams. The Caverns is also a restaurant, whose entrees are named after jazz legends and start at $18.50. You should dress up to come here. 2001 11th St. NW (at U St). ✆ 202/299-0801. Cover $10–$20, but as much as $50 for someone like Shirley Horn, plus a $12 minimum for food or drinks. Metro: U St.–Cardozo.

Madam's Organ Restaurant and Bar *Finds*   This beloved Adams-Morgan hangout fulfills owner Bill Duggan's definition of a good bar: great sounds and sweaty people. The great sounds feature One Night Stand, a jazz group, on Monday; bluesman Ben Andrews on Tuesday; bluegrass with Bob Perilla and the Big Hillbilly Bluegrass Band on Wednesday; and the salsa sounds of Patrick Alban and Noche Latina on Thursday, which is also Ladies' Night. On Friday and Saturday nights, regional blues groups pack the place. The club includes a wide-open bar decorated eclectically with a 150-year-old gilded mirror, stuffed fish and animal heads, and

Late-Night Bites

You can always get a meal at one of a growing number of late-night or all-night eateries.

In Georgetown, the thoroughly French **Bistro Francais,** 3128 M St. NW (☎ 202/338-3830) serves streak frites, omelets, and patés until 4am. On U Street, **Ben's Chili Bowl,** 1213 U St. NW (☎ 202/667-0909), serves up chili dogs, turkey subs, and cheese fries until 4am on Friday and Saturday nights.

Adams-Morgan has the all-night **Diner,** 2453 18th St. NW (☎ 202/232-8800) and the **18th and U Duplex Diner,** 2004 18th St. NW (☎ 202/265-7828), which offers comfort food, like macaroni and cheese, or burgers, until 4am.

Finally, in Dupont Circle, stop in at **Kramerbooks & Afterwords Café,** 1517 Connecticut Ave. NW (☎ 202/387-1400), for big servings of everything, from quesadillas to french fries to French toast. The bookstore stays open all night on weekends, and so does its kitchen.

paintings of nudes. The second-floor bar is called Big Daddy's Love Lounge & Pick-Up Joint, which tells you everything you need to know. Other points to note: You can play darts, and redheads pay half-price for drinks. For what it's worth, *Playboy's* May 2000 issue named Madam's Organ one of the 25 best bars in America. Food is served, but I'd eat elsewhere. 2461 18th St. NW. ☎ 202/667-5370. www.madamsorgan.com. Cover $3–$7. Metro: U St.–Cardozo or Woodley Park–Zoo–Adams-Morgan and catch the Adams-Morgan/U St. Link Shuttle.

INTERNATIONAL SOUNDS

Chi Cha Lounge *(Finds)* You can sit around on couches, eat Ecuadoran tapas, and listen to live Latin music, which is featured Sunday through Wednesday. Or you can sit around on couches and smoke Arabic tobacco through a 3-foot-high arguileh pipe. Or you can just sit around. This is a popular neighborhood place. 1624 U St. NW. ☎ 202/234-8400. www.chi-cha.com. Cover $15 (minimum). Metro: U St.–Cardozo.

Habana Village This three-story nightclub has a bar/restaurant on the first floor, a bar/dance floor with deejay on the second level, and a live music space on the third floor. Salsa and merengue lessons are given Wednesday through Saturday evenings, $10 per lesson. Otherwise, a deejay or live band plays danceable Latin jazz tunes. 1834 Columbia Rd. NW. ✆ 202/462-6310. Cover $5 Fri–Sat after 9:30pm (no cover for women). Metro: U St.–Cardozo or Woodley Park–Zoo–Adams-Morgan, and catch the Adams-Morgan/U St. Link Shuttle.

Latin Jazz Alley This Adams-Morgan hot spot is another place to get in on Washington's Latin scene. At the Alley, you can learn to salsa and merengue Wednesday through Saturday nights; each lesson is $5 for beginners, $10 for intermediate dancers. The club features live Brazilian music Thursday nights, 10pm to 1am. Friday and Saturday nights, from about 10pm to 2am, a deejay plays Latin jazz. Dinner is served until midnight. 1721 Columbia Rd. NW, on the 2nd floor of the El Migueleno Cafe. ✆ 202/328-6190. $5–$10 for salsa dance lessons; 2-drink minimum. Metro: U St.–Cardozo or Woodley Park–Zoo–Adams-Morgan and catch the Adams-Morgan/U St. Link Shuttle.

Zanzibar on the Waterfront One day Washington will get its act together and develop the waterfront neighborhood in which you find Zanzibar. In the meantime, this area is pretty deserted at night, except for a handful of restaurants and Arena Stage. It really doesn't matter, though, because inside the nightclub you're looking out at the Potomac. Yes, this is a club with actual windows. In keeping with current trends, Zanzibar has lots of couches and chairs arranged just so. A Caribbean and African menu is available, and you can dine while listening to both live and deejay music. Every night brings something different, from jazz and blues to oldies. Wednesday is salsa night, with free lessons from 7 to 8pm, though a cover still applies: $5 to get in before 10pm and $10 after. An international crowd gathers here to dance or just hang out. 700 Water St. SW. ✆ 202/554-9100. www.zanzibar-otw.com. Cover typically $10 (more for live shows). Metro: Waterfront.

GAY CLUBS
Dupont Circle is the gay hub of Washington, D.C., with at least 10 gay bars within easy walking distance of one another.

Badlands Twenty-seven years old and still going strong, Badlands is a favorite dance club for gay men. In addition to the parquet dance floor in the main room, the club has at least six bars throughout the first level. Upstairs is the Annex bar/lounge/pool hall, and a show room where karaoke performers commandeer the mike Friday night. 1415 22nd St. NW, near P St. ✆ 202/296-0505. www.bad landsdc.com. Sometimes a cover of $3–$10, depending on the event. Metro: Dupont Circle.

Hung Jury   For the D.C. lesbian insider. Though the address is H Street, you reach this club via an alley off 19th Street. To enter the blue door, you must be a woman or be accompanied by a woman, but Hung Jury welcomes everyone—gays, straights, men, and women. Inside the club is a large dance floor, two bars, a lounge, and a pool table. Open Friday and Saturday nights. 1819 H St. NW. ✆ 202/785-8181. Cover $5–$10. Metro: Farragut West.

J.R.'s Bar and Grill   This casual and intimate all-male Dupont Circle club draws a crowd that is friendly, upscale, and very attractive. The interior—not that you'll be able to see much of it, because J.R.'s is always sardine-packed—has a 20-foot-high pressed-tin ceiling and exposed brick walls hung with neon beer signs. The big screen over the bar area is used to air music videos, showbiz sing-alongs, and favorite TV shows. Thursday is all-you-can-drink for $7 from 5 to 8pm; at midnight, you get free shots. The balcony, with pool tables, is a little more laid back. Food is served daily, until 5pm Sunday and until 7pm all other days. 1519 17th St. NW (between P and Q sts.). ✆ 202/328-0090. www.jrsdc.com. No cover. Metro: Dupont Circle.

3 The Bar Scene

Bar Rouge   Hopping, popping Bar Rouge lies just inside the Hotel Rouge (see p. 44), but also has its own entrance from the street—you must pass under the watchful eyes of the stone Venuses arrayed in front to reach it. As acid jazz or modern international music pulses throughout the narrow room, a large flat-screen monitor on the back wall of the bar presents evolving visions of flowers blooming, snow falling, and other photographically engineered scenes. The place is full of attitude-swaggering patrons tossing back drinks with names like Sin on the Rocks and Love Gun. A lucky few have snagged seats on the white leather-cushioned barstools at the deep red mahogany bar. Others lounge on the 20-foot-long tufted banquette and munch on little dishes of scallop ceviche sopapillas, roasted pumpkin ravioli, and other Latin-inspired tastings served by waitresses in patent leather go-go boots and seductive black attire. Bar Rouge aims to be a scene, and succeeds. But be forewarned: If it looks crowded, you'll probably want to go elsewhere. 1315 16th St. NW (at Massachusetts Ave. and Scott Circle). ✆ 202/232-8000. Metro: Dupont Circle.

Dragonfly   Expect to wait in line to get in here and the other hip clubs along this stretch of Connecticut Avenue. Dragonfly is a club, with music playing, white walls glowing, white-leather chairs beckoning, and people in black vogue-ing. And Dragonfly is a restaurant, with serious aspirations to please sushi-lovers. But Dragonfly is not a dance club, so put on your cool clothes but leave your dancing shoes at home. 1215 Connecticut Ave. NW. ✆ 202/331-1775. Metro: Dupont Circle or Farragut North.

The Dubliner   This is your typical old Irish pub, the port you can blow into in any storm, personal or weather-related. It's got the dark-wood paneling and tables, the etched- and stained-glass windows, an Irish-accented staff from time to time, and, most importantly, the Auld Dubliner Amber Ale. You'll probably want to stick to drinks here, but you can grab a burger, grilled chicken sandwich, or roast duck salad; the kitchen is open until 1am. The Dubliner is frequented by Capitol Hill staffers and journalists who cover the Hill. Irish music groups play nightly. In the Phoenix Park Hotel, 520 N. Capitol St. NW, with its own entrance on F St. NW. ✆ 202/737-3773. www.dublinerdc.com. Metro: Union Station.

Lucky Bar   Lucky Bar is a good place to kick back and relax. But, in keeping with the times, it also features free salsa dance lessons on Monday night. Sometimes the music is live, but mostly it's courtesy of a deejay. Other times the jukebox plays, but never so loud that you can't carry on a conversation. The bar has a front room overlooking Connecticut Avenue and a back room decorated with good-luck signs, couches, hanging TVs, booths, and a pool table. Lucky Bar is known in the area as a "soccer bar," with its TVs turned to soccer matches going on around the world; during the month-long 2002 World Cup playoffs, the bar received permission from the D.C. Alcoholic Beverage Control Board to open at 7am and start selling alcohol at 8am each day (later on Sun) of the championship. 1221 Connecticut Ave. NW. ✆ 202/331-3733. Metro: Dupont Circle or Farragut North.

Mr. Smith's of Georgetown   Mr. Smith's bills itself as "The Friendliest Saloon in Town," but the truth is that it's so popular among regulars, you're in danger of being ignored if the staff doesn't know you. The bar, which opened about 31 years ago, has a front room with original brick walls, wooden seats, and a long bar, at which you can count on finding pairs of newfound friends telling obscene jokes, loudly. At the end of this room is a large piano around which customers congregate each night to accompany the pianist. An interior light-filled garden room adjoins an outdoor garden area. 3104 M St. NW. ✆ 202/333-3104. www.mrsmiths.com. Metro: Foggy Bottom, then take the Georgetown Metro Connection shuttle.

Arlington Row

I wouldn't recommend that you visit Arlington Row if it weren't for one key element: the music. It's live, it's good (most of the time), and it's here almost nightly. So take the Metro to the Clarendon stop and walk down Wilson, or drive up Wilson from Key Bridge, turn left on Edgewood Road or another side street, and park on the street. Then walk to these spots, all of which serve food:

The smallest of the bunch, **Galaxy Hut,** 2711 Wilson Blvd. (✆ **703/525-8646;** www.galaxyhut.com), is a comfortable bar with far-out art on the walls and a patio in the alley. Look for live alternative rock, with no cover.

At **IOTA,** 2832 Wilson Blvd. (✆ **703/522-8340;** iotaclubandcafe.com), up-and-coming local bands take the stage nightly in a setting with minimal décor. There's live music nightly, usually with a cover of $8 to $15.

Whitlow's on Wilson, 2854 Wilson Blvd. (✆ **703/276-9693;** www.whitlows.com), is the biggest spot on the block, spreading throughout four rooms, the first showcasing the music (usually blues). The other rooms hold coin-operated pool tables, dartboards, and air hockey. Cover is usually $3 Thursday through Saturday after 9pm.

Clarendon Grill, 1101 N. Highland St. (✆ **703/524-7455;** www.cgrill.com), wins a best decor award for its construction theme: murals of construction workers, building materials displayed under the glass-covered bar, and so forth. Music is a mix of modern rock, jazz, and reggae. Cover is $3 to $5 Wednesday through Saturday.

Nathans   Nathans is in the heart of Georgetown. If you pop in here in midafternoon, it's a quiet place to grab a beer or glass of wine and watch the action on the street. Visit at night, though, and it's a more typical bar scene, crowded with locals, out-of-towners, students, and a sprinkling of couples in from the 'burbs. That's the front room. The back room at Nathans is a civilized, candlelit restaurant serving classic American fare. After dinner on Friday and Saturday, this room turns into a dance hall, playing deejay music and attracting the 20-somethings Friday night, an older crowd Saturday night. 3150 M St. NW (at the corner of Wisconsin Ave.). ✆ 202/338-2600. Metro: Foggy Bottom, then take the Georgetown Metro Connection shuttle.

Politiki and the Pennsylvania Ave. Pourhouse This welcome addition to the more traditional pubs along this stretch of Capitol Hill has two themes going. Its first floor plays on a Pittsburgh theme (honoring the owner's roots), displaying Steeler and Penguin paraphernalia, and drawing Iron City drafts from its tap and pierogis from the kitchen. Downstairs is a tiki bar: Think Scorpion Bowl and piña colada drinks, pupu platters, and hula dancer figurines. The basement has pool tables, a bar, and a lounge area (behind beaded curtains); the street level has booths and a bar; and the top floor occasionally features live music, dance lessons, and a promised Don Ho night. Now's your chance to wear your Hawaiian shirt. 319 Pennsylvania Ave. SE. ✆ 202/546-1001. Metro: Capitol South.

Toka Café Toka is small, underground, and upscale, affecting a hip New York look, with its sleek decor of white walls and brushed steel accents, aluminum bar stools and glass-topped bar. Toka pursues an NYC ambience, too, requiring no dress code, but catering to a crowd that can afford its pricey cocktails, like the $9 signature drink, the "Tokatini" (orange vodka and Cointreau), and who enjoy bites of fancy food, such as crab croquettes or grape leaves stuffed with duck confit. (Toka is both a restaurant and bar.) Patrons overwhelmed the small space when Toka first opened in 2002; like Topaz and Rouge (see write-ups in this section), Toka works best when it's not crowded. 1140 19th St. NW. ✆ 202/429-8652. Metro: Dupont Circle or Farragut North.

The Tombs Housed in a converted 19th-century Federal-style home, the Tombs, which opened in 1962, is a favorite hangout for students and faculty of nearby Georgetown University. (Bill Clinton came here during his college years.) They tend to congregate at the central bar and surrounding tables, while local residents head for "the Sweeps," the room that lies down a few steps and has red-leather banquettes.

Directly below the upscale 1789 restaurant (p. 93), the Tombs benefits from 1789 chef Riz Lacoste's supervision. The menu offers burgers, sandwiches, and salads, as well as more serious fare. 1226 36th St. NW. ✆ 202/337-6668. Cover sometimes on Tues or Sun nights, never more than $5. Metro: Foggy Bottom, then take the Georgetown Metro Connection shuttle into Georgetown.

Topaz Bar This is Bar Rouge's sister (they are owned and managed by the same companies) and also lies within a hotel, The Topaz. The decor here emphasizes cool sensuality, hence the

Philippe Starck bar stools, blue velvet settees, zebra-patterned ottomans, and leopard-print rugs. A lighting scheme fades into and out of colors: blue to pink to black, and so on. Everyone here is drinking the Blue Nirvana, a combo of champagne, vodka, and a touch of blueberry liqueur—a concoction that tends to turn your tongue blue, by the way. The Topaz Bar serves small plates of delicious Asian-inspired tastes, like shrimp and pork dumplings and stir-fry of sea scallops. 1733 N St. NW. (C) 202/393-3000. Metro: Dupont Circle or Farragut North.

Tryst   This is the most relaxed of Washington's lounge bars. The room is surprisingly large for Adams-Morgan, and it's jam-packed with worn armchairs and couches, which are usually occupied, no matter what time of day. People come here to have coffee or a drink, get a bite to eat, read a book, meet a friend. The place feels almost like a student lounge on a college campus, only alcohol is served. 2459 18th St. NW. (C) 202/232-5500. www.trystdc.com. Metro: U St.–Cardozo or Woodley Park–Zoo–Adams-Morgan and catch the Adams-Morgan/U St. Link Shuttle.

Tune Inn *(Finds)*   Capitol Hill has a number of bars that qualify as institutions, but the Tune Inn is probably the most popular. Capitol Hill staffers and their bosses, apparently at ease in dive surroundings, have been coming here for cheap beer and greasy burgers since it opened in 1955. (All the longtime Capitol Hillers know that Friday is crab cake day at the Tune Inn, and they all show up.) 33½ Pennsylvania Ave. SE. (C) 202/543-2725. Metro: Capitol South.

Index

See also Accommodations and Restaurant indexes, below.

Wickedly honest guides for sophisticated travelers—and those who want to be.

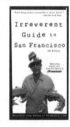

TRAVEL AROUND THE WORLD IN STYLE
– WITHOUT BREAKING THE BANK –
WITH FROMMER'S DOLLAR-A-DAY GUIDES!

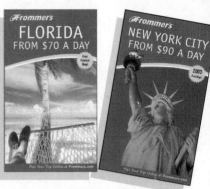

THE ULTIMATE GUIDES TO COMFORTABLE
LOW-COST TRAVEL.

OTHER DOLLAR-A-DAY TITLES

Australia from $50 a Day
California from $70 a Day
Caribbean from $70 a Day
England from $75 a Day
Europe from $70 a Day
Florida from $70 a Day
Hawaii from $80 a Day

Ireland from $60 a Day
Italy from $70 a Day
London from $85 a Day
New York City from $90 a Day
Paris from $80 a Day
San Francisco from $70 a Day
Washington, D.C. from $80 a Day

FROMMER'S® COMPLETE TRAVEL GUIDES

FROMMER'S® DOLLAR-A-DAY GUIDES

FROMMER'S® PORTABLE GUIDES

FROMMER'S® NATIONAL PARK GUIDES

FROMMER'S® MEMORABLE WALKS

Chicago	New York	San Francisco
London	Paris	Washington, D.C.

FROMMER'S® GREAT OUTDOOR GUIDES

Arizona & New Mexico	Northern California	Vermont & New Hampshire
New England	Southern New England	

SUZY GERSHMAN'S BORN TO SHOP GUIDES

Born to Shop: France	Born to Shop: Italy	Born to Shop: New York
Born to Shop: Hong Kong, Shanghai & Beijing	Born to Shop: London	Born to Shop: Paris

FROMMER'S® IRREVERENT GUIDES

Amsterdam	Los Angeles	San Francisco
Boston	Manhattan	Seattle & Portland
Chicago	New Orleans	Vancouver
Las Vegas	Paris	Walt Disney World®
London	Rome	Washington, D.C.

FROMMER'S® BEST-LOVED DRIVING TOURS

Britain	Germany	Northern Italy
California	Ireland	Scotland
Florida	Italy	Spain
France	New England	Tuscany & Umbria

HANGING OUT™ GUIDES

Hanging Out in England	Hanging Out in France	Hanging Out in Italy
Hanging Out in Europe	Hanging Out in Ireland	Hanging Out in Spain

THE UNOFFICIAL GUIDES®

Bed & Breakfasts and Country Inns in:
California
Great Lakes States
Mid-Atlantic
New England
Northwest
Rockies
Southeast
Southwest
Best RV & Tent Campgrounds in:
California & the West
Florida & the Southeast
Great Lakes States
Mid-Atlantic
Northeast
Northwest & Central Plains

Southwest & South Central Plains
U.S.A.
Beyond Disney
Branson, Missouri
California with Kids
Chicago
Cruises
Disneyland®
Florida with Kids
Golf Vacations in the Eastern U.S.
Great Smoky & Blue Ridge Region
Inside Disney
Hawaii
Las Vegas
London

Mid-Atlantic with Kids
Mini Las Vegas
Mini-Mickey
New England and New York with Kids
New Orleans
New York City
Paris
San Francisco
Skiing in the West
Southeast with Kids
Walt Disney World®
Walt Disney World® for Grown-up
Walt Disney World® with Kids
Washington, D.C.
World's Best Diving Vacations

SPECIAL-INTEREST TITLES

Frommer's Adventure Guide to Australia & New Zealand
Frommer's Adventure Guide to Central America
Frommer's Adventure Guide to India & Pakistan
Frommer's Adventure Guide to South America
Frommer's Adventure Guide to Southeast Asia
Frommer's Adventure Guide to Southern Africa
Frommer's Britain's Best Bed & Breakfasts and Country Inns
Frommer's Caribbean Hideaways
Frommer's Exploring America by RV
Frommer's Fly Safe, Fly Smart
Frommer's France's Best Bed & Breakfasts and Country Inns
Frommer's Gay & Lesbian Europe

Frommer's Italy's Best Bed & Breakfasts and Country Inns
Frommer's New York City with Kids
Frommer's Ottawa with Kids
Frommer's Road Atlas Britain
Frommer's Road Atlas Europe
Frommer's Road Atlas France
Frommer's Toronto with Kids
Frommer's Vancouver with Kids
Frommer's Washington, D.C., with Kids
Israel Past & Present
The New York Times' Guide to Unforgettable Weekends
Places Rated Almanac
Retirement Places Rated

Booked seat 6A, open return.

Rented red 4-wheel drive.

Reserved cabin, no running water.

Discovered space.

With over 700 airlines, 50,000 hotels, 50 rental car companies and ,000 cruise and vacation packages, you can create the perfect getway for you. Choose the car, the room, even the ground you walk on.

Travelocity.com
A Sabre Company
Go Virtually Anywhere.

You Need A Vacation.

700 Airlines, 50,000 Hotels, 50 Rental Car Companies, And A Million Ways To Save Money.

Travelocity.com
A Sabre Company
Go Virtually Anywhere.